Black, White and Gray

Black, White and Gray

Twenty-one Points of View on the Race Question

Edited by BRADFORD DANIEL

SHEED AND WARD - NEW YORK

Library of Congress Catalogue Card Number 64–13575

Manufactured in the United States of America

This book is affectionately dedicated to my grandparents

PREFACE

THOUGH CONTRIBUTORS to this volume hold widely divergent viewpoints, certainly all would agree that the complex problems of intergroup and intercultural relations—surely the gravest problem of our time—are not now being clarified. This lack of clarification is, in fact, one of the reasons why the problem grows more serious almost daily.

We must have truth before we can have justice. An informed public can be trusted to act wisely. But the public, assaulted by confusing claims and loyalties, is not, in general, being informed about the basic moral and philosophical questions involved.

The civil strife that has swept our nation in recent years, intensified especially during the anxious months of 1963, has made it vividly clear that there is more involved here than the "Negro Problem," as it has been repeatedly and erroneously labeled. It is, instead, the matter of conscience, the inner and intricate fiber of a great and proud land at war with itself. This is an internal war of many complexities. It resembles in some ways the war of the 1860's which so bitterly divided our nation. Now as then, different cultural patterns blind one segment of our population to the needs and rights of other segments: this both sectionally and regionally.

It is this war, a struggle which today touches all Americans, white and non-white alike, that our contributors have attempted to discuss clearly and truthfully according to their lights within these pages.

We have selected contributors who could give expression to as many different professional fields and viewpoints as possible. The list of authors includes white and Negro, Southerner and non-Southerner. Protestant, Catholic and Jewish viewpoints are also represented.

Foremost, the book was intended to be, and has attempted to attain the direction of, a journal of free voices. We asked contributors to speak informally—personally, even—on the issues best suited to their individual knowledge and insights.

To those who have helped in the preparation of this book, I am deeply indebted and appreciative. Especially I would like to thank John Howard Griffin for his invaluable assistance from the outset; Father John LaFarge, S.J., who did not live to see the completed manuscript reach publication, for his good faith and help; and Robert Penn Warren for his encouragement.

Black, White and Gray provides no concrete answers, no final solutions. Rather, it attempts to instigate a probing, a basis or guide by which the reader may analyze and evaluate (and it is hoped in many cases, re-evaluate) his own conscience, his own heart in these matters. For there is where the ultimate resolutions will originate—in dedicated conscience, within the heart, and in the prevailing spirit of all men, a spirit that will torture each of us until we learn once again to live with dignity and at peace with ourselves.

BRADFORD DANIEL

Winter, 1963

ACKNOWLEDGMENTS

Acknowledgment of the right to reprint material contained herein is made, with appreciation, to the following periodicals and writers:

The Progressive and Harry Golden for "Why the Resistance?"

Ramparts and Father August Thompson and John Howard Griffin for "Dialogue with Father Thompson."

Mademoiselle and Eve Auchincloss and Nancy Lynch Handy for "Disturbers of the Peace: An Interview with James Baldwin."

Commentary and Norman Podhoretz for "My Negro Problem—And Ours."

The Progressive and Lillian Smith for "The Mob and the Ghost."

CONTENTS

Black, White and Gray

"And if we who so far are still free, want to continue to be free, all of us who are still free had better confederate fast, with all others who still have a choice to be free—confederate not as black people nor white people nor pink nor blue nor green people, but as people who still are free with all other people who still are free; confederate together and stick together, too, if we want a world or even a part of a world in which individual man can be free, to continue to endure."

—William Faulkner
Address to the Southern
Historical Association,
Memphis, Tenn., 1955.

"With all the polls and opinion posts, with newspapers more opinion than news so that we no longer know one from the other, I want to be very clear about one thing. I have not intended to present, nor do I think I have presented, any kind of cross-section so that a reader can say, 'He thinks he has presented a true picture of the South.' I don't. I've only told what a few people said to me and what I saw. I don't know whether they were typical or whether any conclusion can be drawn. But I do know it is a troubled place and a people caught in a jam. And I know that the solution when it arrives will not be easy or simple. I feel . . . that the end is not in question. It's the means—the dreadful uncertainty of the means."

—John Steinbeck
Travels With Charley
(New York, Viking, 1962).

Harry Golden

WHY THE RESISTANCE?

HARRY GOLDEN, born in 1902 on New York's Lower East Side, the son of an immigrant, obtained his formal education in the New York City schools and at the City College of New York. Before gaining national prominence as Editor and Publisher of The Carolina Israelite, *issued monthly from Charlotte, North Carolina, Mr. Golden was, at varying times, a hotel clerk, teacher, reporter and promotion man for daily newspapers. In 1952, he received the B'rith Abraham Award for his contribution to Jewish journalism and in 1957 the Man of the Year Award of the YMCA of the Johnson C. Smith University of North Carolina. He is a leading lecturer and has made numerous national television appearances. His books include* Only in America, For 2¢ Plain, Enjoy, Enjoy, Carl Sandburg, *and* You're Entitle'.

WHEN MARVIN GRIFFIN was governor of Georgia, he had a favorite radio message for his constituents. He used to say the problem besetting the South as a result of the Supreme Court decision to end racial segregation in the public schools was caused by "outside" influences and Northern "agitators." Marvin Griffin is the stubborn South in a microcosm—unable and unwilling to understand a social revolution of monumental proportions; a movement generated by twelve million Negroes to end the status of inferiority imposed upon them by state statute and city ordinance.

In 1956, the then governor of South Carolina told his state legislature that all would be well again if only the National Association for the Advancement of Colored People were outlawed. At the same time, the legislatures of two other Southern states declared the NAACP a "subversive" organization.

Even after the sit-in movement, which was really a "revolt" of Negro students who felt the NAACP was not moving fast enough, and even after Martin Luther King's non-violent resistance movement in Alabama, Southern leaders still did not see the problem for what it was. They insisted the demand for civil rights, for equal justice under law, was a conspiracy against the South. "The Negroes do not want integration," these Southerners asserted. "My maid told me so." Even at this late date they do not understand that if the NAACP and all the Northern "agitators" suddenly evaporated, the "agitation" of Southern Negroes for civil rights would hardly miss a beat.

At the bottom of this tragedy, then, is the complete lack of communication between white and Negro. They speak the same words but not the same language. In my city of Charlotte in North Carolina, there was a linotype machine in one of the all-white high schools. For many years seniors who chose could learn this excellent trade. In the "separate but equal" Negro high school no such training was offered. When the white men got together to discuss the Supreme Court decision, they said, "The Negroes want white women," and when the Negroes got together to discuss the problem, they said, "When will we get a linotype machine?" During fifty Negro meetings I attended between 1954 and 1958, I heard that linotype machine discussed fifty times.

Because of this lack of communication the myths that have kept so many of the Southern leaders ignorant about the needs, desires, and rights of the Negro have survived. One of these myths is the legend of the "happy Negro." The impracticable segregationist forgets that for decades the Negro was under duress to be "happy." Working under economic exploitation, the Negro conditioned himself to two modes of behavior, one representing his true self and the other the façade he presented to the white race. He knew he had to present a smile to the dominant white society, and, even more important, he had to make certain that he did not appear too smart, or even aware of the political and historical issues of the day. The "happy Negro" tradition was the Negro's adjustment to his subordinate status. A few years ago Senator James Eastland of Mississippi told a Charlotte audience, "The Negroes of Mississippi are the happiest people in the state." Because of lack of communication, the Senator did not know the songs the "happy" Negroes of his state had been singing for many years: *Nobody Knows the Trouble I've Seen; Father, Let Me Be Rid of This World;* and *Let My People Go!*

Because he did not communicate, the Southerner failed to see another development which future historians might conceivably consider the most important of the entire civil rights struggle in the South. That development is the use by the Negro of that part of the culture the Southerners pressed upon him most insistently—Christianity. There are some twelve million Negroes in the South, half of them only semi-literate, but all of whom have not made a single serious mistake. Under the most extreme provocations, the Negroes have answered simply, "Let's go to church and pray for the fellows who threw the stones or bombed the house." This Christianity is undeviating and profound and sustains the Negro in the face of physical provocation, just as his profound humor sustains him in the face of social provocation.

The provocations of physical danger have been few and far between, but the social provocations occur daily. A Chinese comes from Hong Kong to Charlotte, and opens a chop suey lunch room. The Negro men and women who pass the lunch room have lived in North Carolina for at least ten generations, but they cannot go into that restaurant to get the fifty-five-cent chop suey lunch from the recent arrival from Hong Kong. The movie *Hamlet* with Laurence Olivier comes to town, and the Shakespeare Club at the local Negro college cannot go to see it, not even in the balcony, and this exclusion persists despite the foreclosure of movie house mortgages all over the South. How is that for putting a sense of humor to the proof?

Why should this "happy" man suddenly talk about civil rights—who puts him up to it? asks the Southern politician, as though there were no intervening history since the end of the Civil War in 1865. He fails to correlate the "suddenness" of the Negro's demand for political and economic equality with the parallel "suddenness" of the South's industrialization and equal "suddenness" of the urbanization of his culture. The Negro's demand for civil rights is part of this social upheaval which has transformed a great agrarian civilization into an industrial-urban society. Even as Southerners flock to the cities from the hills and small farms, the stubborn ones insist upon retaining a few dreams of a more placid time. Why does he "agitate" now, why not forty, or thirty years ago? Why now? Here is why *now:*

Before the great industrial-urban revolution in the South, which began in the late 1930's, the Negro saw "separate but equal" poverty all around him. He was a sharecropper and a tenant farmer, and the "white" man was a sharecropper and a tenant farmer. It was hard for the Negro to make his move for equality while white men themselves were segregated; the white Protestant descendants of the Covenanters of Scotland, men and women whose ancestors had helped carve a civilization out of a wilderness, were segregated because they worked in a cotton mill. The "uptown" whites called them "lint-heads" or "burr-heads." When the little uptown boy reached the age of seven, his mother called him aside and said, "The time has come for you to understand that you are not to play with the little boys 'on the hill.' " "On the hill" was the cotton mill, and the white Protestants of the cotton mill went to separate schools and separate churches. When the uptown boy was home from college and he had been seen with a girl from the hill, he caused no concern for his family. There was only whispering and laughter; from the father—"Watch yourself, son, you don't catch something"; and from the mother—"I suppose boys must sow their wild oats." To this extent the whites were themselves dehumanized, and the dehumanization deepened the dehumanization of the "happy Negro."

But toward the end of the 1930's, the Negro began to see a new world springing up. The economic measures of the New Deal were the first break in the racial solidarity of the South. The depression need was so great, and so immediate, that the Southern politicians did not dare filibuster the Roosevelt welfare measures and public works programs into the pattern of racial segregation.

I remember an incident in the early 1940's. A Negro and I

shared a taxi ride, and he reached his destination first. He gave the driver a bill and waited a few minutes as the cabbie fumbled with the change. As we drove off, the cabbie muttered, "That damn Roosevelt, that damn Roosevelt." I asked him why he was mad at Roosevelt and he said, "That damn Roosevelt. When the hell did a nigger ever have a ten-dollar bill?"

Within a few years the Negro saw that the segregated whites, the former sharecroppers and "lint-heads" were leaving the fields and factories and acquiring things, the many wonderful things of American middle-class living. And the Negro wanted "in." When you are in Egypt you step off the sidewalk, smile, and tip your hat to the strangers you pass on the street; but when you are on Mount Nebo and you finally glimpse the Promised Land, from a distance, you want it—and you want it all.

The Negro found his way to Mount Nebo by a circuitous route. He found the path during the Roosevelt Administration. Not the President, however, but the President's wife, Eleanor, was his first "official" champion. During the years he was in office, Roosevelt did little to offend the Southern politician directly. Indeed, when the conservative Southerner complained about "that man in the White House," it was nearly always in terms of "taxes" and "he's too chummy with labor."

It was Eleanor Roosevelt who first sounded the call. When Mrs. Roosevelt visited the mills at race-conscious Kannapolis, North Carolina, and saw the two drinking fountains, one for whites, one for colored, she said, for the benefit of the newspapermen and the edification of the factory owners, "Something must be done to correct this injustice." Southern housewives immediately began to circulate the myth that their colored maids were joining "Eleanor Clubs."

But the Roosevelt Administration itself was far from indifferent. What may have been pump-priming to the white population of the country was something much more to the Negro, who looked upon the New Deal as the legislation which abolished starvation as a general fate. Most important of all was the Works Progress Administration (WPA). It provided some work for millions of unemployed, but for the Negro of the South it was a step of monumental proportions. The paycheck itself may have been only $23.86, but for the first time in the history of the South, the Negro was receiving the same pay for the same job as the white man. For the first time the Negro did not have to work for whatever wages the white men chose to pay him. World War II, with its military service and its veterans' benefits, brought him into the same economic arena with the white man and taught him that a life governed by equity offered him far more than a life governed by white paternalism.

Thus did Eleanor Roosevelt, the New Deal, and World War II put the Negroes of America squarely on top of Mount Nebo; in the South, to fight against the racial segregation sanctioned by law and public opinion; and in the North, to fight against the discrimination in employment and housing.

Why the fierce resistance, then? Why do mobs gather to shout insults and threaten violence to a lone Negro student going in and out of his classes at the University of Mississippi? Why is it necessary for Senators like Russell of Georgia, Fulbright of Arkansas, Hill and Sparkman of Alabama, Stennis of Mississippi, and Ervin of North Carolina, men with good minds and kind hearts, to "holler nigger" every time they return to their states to run for re-election? Why the need for even this token declaration for racial segregation, a policy that is not only irreligious and immoral, but also illegal?

Many arguments have been advanced for maintaining the status quo of segregation, and they are all pretexts. "States' rights" is the most common of these pretexts. On the same day Senator Strom Thurmond of South Carolina spoke of the sacredness of "states' rights" in opposing government aid for education, it happened to be payday for the farmers of South Carolina participating in the Federal government's soil-bank program. (There are no states' rights in segregation, only people's wrongs.) The Southern Senators have filibustered for "states' rights" only when the legislation involved the Negro. They have remained silent about the principle when it involved roads, hospitals, farm subsidies, school lunches, and the construction of airports.

Only a few embattled editors, college professors, and social workers have seen the racial problem for what it is: the need to continue the caste system of the South. This caste system has been the key to political success, and in the process the politician has succeeded in making the sanction of racial segregation the test of loyalty to the South itself. When Jack O'Dowd, an editor in Florence, South Carolina, wrote "The Supreme Court Has Spoken," he was called a traitor and was forced to leave his home state. When Dr. Chester Travelstead, dean at the University of South Carolina, spoke out for integration in 1956, he was accused of being a renegade and was forced to resign. It is this fear of being called a traitor that has prevented thousands of Southerners from speaking out since 1954.

The Southern politicians who called for racial solidarity gained seniority in the Congress and perpetuity in the state legislatures. Election issues were simple and uncomplicated: "Holler nigger first and loudest." The politician gave something of value in return, because the segregation of the Negro provided psychological status to millions of white tenant-farmers and industrial workers, well aware they were at the bottom of the list of per capita earnings among all the workers of the nation.

Low-income whites felt, and feel, that the Negro stands between them and social oblivion. As long as they can say, "Stay out of our schools, parks, restaurants, and theatres. Sit in the back of the bus," they have achieved some degree of self-esteem and proof of individual worth.

The upper middle class of the South turned on the Negro after the Supreme Court school decision of 1954 for the same reason, but in reverse. If low-income whites lost their Negro, where would they now find their self-esteem and proof of individual worth? For one thing, the low-income whites would probably join a labor union. Only a few months ago the Textile Workers Union lost another election in a Tennessee plant because management circulated a photograph of Walter Reuther of the United Automobile Workers handing a check to Roy Wilkins of the NAACP. The caption read, "This is what happens to your union dues."

Since we are a school-oriented society, the integration of the public schools would result in the collapse of the entire segregation pattern. The low-income white would say, "I am a doffer in a mill and I get a dollar twenty-five an hour; a doffer in a mill in Massachusetts or in Pennsylvania gets a dollar eighty-five an hour; while you kept the Negro segregated I was willing to work for sixty cents an hour less, but now he is going to school with my kids, and I want that extra sixty cents an hour." You multiply sixty cents an hour by one million six hundred thousand industrial workers, and you will see there is much more to racial segregation than, "Do you want your sister to marry a Negro?"

That the evil is based almost entirely on the need for a caste system is proved every moment of day-to-day living in the South. A Negro with a white coat and a black leather bow tie has ready access to every room in the hotel where Nobel Peace Prize-winner Dr. Ralph Bunche cannot get lodging for the night. A Negro wearing a turban will be accepted everywhere. I once secured a room for a Negro clergyman in the finest hotel of my city, although the clergyman did not wear a turban. I merely said that my friend was a Hindu who did not look Hindu because he had become a Methodist. I told the hotel manager that when a Hindu becomes a Christian, he lays aside the turban. The hotel manager sent a bowl of fruit up to the Negro clergyman, who was born in Decatur, Georgia. There is more tragedy than humor in this illusion that a turban makes a man different.

The struggle against racial segregation has been dramatized by the picture of a well-dressed Negro walking to and from his classes on a college campus surrounded by Federal marshals. But racial segregation also exacts an awesome price in human resources and early death. Tuberculosis, twelfth cause of death among whites, is second among Negroes; four Negro women die in childbirth for each death among white women; and Negro infant mortality is five times greater than among white infants.

Not the least of the tragedies is the denial of humanity, withholding from the Negro inherent rights which are not ours either to give or withhold—the right to communicate his worth and the right to interchange ideas. The segregationists love to emphasize the role Chief Justice Earl Warren of California has played in this great civil rights movement. The segregationists, however, ignore the fact that the Supreme Court decision to end segregation in the colleges of the South was drafted by Fred M. Vinson of old Kentucky.

The Attorney General of Texas had argued that a separate law school for Negroes had adequate facilities. In ordering the all-white University of Texas to admit the Negro students, Chief Justice Vinson ruled that the separate Negro law school was not equal because education also involves the reputation of the faculty, status of the alumni, prestige of the university, size of its library, and the ability of the students to communicate with one another—to communicate, that is, with future lawyers, future judges, and future community leaders.

I am reminded of the Negro doctor who traveled from Charlotte to Washington, D.C. As usual, the railroad gave him a drawing room, even though he had paid only for a lower berth. The railroads followed this policy in an attempt to make the segregated Negro as comfortable as possible and to keep him out of the men's room and smoking car. Every hour or so, the conductor knocked on the door of the drawing room and asked, "Is everything all right?" The conductor asked, "Is everything all right?" at least three times during the course of the evening, and finally the Negro doctor answered wearily, "No, everything is *not* all right. I want to be where the people are."

John B. Connally

LET US DO IT OUR WAY

JOHN B. CONNALLY is Governor of the State of Texas. Born in 1917 at Floresville, Texas, he attended the public schools of Floresville and San Antonio. In December, 1938, in advance of his graduation from the University of Texas Law School, he was admitted to the Texas Bar with an LL.B. degree. He has been a practicing attorney for more than twenty-five years. In 1939, he was employed by the then Congressman Lyndon B. Johnson as Congressional secretary. He is a leading Texas businessman and has served with distinction as a director of many of Texas' largest industries. Volunteering for temporary duty with the U.S. Navy in 1941, Connally served with the Allied Forces Headquarters, North Africa, in Algiers. He was awarded many combat decorations, including the Legion of Merit and the Bronze Star. In December, 1960, he was named Secretary of the Navy by President John F. Kennedy. He served in that capacity until resigning to seek the governorship of Texas. The following article is the address that Governor Connally made in Texas before attending the 1963 National Governors Conference in Florida.

GOOD EVENING, fellow Texans. I want to talk to you tonight about a matter of grave concern to all Texans.

Tomorrow, I will be in Miami speaking as a voice for Texas at the National Governors Conference. This conference is a convocation—a meeting of the chief executives of all the states of this great nation. Each year, for some fifty-five years, governors have gathered together from North and South, East and West, Democratic and Republican, to discuss our problems, our progress. Our program deals with the day-to-day operations of our state governments—financing our schools and colleges, improving our hospitals, traffic safety, civil defense, economic development, and the like. We meet in fellowship to share our experiences, our experiments, in order that we may learn to serve better the people of our states.

Though it is not on the program, the primary topic of discussion there—as it is throughout the nation today—will surely be that of the uncertainty and unrest on civil rights. As your spokesman, I want to talk to you tonight about civil rights in Texas—the integration issue. I want to tell you personally of my convictions before I leave Texas, and before I advance any views at the National Governors Conference. (*Editor's Note: It was decided at the 1963 Governors Conference to table a conference discussion of civil rights until 1964.*)

I'm sure that most Texans share a feeling of compassion for the President of the United States as he bears the brunt of a massive burden as the leader of 180 million Americans, certainly one of the heaviest burdens of any president in our history.

As chief executive of the nation, he faces problems of frightening magnitude. He must deal with Khrushchev in a continuing struggle for the very preservation of the free world under constant threat of H-bomb annihilation. He must deal with a dictatorship in Cuba, less than a hundred miles from our shore. He must deal with a ruthless Communist China. He must contend with a cantankerous de Gaulle in efforts for a united West. He must deal with growing economic and political effects on this nation of the European Common Market. And in a new dimension that no American leader has ever had to face, he must chart this nation's course in space, as well as on earth.

As if this burden were not enough to bear, he now carries the crushing weight of one of the most serious and perplexing domestic issues of this nation in almost a century—the churning issue of civil rights. It is a heavy care for any man. I do not envy him his responsibility.

Regardless of our political views, Democratic or Republican, we can have understanding sympathy for the massive tensions of our times, and sympathy for the conscience-heavy judgments necessary in these times to tax every resource of wisdom of any man who holds the presidency. I would say these same words if the man in the White House were a Republican.

In the civil rights issue, the President of the United States faces a problem that varies in intensity and complexion very widely throughout our nation. The situation in Maryland is far different from that in New Mexico. We therefore as Texans should be tolerant and restrained in judging necessary actions or needs in areas remote from us. This often demands very broad understanding, but we are capable of it. I cannot and should not sit in judgment from the capitol in Austin on actions taken in forty-nine other state capitols or the one in Washington.

But, as governor of Texas, it is my responsibility—and one in which I take pride—to reflect the sentiments and convictions of ten million citizens, in view of national developments which deeply affect us and our lives. To do less, I would fail in my obligation to be the spokesman, the advocate, of our people. It is in that spirit that I address you tonight.

In our land today, headlines reflect the harsh voices of extremism on civil rights. Spokesmen are plentiful and eloquent in pleading diametrically opposed views. The din of controversy has risen to a disquieting level. And throughout it all, most Texans I know have quietly, patiently listened with remarkable restraint and fairmindedness. This, to me, is a tribute to the common sense of the people of Texas. And I am proud.

But the din becomes louder, without tranquility in view. Texans are disturbed, I believe, over the fact that all is not well in our nation.

I am speaking out to you tonight on civil rights because I am convinced that the voice of reason must be raised—clearly, strongly—to reflect the feeling of the vast majority of Texans.

The issue of civil rights is too vital to be left to the discordant, divisive elements of either the extreme left or the extreme right. The reasonable, responsible people of this state must not abdicate in favor of the forces of passion—or those who would exploit strife for selfish gain.

We Texans are a unique people. Ours is a distinctive heritage.

On the floor of the rotunda of the capitol in Austin are emblazoned the seals of six great nations. We alone of all Americans have lived under six flags. We have lived under tyranny, and in revolt. We have tasted the wines of victory and the dregs of defeat. This heritage was not forged by any one race, or color, or creed; it was forged rather by a new breed of man—a breed known as the Texan. A breed composed of Protestants, Catholics and Jews, a breed originating in a host of colonial states, in Mexico, Scotland, Ireland, France, Germany, Czechoslovakia, Poland, Italy and a dozen other lands. A breed proudly bearing names such as Austin, Houston, De Zavala, Crockett, Dowling, Solms, and Jones and Smith.

At one time or another in the past, we Texans have all known what it meant to be different—to be part of a minority. This heritage gives us an unusual insight into the problem of civil rights. I like to think that it gives us warmth and understanding in these difficult times.

To discuss meaningfully civil rights in Texas, we must first evaluate our own situation here in the state. And I am particularly pleased, at a time when all communications media are filled with strife and rumors of strife elsewhere, that Texans can point with pride to achievements rather than crisis.

Many of you listening tonight may have little awareness of how much progress has been made in Texas toward insuring equal civil rights for racial minorities. I'm going to review this progress briefly.

In education, the most important, the most vital area of interest to all Texans, tremendous strides have been taken:

—Sixteen of our twenty-one public senior colleges and universities are now desegregated.

—Twenty-six of our thirty-three public junior colleges have desegregated, and others are prepared to do so.

—As of today, 212 Texas public school districts have taken steps toward desegregation. Fifty-three per cent of the Negro school children in Texas now live in school districts which have programs of desegregation actually in operation. More districts are desegregating every week.

Equally dramatic progress has occurred in other areas:

—Seventy-five per cent of our restaurants serve all citizens regardless of race.

—Eighty per cent of our hotels shelter all citizens regardless of race.

—Eighty per cent of our theaters admit all citizens regardless of race.

But this is not the whole story. Across the length and breadth of this state desegregation proceeds apace in parks, playgrounds, swimming pools, libraries, and churches. In every corner of Texas the horizons of equality extend to more and more citizens of our state.

I'm proud of Texas and of Texans for this kind of progress, progress which is continuing day by day. I'm equally proud of another kind of progress that has come particularly in recent months.

During the past few months you have heard names such as the Reverend C. A. Holliday, Dr. Joseph Chatman, Joe Scott, the Reverend Marvin Griffin, Dr. Vernon McDaniel. These men are serving on the highest policy boards of this state. All these outstanding Texans happen to be Negro. They are qualified by background, experience and leadership for distinguished public service.

There are other names you haven't heard of, equally outstanding Negro citizens who have assumed increasing roles of responsibility in the affairs of our state and local governments.

But let me make one point clear: I did not appoint any of these citizens because they are Negro. I appointed them because they were outstanding Texans who were qualified through education and experience to render service to the people of this state. I have not —and I will not—appoint any man to any position merely because he is a Negro.

Now I realize that our progress leaves much to be desired. But as a Texan, I'm proud to point to this progress, and to hold high the banner of this sovereign state and to repudiate any who would ridicule or minimize achievements in Texas.

Now how has the past progress been possible? To me, this question is every bit as important as the progress itself, because it points the way to meaningful progress ahead. It has been possible because reasonable men—men of good will, men of humility—have worked quietly, conscientiously to make it so. They are not men who have sought headlines, nor men who have dealt in inflammatory phrases or passions, but rather in the quiet understanding of human dignity.

They are men who seek harmony and first-class citizenship for all our people—nothing more. As governor of Texas for the past six months, I have had a hand in some of these endeavors. I have done so quietly, without publicity, because in my judgment this is an issue that calls for sincerity, not sensation. But principally, the job has been done not by me at all, but by unassuming, unsung leaders of cities, towns, and villages throughout this state.

Now who has done this job? It has been your mayors, your commissioners, your judges, your public school boards, your local businessmen, lawyers, ministers and educators. It is they who have had the courage and good citizenship to step into the breach in this trying time. They have seen their duty and they have done it magnificently. Ten million Texans owe a mammoth debt of gratitude to these men—men of both races—for their dedicated and untiring endeavors. While others have talked, they have done.

A few weeks ago, I spoke to a gathering of Negro Texans in Austin at a meeting of the United Political Organization, an organization dedicated to the improvement of the legal, educational, and economic opportunities of their people. It was a distinguished gathering of some of the state's most accomplished citizens. There were outstanding members of every business and profession.

The meeting honored Negroes who have assumed roles of leadership in Texas, and it was an occasion to do honor to this state. Speaking to these Texans, I said, in part: "I believe that most Texans share my confidence that we will go the rest of this journey to the common destiny that is ours if we follow the road of cooperation and avoid the perilous path of unreasonable coercion."

This statement brought enthusiastic applause from these fine Texans. And I'm proud that it did.

Two days later, speaking in Dallas to the State Bar of Texas, I told that group of advocates and practitioners of law and order in our society about the meeting in Austin, and repeated to them, word for word, the same sentences as in Austin. In Dallas, as in

Austin, this statement brought enthusiastic applause from these fine Texans.

This to me underscores and dramatizes the philosophy and spirit of our success in civil rights. We have avoided the cold, arbitrary tool of governmental edict. So you see, I go to Florida with pride in our achievements.

But as I represent you at the National Governors Conference the next few days, the spotlight of national attention is focused on controversy presently swirling about proposed federal legislation to deal with the problems such as those which we have been solving in Texas. I want to make clear to all Texans tonight my views on this legislation.

I believe the record of my administration leaves no doubt that I will do all within my power to meet in good faith our state's responsibilities, including those in the field of civil rights. But as an attorney by education and practice for more than a quarter of a century, I am deeply concerned over some of the provisions of the proposed legislation.

I am disturbed because I fear that these provisions could carry potential danger to thc people of this state that is far greater than any now envisioned. They would be laws which in my judgment would strike at the very foundation of one of our most cherished freedoms—the right to own and manage private property, a right as dear to a member of any minority group as to any other Texan. I speak specifically of the proposed federal law which would deprive the owners of private business of the right to decide whom they would serve, and of the accompanying proposal to give broad powers of enforcement to the attorney general of the United States.

Let me make clear once again: I can conceive of no Texan disagreeing that every citizen of this state shall have full and equal legal rights as guaranteed under the Constitution.

But I cannot accept nor support the proposition of violating one person's rights to bestow privilege on another person, regardless of the color or race of either.

I therefore respectfully oppose these proposals of the national administration, as the spokesman for Texas.

Regardless of my view on the pending federal legislation, its fate obviously will ultimately be decided by the national Congress, and not by me. If this legislation does become law, I of course will uphold that law in accordance with my oath of office.

But no matter what happens in Washington, it will not change the character of the problem, nor provide the real answer. For the problem is not in Washington—it is in the tens of thousands of communities throughout the fifty states where we live and work every day.

The voices of irresponsible demagogues are loud and demanding on what the individual states should do. Radical extremists on both sides advocate widely divergent actions. Some would have the state used as an instrument and a force of oppressive action against the whites. Other equally militant voices would have the state used as an instrument of force and oppressive action against the Negroes.

As governor of Texas, I vigorously reject both approaches as wholly distasteful and unacceptable to reasonable, responsible Texans.

As I said earlier, this entire question is too important to be left in the hands of extremists on either side, and I do not intend to see that ever come about in Texas. Regardless of what happens in Washington today, next week or next year, progress in civil rights is a continuing responsibility of this state. As long as I am governor, I intend to see that we live up to this responsibility. But in our own Texas way.

What is the Texas way that I advocate and pledge to support?

Well, let's look at the real basic desires of the minority group citizen of our state:

First and foremost, he asks equal treatment under the law. And as governor of Texas, I'll do everything within my power to see that he has this constitutional right. And I don't know of any Texan who would think it should be any other way.

Second, he asks equal voting rights—freedom at the ballot box. And as governor of Texas, I'll do everything within my power to see that he has that constitutional right. And I don't know of any Texan who would think it should be any other way.

Third, he asks free and equal access to public facilities maintained and operated by public taxes, including his. As governor of

Texas, I intend to do everything within my power to see that he has that constitutional right.

But there are two more critical needs of the minority group Texan that really go to the heart of the matter—for they determine what kind of life he and his family enjoy, and what kind of productive citizen he is in our society, and whether he makes a contribution to the state or whether he requires the support and aid of the state.

I refer to the twin necessities of education and economic opportunities. Unless we have achieved these goals, equality under the law is but a pretense.

We in Texas recognize that we cannot have a system of second-class citizenship for any minority group. By the same token, we must recognize that we cannot have a system of second-class education for any group. We need, indeed we must have, a system of education which affords to each child, irrespective of race or color or creed, opportunity to develop to the fullest extent possible his God-given talents and abilities.

If we in Texas are to meet the challenges of the space age, we will need to utilize the educational opportunities of all our children. We are entering an age of great change, an age of technology, an age in which there will be a tremendous demand for scientists, technicians and skilled workmen. We cannot afford to waste the brain power, the unused educational capabilities of a single child. To each we must provide an education of the first class.

But educational opportunity alone is not enough. It does us little good to train a Negro or a Latin American youth to be an automobile mechanic or a bricklayer or an office worker or a mathematician or a physicist unless we provide him also with the opportunity to utilize his skills, his training, his abilities. We need to recognize that ability is not limited to a particular color. It covers the broad spectrum. We need to utilize it wherever it is found. Our society faces vigorous economic competition, both from other free societies and the totalitarian world. In this competition we cannot afford the economic waste attached to discrimination solely because of color. This is not solely humanitarianism, it is but good business sense, the same type of sense that helped build the best economic system on the face of the earth.

Let us face the fact that when we restrict the educational and economic opportunity of any citizen, we restrict also his opportunity to become a fully self-supporting participating member of our economy and our society. In so doing, we impose upon our governments at the state and local level unnecessary additional burdens for social welfare expenditures.

You cannot bestow education by administrative edict. Neither can you assure economic opportunity solely by legislation.

How then do we do it? We do it as it has been done all over this state: by allowing individual citizens of good will of the community to sit down together—men and women who know each other, who have mutual respect and confidence—to discuss calmly and without tension the steps necessary to make fully participating citizens of everyone. We do it by talking out our differences—through persuasion and cooperation, not passion or compulsion.

And this is the path I propose for Texas to continue to travel. Some have asked why I haven't appointed a state action committee on civil rights. I have purposely avoided that course, for the very reason that I am deeply convinced that civil rights is a local issue. It must be faced and be solved locally. This is the only way to achieve meaningful progress.

Can Texas continue to meet the challenge in this way? I am convinced that we can and we will. Not in decades have we had such a chance to give dramatic support in deeds of our dedication to the sacred principles of local self-government. If we truly believe in the doctrine of states' rights, we never shall have a better opportunity to demonstrate it to the glory of Texas. And I know that we will.

This is the path I want to continue to travel—the path of persuasive progress. If the necessity should become clear, of course, I will appoint a state commission to deal with civil rights in aiding local communities.

But I don't want to set up such a committee. The job should continue to be done without anybody from Austin telling you what to do, and without anybody from Washington telling us we have to do it.

Basically, Texans are sound, reasonable people who can be counted on to do what is right. They can be led, but they don't like to be shoved.

As I depart to represent the people of Texas at the National Governors Conference, I want to ask your help in this vitally important matter. You, and only you, can help assure full civil rights for all.

Help to meet the challenge of civil rights, in your neighborhood, in your community; join me as a reasonable voice for progress.

Ours is the opportunity to stand tall in the proud Texas tradition as the state of good will, without compulsion of law.

Finally, let us not view this issue as just a problem; rather, let us in Texas make of it a great opportunity to educate and elevate our people to the end that all of us may recapture the bold faith of those who began this noble experiment founded upon the worth of an individual human being. In the end, this will not be done by constitutions, laws, ordinances or edicts, but by a resolute people determined not to betray our historic and religious heritage. There must be a moral basis for asserting the worth of the individual, the essentiality of freedom. This basis is, I think, simply the belief that man is the child of God; that he holds within himself some portion of divinity. There is cause for concern that faith—the heart and meaning of freedom—has become less a part of our everyday life. We profess less, and perhaps share less, the religious faith of an earlier time which bade us love and trust one another, and accordingly respect each other's freedom. The poet speaks of "freedom's holy light." And it must be a holy light, or it will be no light at all. It can glow only in a cherished faith that each man contains within himself a spark of the divine.

A great jurist of our country once stated his faith in these words: "The spirit of liberty is the spirit which is not too sure that it is always right; it is the spirit which seeks to understand the minds of other men and women; it is the spirit which weighs their interests alongside its own without bias; it remembers that not even a sparrow falls to earth unheeded; the spirit of liberty is the spirit of

Him who, nearly two thousand years ago, taught mankind that lesson it has never learned, but has never quite forgotten; that there may be a kingdom where the least shall be heard and considered side by side with the greatest. That is the spirit of an America which has never been and which may never be; nay, which never will be except as the conscience and courage of Americans create it; yet it is the spirit of that America which lies hidden in some form in the aspirations of us all."

Roy Wilkins

WHAT THE AMERICAN NEGRO WANTS
An Interview by Editors of *U.S. News & World Report**

ROY WILKINS joined the staff of the National Association for the Advancement of Colored People in 1931 and has been its executive secretary since 1955. Born in St. Louis, Missouri, in 1901, he grew up in St. Paul, Minnesota, then attended the University of Minnesota. From graduation in 1923 until joining the NAACP staff in 1931, Mr. Wilkins was managing editor of the Call, *a weekly newspaper for Negroes published in Kansas City, Missouri.*

MR. WILKINS, *can you explain for us the direction policy is taking in the National Association for the Advancement of Colored People?*

Our policy reflects the dominant mood of the Negro today. That mood is one of impatience with the pace of desegregation, or, as we say, impatience with the speed with which the Negro comes into the status of full citizenship. It is a very great impatience, I think, spurred by the resistance to implementing the 1954 Supreme Court decision against segregated public schools.

Would you say the Negro's impatience is growing?

I think it is. It's a mixture of impatience and cynicism. The Black Muslims, of course, are an outgrowth of this sentiment.

The Muslims' idea of black for black has always been around in

* This article is reprinted from *U.S. News & World Report,* published at Washington, April 29, 1963.

one form or another. Some of you may recall the Garvey movement of the 1920s—a movement whose leaders claimed 2 million followers. Even if you cut that in half, it's a million, or about 10 per cent of the Negroes at that time. Other estimates had the total nearer 100,000.

The idea of us all getting together—putting our money together and building ourselves an economic structure and electing Negroes to office, running our own affairs, making ourselves rich instead of making the other man rich—has always had an appeal.

Is that a form of apartheid—separateness?

You can call it a form of apartheid, but it didn't reach that kind of dignity in terms of a political-science concept. It was a gesture of desperation born of frustration. I wouldn't say it was apartheid in the sense that it was a conceived-of policy. You might call it counter-apartheid, perhaps.

Now the Muslims have come along and sharpened up the concept by giving it religious and cult overtones.

How seriously do you regard the Muslims?

They aren't serious in numbers. They aren't serious, as yet, psychologically. The American Negro, whatever else he is, is pretty thoroughly American. He's under a lot of handicaps, and he feels terribly frustrated and down at times, but, if I know anything about him, he believes in this country and he believes some way he'll make it.

Along comes a man who says, "Give up Christianity, give up American citizenship, give up the idea of integration, give up the idea of association with white people, working with white people, talking to white people, or expecting any reason from white people, and cut off everything and come with us." The American Negro can't very well accept this philosophy, which goes counter to everything he's been working for and talking about—that is, integration into the American scene as an American citizen.

Do the Muslims propose violence?

No. They want the U.S. Government to give them two or three States, and establish their own Negro country within the United States. But they don't name the States. They don't spell it out the way the Communists did in their heyday.

The Communists in the '30s and '40s drew maps showing counties in the South—the "black belt" counties—over which they wanted Negroes to have hegemony. They wanted the Government to get out and wanted, in effect, to have the land turned over to them.

The Muslims do not spell it out quite that way. Also, the Muslims are a well-disciplined group. They are well behaved. They do not believe or indulge in violence. They do not preach going out and throwing bombs or beating up anybody. They are well dressed, quietly dressed. The youngsters wear ivy-league-cut clothes.

Are the Muslims young people for the most part?

I would say that most are under 40.

Do they attract middle-class Negroes?

I don't know. They don't give out membership figures or breakdowns. They specialize in recruiting the frustrated and the disappointed—the people largely without hope. They recruit people in jail, people who feel that "the white people are all against us, the NAACP is crazy, and Adam Clayton Powell, even, is all wrong. What's he doing wasting his time in Congress? You never get anywhere there. You never get anywhere in the courts. What we black people have to do is stick together and build our own institutions."

Where do you think they're going with all this?

I don't know.

Mr. Wilkins, has your association officially expressed disapproval of the Muslims?

Oh, yes. Years ago. Of course, ideologically, we would have to disagree with them on integration. We believe in integration; they believe in separation. Aside from that, we had to disassociate ourselves from a group that was anti-Semitic and antiwhite.

Does the militancy of the Muslims compel the NAACP and other organizations for Negroes to be a little more militant?

I don't think so. You see, the Muslims don't concern themselves with problems of the day. They don't fight in Greenwood, Miss., for example, to get Negroes to register and vote. They don't even register and vote in Harlem, where they are. They say they're through with white civilization. You don't hear of them carrying on any civil-rights program.

Why are Negroes so dissatisfied when the federal courts have consistently upheld their rights?

I think much of their dissatisfaction goes back to that 1954 school decision—the Brown v. Board of Education case. I feel that the Negro had the right to conceive of that decision as getting rid of the doctrine of "separate but equal" facilities for Negroes. That's what the decision said. The Negro was prepared for reasonable progress toward implementing the decision, provided it began and was in good faith.

Hasn't that occurred?

No. Instead of that, resistance broke out—extreme resistance. Now the Negro sees—nine years after the Court decision, come May 17, 1963—still more than 2 million Negro youngsters in segregated schools and school districts, having to fight every step of the way, county by county and school district by school district. Even where there is integration, it's only token. So some Negroes are coming to say: "Why do you put so much stock in the courts? Who cares what the Supreme Court says, because it doesn't have any effect on me, anyway?"

DELAYS IN THE SOUTH

Does your statement apply to cities such as Washington, D.C., or New York or Philadelphia?

No. It applies to Virginia and similar States. Although Virginia is improving, it's still token. I'm talking about North Carolina and Florida, about South Carolina, which has only one student at Clemson, and about Georgia, which has a few in Georgia State, a few in Georgia Tech, one in Emory, two or three at the University of Georgia, and eight or nine kids in high school in Atlanta.

Louisiana has Negroes in Louisiana State University—one of the earliest to take them in, and they live in the dormitories there. Negroes are in several other State colleges and a few are in grade schools in New Orleans, and that ends integration in Louisiana.

Arkansas, if Governor Faubus had kept quiet, was going right along on its own. The State University there desegregated without a lawsuit. Fayetteville desegregated its high school in September,

1954, without a court order. But Arkansas, even so, has token integration.

West Texas and central Texas might be said to have token integration. East Texas has almost none.

So when we say token integration, that's what I'm talking about. I'm not talking of West Virginia, where all of the counties with biracial school districts now have integrated schools, nor of Missouri, which is 85 to 90 per cent integrated. Nor am I talking about Kentucky, where there is about 50 per cent integration in a slow, steady process.

In Washington, D.C., there has been full integration since 1954, but there seems to be voluntary segregation. Is that another problem as you see it?

Yes. They speak of "resegregation." Well, you've had a large influx of Negroes into the capital, and now 53 per cent of the city's population is black.

And 84 per cent of the school population is Negro, because so many white families have moved to the suburbs—

That's right. Yet, I believe it is true that more youngsters are getting a better education under the present system in Washington than did before the Supreme Court decision. It may be that some youngsters got a better education under the previous system than they would get under this system. But more kids are getting a better education now, because the lower and middle groups get better schools.

Did you expect progress on school integration in the South to be faster than it has been?

I did indeed. I wasn't so naïve as to think the Court's decision would be self-enforcing. But I did believe that, with reasonable representations on the part of the Negro public as to what it wanted, and through conferences with school and public officials, plans would have been worked out for a steady implementation of the Court's ruling, even though at a relatively slow pace.

This has not happened. And this is the reason why some Negroes may lend an ear to appeals for less diplomacy and more action.

Won't the vote help Negroes to get more action?

Most Negroes can't vote in the South. And voting takes a long time to change conditions, too, you know.

It has been suggested that the Negro would have made more progress faster if, instead of aiming at integration of schools, he had aimed first at gaining the vote. Do you think that idea has any validity?

I have a standard answer to that—one which I think is very valid. That answer is: It doesn't really matter what area the Negro selects for attack, that area becomes the area of great resistance. And the white Southerners say, "Why didn't you pick something else?"

Actually, the NAACP began its campaign against disfranchisement in its first Supreme Court case in 1917, challenging the "grandfather clause." On our third try in the highest court, the white primary was declared unconstitutional in 1944.

Personally, I think we did right in moving on schools. I think education is basic. One of the tragedies right now lies in the consequences of the deprivation of educational opportunities for the Negroes who grew up in the South and have now emigrated to the North. I see great tragedy and heartache for those now entering a space age when they don't even have the education for the automotive age.

But suppose we Negroes had said "No" to the idea of attacking school segregation first and had said, "We'll go for voting first." Then the Southerners would trot out all the old arguments: "Do you think we're going to have a Negro mayor, or chief of police? Why, you're crazy. You should pick out something else."

So, say we pick out housing. Then they say: "We aren't going to have Negroes living next door to us. They'll ruin property values." Actually, it must be said that there is more integration of housing in neighborhoods of some Southern cities than in the North. Whites and Negroes have been living side by side for years in such places as Charleston, S.C., or even Sumter, S.C., in the State where the Civil War began. But on Long Island, N.Y., it causes white folks to have the heebie jeebies when a Negro moves in next door.

All right, so you don't pick housing, but instead you pick fair-employment practices. Then you run into the argument that you are trying to coerce employers, telling them whom to hire.

So the answer is that no matter what right the Negro picks to demand, it is called the thing he should not have picked.

So what are the Negroes going to use to get action? The boycott?

They've been using the boycott for some time. In the NAACP we call it selective buying. We have a campaign on now in Jackson, Miss., and we've run successful campaigns in Savannah, Ga., in Macon, Ga., Durham, N.C., St. Petersburg, Fla., and a variety of other places—some you never even hear about.

Have these boycotts proved effective?

They've been very effective.

Will the use of boycotts spread?

I think it is spreading.

How much economic power do Negroes have?

Well, the Negro market has been estimated at about 15 billions a year—about as large as our Canadian market. This is not to be sneezed at.

Is this economic power growing?

It's growing and will grow more if we can get more and better jobs for Negroes. But the Negro unemployment rate is now more than twice the rate among whites. It's about 14 per cent among Negroes and less than 6 per cent among whites. And automation is pushing the Negro out of more and more jobs.

The South abandoned its plantation economy, went either to mechanized farms or diversified farming, or went industrial. The Negro was kicked off the land.

So where does he go then? He goes to a Southern city. But he can't get a job there, first of all because he's black, but also because he has no skills. He doesn't know any job but farm work, you see. So he drifts north.

What happens when the Negro goes to a Northern city?

Sometimes he gets a job, and sometimes he doesn't.

When Negroes can't get jobs up North, why don't they go back to the South?

I would say one third of those who have left the South would go back tomorrow if conditions in the South were changed. They would like it down there if things were different. They're like a lot of white people in the North who don't like cold winters.

I got a letter from a man who is a member of the NAACP in a town in Louisiana. He is an electrician. A few years ago he went to Seattle. His daughters were ready to go to high school and he wanted them to have a good education.

Incidentally, in the past, Negroes not only went north for jobs, but also to get a better education for their children. A lot of them will endure a lot of things for that. They are enduring reprisals today to desegregate their schools in their South.

But this man didn't like Seattle. It was too cold. So he finally decided to leave and go back to Louisiana. There he went to see his old banker. When he told the banker he didn't like it up North the banker was delighted and told him, "You can have anything now."

This man got a loan from the banker, went back into the electrical business again, and now he's very happy.

I think the South is throwing away an opportunity. The Southern people should realize that the Negro is an asset and has value to them—that he's part and parcel of the South.

But the South is losing the Negro. You meet Negroes in the North who are successes in business or in good jobs. Why shouldn't a Negro be as good a policeman in Augusta, Ga., as in Ohio? Or as good a cashier in Jacksonville, Fla., as in New York City?

EXPORTING RACE PROBLEMS

But the South doesn't have all the race problems—

No, it doesn't. The South has transplanted some of them—shoved them up North. It has become fashionable to say that this is no longer a Southern problem but a national problem. When the North points an accusing finger at the South, the South says back to the North: "Why don't you clean up your own back yard?" The North is no angel in this matter, but, in all fairness, it must be admitted that its back yard does contain many problems exported by the South.

Yet, in the North, there is a difference. It is still possible for a

Negro in the North in many places to go to a desegregated school and get a good education. Even where Northern schools are segregated by residential patterns, it's often somewhat better than where schools are segregated by law.

The North, bad as it is, hypocritical as it is, still offers an improvement over the South.

No. I'm not anti-South. I'm just antidiscrimination.

I'll tell you, I think the South is more of a devil in this than appears on the surface. I'm not talking just about the outward treatment of the Negro. I'm talking about the lack of preparedness of Negroes who grew up in the South.

You see, most of the Negroes in the North are end products of the system in the South. For years, the South has cheated Negroes out of any kind of training for citizenship or any opportunity to advance their economic skills or their artisan skills. Now, you say, "These people are not good citizens." Why, they never had any opportunity!

NEGRO CRIME AND JUSTICE

Does that account for the crime rate among Negroes?

It accounts for a great many things.

Now, I don't want to use deprivation as a blanket excuse, because I think people ought to have some restraints on their conduct, regardless of how much they suffer. Whether they kick you around or not, you ought to learn good from bad.

But I do say that this kind of treatment has weakened those restraints among Negroes, and made it easy for them to defy convention, to rob, to steal. Even the Southern system of jurisprudence encouraged this because it said, in effect: "Negroes will steal. If they steal just a little, we won't punish them. If a Negro steals from another Negro, that's no crime. If he kills another Negro, why that's just a misdemeanor. But, if he kills a white man, why, that means electrocution." Well, that type of justice doesn't breed respect for law.

Is that situation changing?

I think it is. The Southern courts now are better. Some Southern judges are better. And there are more Negro lawyers.

Mr. Wilkins, what about Negro family life?

I can see how some people would point a finger of scorn at some manifestations of Negro life. But I think, by and large, they are not doing too badly. Personally, when I consider the terrible obstacles, I am proud of most of them.

Are they disciplining their children?

I think they are disciplining their children, where they have a family life. But it's hard in those cases where there is no man in the family.

You see, Negro family life has been matriarchal from slavery days. This is a direct heritage of slavery—where there was no marriage, no family life, no holding of families together. And this had come down, you see, so that it has been the woman who ran the Negro family. And often it has been the woman who got employment. If a man couldn't get a job as a machinist, a woman could always get a job as a washwoman, a cook, or a domestic.

Doesn't the Negro father take much interest in his family life?

He does if he is there. But so many Negro fathers are not at home. They drift off, or they are separated, or they are working in one place while the family lives in another.

This is a result of the system that makes it harder for a Negro to get a job. He often has to leave his family behind while he goes scouting around in some other town for a job. When he gets a job, he may send for his family, and settle down and rear his children. Or he may not. At least, it's harder for Negro men to keep their families together than it is for white men.

So, when you ask me about Negro family life, I have to tell you that, of course, there are a lot of Negro women on relief with illegitimate children, although they are not alone in this—white women also have such children. And there are a lot of juvenile delinquents.

But the vast, solid majority consists of fine Negro families—people who respect conventions, and who believe in rearing their children right and making sacrifices and working at whatever job they can get, buying homes, paying their debts, supporting churches. These are the backbone of the Negro community.

FEARS OF INTERMARRIAGE

One thing that seems to disturb people is the idea that Negroes seek intermarriage with whites—

I don't know what may happen in the distant future, but I am confident that the Negroes have no goal of intermarriage. If they had, they would have been rushing to marry whites in New York, in Illinois, in Michigan and in all the other States—about 35 in all—where intermarriage is not forbidden by law. But, instead, you have a very few, an infinitesimal number of intermarriages. I think that is the best answer to this question.

Furthermore—women being far more canny at this marriage business than men—white women are not going to marry men who, they've been told since childhood, are inferior, can't earn a good living. The woman naturally wants somebody who's going to have social standing, whom she can introduce to her friends with pride, and whom her family will accept.

What is the attitude of Negroes toward intermarriage?

It disturbs some Negroes, too. I know of a Negro mother who was greatly disturbed because her boy was going with a white girl. Finally, the two mothers got together and talked about it. And it wasn't a question of one feeling that her family was better than the other one. They just felt that, in the first place, the kids were too young to understand what they were up against. The colored mother was more disturbed than the white mother. The youngsters finally broke off.

Was this colored mother typical, would you say?

I would say "Yes." You'll find some Negroes who consider it to be a great thing to be allied with a white family. But they are in the minority.

Is a white person who marries a Negro accepted in Negro circles?

I'm afraid that I have to admit that such a white person has a tough time. However, the acceptance depends on the sophistication of the groups concerned. Sometimes there is no resentment. Even the Japanese and Korean brides brought back by Negro soldiers had a hard time in Negro neighborhoods, in Negro social circles—to say nothing of the white circles.

Why is that?

Well, the only thing I can say is that Negroes are just as conservative as American white people.

And then there is this: Among Negro women there is great competition for a good Negro husband—a man who can give some promise of making his way in the world and winning some prestige. Negro women, as women all over the world, are looking for security and prestige in marriage. Potential husbands of this caliber are scarce. So, when a white girl comes along and takes one of those Negro men away, that's one possible husband gone. This is one reason why intermarriage meets some hostility in the Negro community.

There seems to be considerable interest in Africa among American Negroes. Do many American Negroes aspire to go to these new countries being formed in Africa?

Some have gone over. Some of them have gone on a purely patriotic basis, because they wanted to go. Some of them have gone on the old American urge to make a fast buck. They've gone to East and West Africa and attempted to set up businesses. Others are teachers, or members of technical teams.

But there is a very great emotional interest in Africa on the part of American Negroes. They are very proud of the new African states. This is one of the things that contributes to Negroes' unrest and dissatisfaction in this country. They read about and see pictures of and meet Negro ambassadors, prime ministers and business leaders from other countries.

They see pictures of Negroes working in oil refineries in the Congo and doing technical work and being locomotive engineers. And they remember that there are very few Negroes in such jobs here. Why, you can't even find one Negro locomotive engineer in this country.

How about jobs in this country? Are Negroes making much progress toward getting better jobs?

They are not getting enough better jobs.

Haven't Negroes made tremendous strides in the last thirty years?

Oh, yes. But, you see, their progress has to be measured against the accelerated progress of white people. I think the Negro's median wage is now slightly less than 50 per cent of the white median wage, whereas it used to be down around a third. So, although the Negro has improved his wage earnings, he is still far behind. The white wage has gone so far ahead of his.

Negroes are largely concentrated in the unskilled categories, and those unskilled categories are the ones that have lost out to automation first, naturally.

Where is all this going to lead for the Negro?

It leads to a big problem, and the NAACP plans a conference soon on unemployment problems.

Now, the Government has initiated a retraining program for workers. It's small, but it's an indication of where you can go. Yet, already, the Negroes have run into trouble on this retraining business.

How?

They and the retraining program got caught in a hassle between two candidates for Congress from the same district in Mississippi. One of them had tentatively endorsed a retraining program and, as soon as the other one found out about it, he came out against it, saying his opponent wanted to train Negroes to take over white jobs. The Federal Government didn't want to get caught in this fight, so it dropped the plan.

HIRING NEGRO CLERKS

Many large companies in the North tell us they have trouble getting clerical help, for example. Are Negro girls getting such jobs in the North?

Yes, I think Negro girls are working in more and more of these offices. Here's an example: The Metropolitan Life Insurance Company had no Negroes employed in its New York office until New York State passed its fair-employment law in 1945. Then Metropolitan did what the South should do. It said, "Well, it's the law." And the company began hiring Negroes for clerical work. Now they have Negroes in supervisory jobs.

In the early days—the late forties—some of Metropolitan's Negro girl employes joined a swimming club that had a contract to swim in a pool in a hotel. When the hotel tried to bar the Negroes, the Metropolitan said: "We have a contract to use this pool, and either these Negro girls swim or we sue." That settled it, right there. Now, if somebody in the South would do something like that—

What we need, gentlemen, is a few men in the South with some guts who would simply sit down around a table and say: "Now, look, this is what's got to be done and let's do it. Let's do it without a lawsuit, without Bobby Kennedy coming down here and beating us over the head, without the NAACP driving us or the North pressuring us. We have said we'd do it if they didn't push us. So, let's do it."

What kind of men are you talking about—officials, Governors?

I think the industrialists, the businessmen, the people who really run things. You will have to bring in the mayors and the Governors eventually, but these businessmen are the kind of people who decide things.

These are the kind of people who decided, for example, that in Little Rock they'd had enough. They were the ones who decided in Norfolk and Charlottesville, Va., that the schools were going to be desegregated. And it was these people in Tuscaloosa, Ala., who held a meeting and said, "If desegregation comes to Alabama, we're not going to have it like it was at Oxford."

Now, of course, there they face a formidable opponent in Alabama's Governor George Wallace. But at least they have made their wishes known in the business community, and my bet is that they are going to win. Segregation conflict is not good for business.

Do you see this kind of thing spreading in the South?

No, I don't see it. But I wish for it. I think whatever solution is arrived at, in order to be effective it will have to have the approval of this kind of citizen.

NEGRO AIM: NO COLOR LINE

What does the Negro regard as the solution? What does he really want?

Generally, the Negro wants the color line wiped out, because it restricts his rights and opportunities. That's his general objective. And, to be effective, this has got to be on more than just a token basis.

In 1962 in a public statement you said to the Kennedy Administration: "We've come to collect what you promised us in 1960." What do you feel they promised you? And have they fulfilled that promise by now?

The 1960 platform was the best civil-rights platform ever adopted by the Democratic Party or any party, although the Republican platform came very close to it in 1960. Both of them were very good platforms. The Democrats promised to work for a Fair Employment Practices Act, to put the Civil Rights Commission on a permanent basis; they promised to use legislation, if necessary, to bring about school desegregation. They promised a number of other things.

The Kennedy Administration worked hard on the voting problem—very hard. They filed almost thirty cases to protect the right to vote under the 1957 and 1960 civil-rights acts, which were passed under the Eisenhower Administration.

Bobby Kennedy has worked like a beaver on this voting. He also worked at those emergencies that developed—like the attacks on "Freedom Riders" in Alabama and Mississippi, and the attempt to bar a Negro from the University of Mississippi. He tried to move into that disgraceful situation in Prince Edward County, Va., where they have shut down their whole public-school system rather than educate Negroes on an integrated basis. It's really refreshing to see a man as high in Government as the Attorney General showing outrage at such things.

Finally, the Administration redeemed its pledge on housing after a fashion by issuing the housing order of November 20, 1962. I say "after a fashion" because the order is so limited, so inadequate. But some of their pledges remain wholly unredeemed. The idea of a Fair Employment Practices Commission has gone by the board. If you reread the 1960 platform, you can pretty well check off what has been done and what has not.

Negroes in recent years have voted heavily Democratic. Are they likely to shift that political allegiance?

They might. However, my meaning was exaggerated in the newspaper accounts of a speech I made here recently. I was quoted as saying that the Negro vote is likely to shift to Republican. I don't mean to predict a wholesale shift. I only used that as an illustration of one of several avenues that the Negro might choose to achieve his aims.

Why are Negroes mostly Democrats? Do they relate their troubles in the 1930s to the Republicans?

Not only that. Since Franklin Roosevelt came in, in 1932, the Democrats have had a chance to consolidate their gains among Negroes. They have had all kinds of patronage and prestige jobs to give out on the national, state and local levels. Negroes have become integral parts of the Democratic city machines. You're not going to jar them loose from that very easily.

But it is conceivable that they may shift a bit, and I think it would be helpful. I'm not talking now as a Democrat or as a Republican, but purely as a civil-rights advocate. It doesn't help the Negroes' strategic position to have their voters 79 per cent in the camp of one political party.

Why?

That party begins to take the Negroes and their desires for granted. And at the same time the Republicans say, "How can we expect to get them back?" But, if the Negroes were divided, say 55 per cent or so in one party, then there'd be something for the Democrats to try to hold and for the Republicans to scramble for.

How would Negroes react to Nelson Rockefeller as a presidential candidate?

I would estimate that the Rockefeller name would be very persuasive with Negroes, just as it was in his first campaign for Governor of New York.

Why?

Negroes remember a good many things about the Rockefellers:

the Rockefeller Foundation's General Education Board; the Laura Spelman Rockefeller College for Negro girls in Atlanta, Ga.; the University of Chicago, which was practically built by Rockefeller money and which has had Negroes on the faculty for a long time, and has had some distinguished Negro graduates. And, don't forget, it was Standard Oil which opened its rest rooms to Negro travelers in the 1930s. By and large, Negroes tend to believe that a Rockefeller is something special. Yes, the Rockefeller name has some magic among Negroes. I wouldn't predict anything, of course. . . . But, if you ask me, "Would the Rockefeller name have an influence among Negro voters?" my answer has to be "Yes."

What can the Republicans do to win back the Negro vote?

Well, the Republicans are naïve if they believe that they can get back in one year the Negro votes that they threw away in 1932. They can get back some of them. Dwight D. Eisenhower got 17 per cent of the Negro vote in 1952 and 38 per cent in 1956. But the Republicans refused to go after the rest of the Negro vote. If they had, then Richard Nixon might have won in 1960. But the Republican Party leaders didn't work for the Negro vote. They have been very inept on this. They seemed to think the Negroes were "due" to come back to them—because of Abraham Lincoln, or something.

How does the NAACP stand in relation to Adam Clayton Powell, the Negro Congressman from Harlem?

We've had a little exchange of views with Mr. Powell recently. He made some speeches suggesting that Negroes ought to consider boycotting the NAACP because we have white people in policy making positions—specifically, because we have a white president. Well, Mr. Powell is just talking through his hat. He doesn't know enough about the NAACP and its inside workings to know who supports it and who runs it.

Does Representative Powell belong to the NAACP?

He's a life member.

Is Mr. Powell slipping, politically?

He's not slipping politically. At least, if he is, it is not discernible. You know, in his last election he didn't print a single campaign poster, make a speech or send out a piece of literature. Yet he got 40,000 more votes than his two opponents combined.

What is the basis of his political strength? Is it the church of which he is pastor?

Well, the church is partly the base of it. But Harlem has become used to Adam Powell, and they like the way he talks. Negroes like a man who, as they say, "talks back to the white folks." You see, most Negroes are in no position to talk back to white folks, but Congressman Powell is and he does. That is the reason he's a hero up there in Harlem.

And he does things with a flair, too. He has a way about him. There's a New York newspaper that has just printed a series of articles about him. The first article dwelt upon his charm. Recently, at a Powell rally, one of my staff members sat near some women who kept saying: "Isn't he beautiful? Isn't he wonderful?" They didn't know whether he was talking in Swahili or English and didn't care—just how he looked. This series is very revealing. It helps you to understand why you can't unseat Adam Powell in Harlem. An attack from an outsider just enhances his standing in Harlem.

Some Negroes have complained that the NAACP is not tough enough. And yet, to some white Southerners, mentioning the NAACP is like waving a red flag. How do you account for that?

I account for it by saying that we in the NAACP are the real radicals, the real tough guys, because we espouse the tough ideas—not the tough language. The idea of outlawing racial segregation, deeply imbedded as it had become, was the toughest idea since the drive to abolish slavery. It struck home. It was a root battle. It was ours and we brought it off. Only a truly radical crusade could have brought about the present upheaval and flux.

How do you regard CORE—the Congress of Racial Equality?

I regard CORE as a sort of striking force—like General Patton's spearhead across Europe into the heart of Germany. But the white Southerners who regard the NAACP as most dangerous to their viewpoint are correct. And, if they ever get to believe that the NAACP is the kind of organization they can agree with, then we will have lost something, or they will have abandoned segregation and come over to our side.

HOW SOUTH IS CHANGING

Mr. Wilkins, do you foresee any substantial changes in the South's attitude on Negroes?

I do, and the changes are occurring. They are not very fast, but they are occurring. There are Southerners now who say that integration is going to happen and we ought to help it to happen "our way" rather than, as they say, the "Kennedy way" or the "NAACP way."

I think changes are taking place in the South, and I think the problem is going to be solved in the South.*

Orval E. Faubus

ADDRESS TO THE ILLINOIS PRESS ASSOCIATION

ORVAL E. FAUBUS is Governor of the State of Arkansas, currently serving an unprecedented fifth term. Born in 1910 in Combs, Arkansas, Governor Faubus attended rural schools in that region and was graduated from State Vocational School. He was a rural school teacher at eighteen. From 1939 to 1942 he served as Madison County Circuit Clerk and Recorder, his first elected office. Resigning this post to volunteer as a private in the Army, he served four-and-one-half years with the 35th Infantry Division, separating as major in 1946, after having received numerous battlefield citations including the Bronze Star. He was appointed Acting Postmaster at Huntsville, Arkansas, in 1946. A journalist by training, he purchased the Madison County Record *in 1947 and* The Arkansas Statesman *in 1960. He is still owner and publisher of both publications. From 1949 to 1953 he served as Highway Commissioner, Administrative Assistant to former Governor Sid McMath, and Director of the Highway Department. Installed as Permanent Postmaster at Huntsville in 1953, he resigned in 1954 to run for governor. He won that election and has been Governor of Arkansas ever since. In 1962, he was elected Chairman of the Southern Governors' Conference.*

YOU ARE AN AMERICAN; you love your country. You think it is the greatest and the finest nation on earth. You feel, of course, that there is plenty wrong with it, but, after all is said, you somehow have confidence that we will always come out on top in this country. You seldom think consciously about it, but you feel you have the protection of such a charter of freedom as men have never before known—the Constitution of the United States. It guarantees to you a system of government and a mode of economic life which, whatever the faults or defects, has brought you the highest degree of freedom and abundance among all the world's inhabitants.

Then, one day you pay a visit to your child's school room. The teacher is expounding to the class, including your child, some theories that sound strangely alien to you. They are alien to sound American thinking, but this teacher does not label them as such. The teacher seems to be telling your child and your child's fellow students that these theories are the right ones, the best ones.

You realize that it is all right to teach theories of different kinds, because that is the guarantee of academic freedom; but to propound alien theories as the right ones seems to you to be going a bit too far.

Therefore, you are troubled, and you go to the principal or the superintendent, and you say: "Who is this teacher? He sounds like a communist to me, or at least a fellow traveler."

The principal answers: "He is."

You, of course, are astonished, and ask: "Then, what is he doing here in a local public school that I help support with my taxes?"

"We fired him," the principal says. "We have a law in this state that a teacher in one of our schools who is called before an investigating committee and hides behind the Fifth Amendment to conceal his communist connections is subject to immediate dismissal."

"Then how did he get back in school?" you want to know.

The answer: "The Supreme Court of the United States made us reinstate him in his job, with back pay, too."

This happened in a New England state.

Later on, you need an attorney to handle a small legal matter for you. You pick one at random from the accredited list in your state, and go to see him. You aren't talking to him long before you realize that if you give this man your case, you will have a communist representing you. You leave his office, and go to the state bar association. You demand to know how this young man, not long out of law school, can be an accredited attorney in your state—particularly in the face of all we know about the communist conspiracy.

The bar association official patiently explains to you that the bar examining board in your state has had a rule for some time that any would-be lawyer who is a known communist, or who refuses to say whether he has communist connections, is not admitted to the bar and permitted to practice before the courts. "But," he says, "that was the rule. Now the Supreme Court of the United States has stepped in and told us, a sovereign American state, that we cannot set the standards for who shall and shall not practice law before our own courts. In other words, the court says we can't keep a man from taking the bar examination in this state because he is a communist."

This happened in California.

Then, we take the cases in a number of states, including Kentucky, Tennessee, and Pennsylvania, wherein the duly elected representatives of the people took action to guard against subversion within their boundaries. Laws were enacted prohibiting the advocacy of the overthrow of the respective state governments, as well as our national government, by force and violence. These states recognized that under the guarantees of liberty under the Constitution, anyone has the right to advocate a change or overthrow of any existing political order through the accepted and recognized democratic methods. However, the legislators felt that they were within their rights, as representatives of a free people, to stop the advocacy of the overthrow of their governments by violent means.

After the enactment of the laws, certain communists were arrested and charged under the provisions of the acts. After a fair trial, according to the laws duly enacted, and the scrupulous observation of the Anglo-Saxon precepts of law, they were found guilty. Whereupon, these known communists appealed to the higher state courts, where the convictions were upheld. Further appeal was taken to the United States Supreme Court, and their convictions were set aside and the laws declared null and void. Therefore, the states have been prohibited from taking any steps to prevent the advocacy of the violent overthrow of their existing forms of government.

This happened in the states I mentioned, and others.

We now come to the decision of the United States Supreme Court of May 17, 1954. I will pass this for the moment, for I wish to refer to it later.

At this time, I wish to refer to two more recent decisions of the U. S. Supreme Court.

There is a basic precept of law which has been firmly implanted in the minds of all people of all sections of this nation, from the lowest to the highest ranks of society, and that is that no person under our Constitution and the laws of our states or nation can be placed in double jeopardy. A recent decision of the U. S. Supreme Court has nullified this, another of the constitutional guarantees of freedom under our Bill of Rights.

And then, more recently, just a few days ago, another decision of the U.S. Supreme Court has knocked out or jeopardized another of the liberties which we thought was guaranteed to us by the Bill of Rights.

Remember the history of James Otis and the Writs of Assistance—how, as a great orator of the American Revolution, he stated that "a man's house is his castle," and that so long as a man took refuge in his own home, he should be as safe from molestation as a knight in his castle? Following the Revolution, under the laws adopted by the people under the Constitution, the privacy of any home could not be invaded by any official without due process of law—the acquisition of a proper search warrant.

I now quote a brief item from the recent May 18th issue of *U. S. News & World Report:*

WHEN SEARCH WARRANT ISN'T NEEDED

Washington. No warrant is needed by a public health officer searching your home for rats. So said the Supreme Court by a 5-4 decision. Such power, said the majority, is necessary for maintaining community health. Said dissenting Justice William O. Douglas: "The decision greatly dilutes the right of privacy."

This ruling is all that is needed by any tyrannical form of government that might spring up in Washington. It can merely clothe its agents in the guise of health inspectors, and they can enter homes for any reason to look for anything, under the pretext that they are looking for cockroaches, in the same manner as the infamous secret agents of Hitler, or the secret police of communist Russia.

This ruling can cause other difficulties, and I cite the following news story from a Little Rock newspaper of May 12th:

IMPOSTOR WARNING ISSUED

In an effort to head off anyone from impersonating city health inspectors, Dr. J. N. Laman, North Little Rock health officer, said today rules of the health department prohibit personnel from invading a resident's privacy. Dr. Laman said a resident had telephoned the department to complain that someone posing as an inspector tried to enter his home. The incident occurred since the U.S. Supreme Court's ruling that a health inspector can inspect a residence without first obtaining a warrant, Dr. Laman said.

"Despite the court's ruling the North Little Rock department will abide by its policy," Dr. Laman said. He cautioned citizens to demand credentials from anyone attempting to enter their homes as an inspector.

"City inspectors may inspect a person's residential or commercial premises, but cannot enter a home unless summoned," Dr. Laman emphasized.

There are ten amendments in the Bill of Rights to the Constitution. All close students of history tell us that it became readily apparent that the Constitution, after its adoption by the Constitutional Convention, would not be ratified by a sufficient number of states to put it into force, unless it was clearly understood by the people that it would immediately be amended by the very first Congress. A number of states ratified it with this understanding. In fact, the acts of ratification in some states provided that it was effective only upon a successful adoption of certain amendments.

That is the reason why the very first session of Congress adopted the first ten amendments to the Constitution of the United States, and these ten amendments have since that time become known as the Bill of Rights.

The first amendment contains this phraseology: "Congress shall make no law prohibiting the right of the people to petition the government for a redress of grievances."

Shortly after the September crisis in Little Rock in 1957, two students in a large school in Illinois petitioned the school authorities for segregated classes. A number of other students signed the petition. Whether this was for a prank or whether it was a sincere expression of those students, matters not. As a result of their actions, the two circulators of the petition were immediately suspended from school, and were arrested by the authorities. Charges were placed against them, and they were threatened by the judge on the bench, when they appeared before him, of even further reprisals, should they give countenance to any such activity in the future.

What a contrast with the rulings of the courts, where the right of a citizen to be a communist, and to advocate not just the overthrow of the government, but the overthrow by violent means, which has been upheld by the courts time and again!

The second amendment says: "A well regulated militia, being necessary to the security of a free state, the right of the people to keep and bear arms, shall not be infringed."

I think this amendment was very clearly violated in the federalization of the Arkansas National Guard in September, 1957, in order to deprive the state and its people of the use of said militia. Never before in the history of the republic had such action been taken by the federal authorities.

The third amendment says: "No soldier shall in time of peace be quartered in any house without the consent of the owner, nor in time of war, but in a manner to be prescribed by law."

The sending of 1,200 federal troops of the 101st Airborne Division to Little Rock to occupy any place they saw fit seems to me to be clearly an infringement of the rights guaranteed to the states by this amendment to the Constitution. The federal troops quartered themselves in state property, without permission, and encamped upon and occupied the school grounds of Little Rock institutions, which are supported by state and local monies.

The fourth amendment says in part: "The right of the people to be secure in their persons, houses, papers, and effects, against unreasonable searches and seizures, shall not be violated."

The recent ruling of the Supreme Court, already mentioned earlier, is the first major infringement upon this article in the Bill of Rights.

The fifth amendment reads in part: ". . . nor shall any person be subject for the same offense to be twice put in jeopardy of life or limb."

A recent ruling of the Supreme Court, already mentioned above, infringes upon this basic right of the people, as guaranteed by this amendment to the Constitution.

Amendment six says in part: "In all criminal prosecutions, the accused shall enjoy the right to a speedy and public trial, by an impartial jury of the state and district wherein the crime shall have been committed."

You are all aware of the recent efforts of certain so-called civil rights advocates in the Congress to pass a law taking away the right of trial by jury. This would clearly have been an infringement of this constitutional guarantee.

Amendment nine reads: "The enumeration in the Constitution of certain rights shall not be construed to deny or disparage others retained by the people."

And the tenth amendment reads: "The powers not delegated to the United States by the Constitution, nor prohibited by it to the states, are reserved to the states respectively, or to the people."

We come now to the Supreme Court decision of May 17, 1954. In this connection, we hear a great deal of the phrase, "supreme law of the land." Who makes the laws of the land?—The Congress, for the nation, and the legislative bodies, for the respective states. These are the only law-making bodies. No law can be changed, and no new law can be made, except through the functioning of Congress or the state legislatures.

If we are to accept the phrase, "supreme law of the land," as coming from the U. S. Supreme Court, then what was the law of the land on *May 16,* 1954? The law of the land and the laws of the states were that *separate but equal* facilities were constitutional.

If *separate but equal* was the law of the land on May 16th, then what brought about the change in the law from one day to the next? Had our Constitution been abolished, and a new one written? Had our Constitution been amended, as is provided for in that document itself? Had Congress changed the law, thus making necessary a new interpretation by the court?

None of these things had occurred. Therefore, if the law changed from one day to the next without any of these actions taking place, then the court must have made a new law itself. And we, all of us who are informed citizens, know beyond any peradventure of a doubt, that the making of laws is not within the scope and jurisdiction of the court, and that the courts have no authority in this field whatsoever.

We must then accept as a basis for the court's ruling that it, the membership at that time, had decided that all of the previous rulings, over a period of almost 100 years, had been in error, and that the court at that time was taking upon itself the grave responsibility of correcting this error, without any action by the people's representatives or the people themselves. If this was the basis of the court's ruling, might not this ruling also be in error? And, if that be the case, may not the people oppose the ruling as being in error?

I say that the people may—that they have that right, as free citizens of this republic, just as did the citizens of the republic in the 1850's, when they properly opposed the Dred Scott decision, which was later overruled and nullified.

Samuel B. Pettengill, former member of Congress from Indiana, has been quoted in the December 8, 1958, issue of *Human Events* as having this to say:

> But more important than integration or segregation is the preservation of the Constitution against the brain-washing of the American people now going on, to support the curious notion that a decision of the U.S. Supreme Court—any decision—is "law." President Roosevelt said in 1930: "The preservation of home rule by the states . . . is a

fundamental necessity, if we are to remain a truly united country. . . . We are safe as long as the individual home rule of the states is scrupulously preserved and fought for whenever it seems in danger."

Again Congressman Pettengill said:

It is a maxim of the law, centuries old, that the intention of the law giver is the law. As the Supreme Court once said: "The whole hope of constitutional construction is to give effect to the intention of the framers of the instrument and, additionally, to the intention of the people in adopting it."

As evidence that the proposing of the fourteenth amendment by the Congress was not intended to forbid the establishment and maintenance of segregated schools, the Congress at the same time passed a law requiring segregated schools in the District of Columbia. Also, the state legislatures, in ratifying the fourteenth amendment, passed statutes requiring or permitting segregated schools.

There is not a word in the Constitution which gives the Supreme Court the power or right to enact laws or to amend the Constitution by giving it a meaning which the proposing Congress or ratifying state legislatures, or the people, did not intend it to have.

Congressman Pettengill also said:

The only persons who have the power or right to amend the Constitution are the people, in the manner set forth in the Constitution. The only persons who have the power or the right to enact federal law are the members of the House and the Senate, and the President by his approval, or, in case of treaties, the members of the Senate. This is what is meant by government of law, and Congress has never said that segregated schools are against the law.

Thomas Jefferson wrote:

It is a very dangerous doctrine to consider the judges the ultimate arbiters of all constitutional questions. The Constitution has elected no such single tribunal.

Jefferson further wrote:

> The germ of dissolution of our federal government is in the constitution of the federal judiciary; an irresponsible body, working like gravity by night and by day, *gaining a little today and a little tomorrow,* and advancing its noiseless step like a thief, over the field of jurisdiction, *until all shall be usurped from the States,* and the government of all be consolidated into one. To this I am opposed; because when all governments, domestic and foreign, in little as in great things, *shall be drawn to Washington as the center of all power, it will render powerless the checks provided of one government on another, and will become as venal and oppressive as the government from which we separated.*

George Washington had this to say about the division or distribution of powers:

> If, in the opinion of the people, the distribution or modification of the constitutional powers be in any particular wrong, let it be corrected by an amendment in the way which the Constitution designates. But let there be no change by usurpation; for, though this in one instance may be the instrument of good, it is the customary weapon by which free governments are destroyed.

The point which I wish to make from all this wisdom of both the past and the present is the inescapable fact that the safeguards of liberty enacted for the protection of the people are fast being whittled away by the illegal usurpation of powers by the federal government, principally the U.S. Supreme Court.

Now, what of the racial question, in relation to these problems? It is merely one facet of the problem. It is just one of the many points of conflict. Because of its inflammatory nature, it has been highlighted out of all proportion to its true relation to the overall problem of the division of powers and the retention of constitutional government.

The way most of us feel in the South, and the way most segregationists feel, is fairly well stated by Noel Smith, editor of the *Baptist Bible Tribune* of Springfield, Missouri:

The Negro has as much moral and constitutional right to be on this continent as the rest of us. If anything, he has more right. He was brought here against his will, in the chains of slavery. In the North and East, and very especially in the South, he has since he arrived here been the black, sweaty burden-bearer. He has on the whole borne more than his share of the heavy load. And most of the time he has borne it with rhythm in his step, faith in his heart, and music on his lips.

I not only respect this man, I have—and always have had—a deep and genuine affection for him. I have no patronizing attitude toward him. I recognize the inherent dignity of his person. His "place," so far as I am concerned, is wherever his character and ability lead him. I want him to get the same value for his tax dollar that I get for mine. I want his child to have the same advantages and opportunities that mine has. Since the Creator Himself is no respecter of persons, neither am I.

And if whites and Negroes wish to live together, eat together, and attend school and church together, I am in favor of their being permitted to do so. Under the spirit and letter of our Constitution they have that right.

But I am opposed to the Supreme Court of the United States forcing whites and Negroes to associate themselves together in this way against their mutual desires and against their mutual interests. I believe in the right of voluntary association. I am opposed to the Supreme Court's proposition of legal compulsion.

As to the South, the radicals and egghead intellectuals are all the time screaming how the "poor Negro is persecuted" down there. Here is the way the poor Negro is persecuted in the South.

I have before me *The Negro Year Book for 1949.* It was published by Macmillan. I wrote the publishers for a later copy and they replied that the book was not now being published. This book was edited by Florence Murray, a brilliant Negro newspaper woman.

Here is what we find in this *The Negro Year Book for 1949:*

On page 200 we have a list of Negro banking institutions. Fourteen Negro banks are listed in the United States. All but two are in the South. The two exceptions are Citizens & Southern Bank & Trust Co., Philadelphia, and Industrial Bank of Washington, D.C. The Citizens Trust Co. of Atlanta has total deposits of $3,793,718, capital of $100,000 and total assets of $4,009,666. The total capital of Southern Negro banks is $1,170,279, while the total capital of the Philadelphia and Washington banks is $225,000.

On pages 205–209 are listed the local Negro business leagues and chambers of commerce. There are 124 such organizations in the United States. All but sixteen of them are in the South. Ohio has the largest number north of the Ohio River; it has four—the exact number in Arkansas. Governor Williams' Michigan is listed as having but one. The *Chicago Tribune's* Illinois has but three. Chief Justice Warren's California has but one. Georgia has eight, and Texas has forty-two. Not a single one is listed in Indiana—which includes Indianapolis, to which the Negroes have been going from the South since the button-shoe age.

And on page 201 of the book we read this: "Among the larger Negro-operated (insurance) companies which had more than twenty-five million dollars worth of insurance in force in 1944 were the Atlanta Life Insurance Company, Atlanta, Ga., with more than 101 million dollars; the North Carolina Mutual, Durham, N.C., more than 89 million dollars; the Supreme Liberty Life, Chicago, Ill., more than 83 million dollars; the Universal Life, Memphis, Tenn., more than 38 million dollars; the Pilgrim Health and Life in Augusta, Ga., more than 36 million dollars; and the Africo-American Life, Jacksonville, Fla., more than 25 million dollars."

The Negro's own records show here—and everywhere else—that the greatest progress the Negro has made—and is making—has not been in Africa, not in any country dominated by Great Britain, not in the East, not in the North, not in the West, but in the South.

In the South the Negro not only has made more social and economic progress, enjoyed more freedom and liberty, more security, and realized more dignity of person than he has ever known anywhere on earth, but it is also in the South that the Negro has found the only people he has ever known that really love him.

Now, what of the physical aspects of the Little Rock situation, and the racial question in Arkansas? In the state at large, more public schools have been voluntarily and peaceably integrated than in nine other Southern states combined. There are more Negroes in one public school in Arkansas than there are in the integrated schools of the entire area of the so-called moderate state of North Carolina.

The University of Arkansas and all institutions of higher learning, except two, have been peaceably integrated. My own son attended one of these state-supported, integrated colleges.

All forms of transportation have been integrated in Arkansas for some time.

Both the Democratic and Republican parties of Arkansas have had Negroes as members of their state central committees.

In the field of state service, the McRae Sanatorium for Negro tubercular patients is one of the best run facilities in the state, under the able leadership of a Negro doctor and a staff made up entirely of Negro personnel. A. M. & N. College for Negroes at Pine Bluff, Arkansas, receives the highest appropriation per student of any institution of higher learning in the state. The Negro school for the blind and deaf is one of the finest in the South, and is ably administered by a Negro superintendent and Negro personnel. The school for delinquent Negro girls at Fargo in Monroe County has entirely new and modern facilities, finer than are provided for any white institution of a similar nature in the state. The school for delinquent Negro boys has had a number of improvements during my administration, and is now being almost entirely rebuilt after the disastrous fire which resulted in the tragic loss of twenty-one lives.

In this connection, I wish to state that the board was composed of both Negro and white men. The superintendent and all personnel were Negroes. If there is any blame to bear or credit to receive for the administration of this institution, or anything that has happened there, the blame or the credit must rest with the Negro personnel.

A great deal has been said about civil rights in the voting field. There has been no difficulty in this area in Arkansas for many years past. Each and everyone votes freely in Arkansas, and there has never been the slightest incident involving voting rights since I entered actively the field of state politics some ten years ago. In fact, Negroes have been elected to office on the local level in Arkansas for some years.

I am sure that many of you and millions of others are not aware of the excellent relations which have existed between the races in Arkansas. Many of you are likewise unaware of the great progress that is being made by all people in the state, regardless of race, creed, or color. All of these facts which I have just cited to you were freely available to the host of reporters that swarmed over the state, and who have continued to visit the state since September of 1957. Either they declined to relate the facts, all of them, as they found them, or else certain facts were deleted by their editors after the receipt of their stories. This situation has come to be known as the Paper Curtain. It exists not only in the South, but throughout the nation.

A striking example of this was a recent occurrence in the city of Washington. I was privileged to attend the dinner given by the Good Government Society, at which the George Washington awards were made to Senator John L. McClellan of Arkansas and Admiral Lewis Strauss. There were more than 800 people in attendance from all over the country. The oration of the evening was made by Senator Barry Goldwater of Arizona. The presentation to Senator McClellan was made by Congressman Charles Halleck of Indiana, the Republican leader in the House. The award to Admiral Strauss was made by Senator Harry Byrd of Virginia.

These are prominent men of ability. Many things were said which I, as a citizen, as a public official, and as a newspaper man, thought were newsworthy. I looked in the newspapers of Washington, D. C., the next day to see what had been said about the meeting. Not one single word could I find of this most newsworthy event.

Why? I can reach only one conclusion at the moment. They did not say the things which were pleasing and suitable to the pseudo-liberals and fuzzy-minded left-wingers who today are writing most of the news and publishing most of the big newspapers and magazines of this nation. I have been a close observer of this situation now for some time. There is too much effort on the part of the national press in both the newspaper and magazine field to write the news as they want it to happen, and not as it occurs. They color, slant, and distort the stories to conform to their personal views and ideologies, instead of reporting the facts as they are.

This trend is nation-wide, and has progressed to an alarming extent.

I remember that when I was elected Governor of Arkansas in 1954, having emerged from a bitter campaign and charges of communistic leanings, growing out of my brief connection with the "Red" Commonwealth College, I received far more favorable publicity at that time than I have since. The many worthwhile accomplishments that may have been made for the State of Arkansas during my administration have gone unnoticed. In this I do not refer to the state vs. federal power struggle, in which I have been engaged for more than a year.

I recall that on my first trip to Washington, I was put in touch with people who introduced me to Drew Pearson. I was invited to appear on his nation-wide television and radio program. I was introduced to other writers, some of national fame, and I received generally favorable notice by the ultra-liberal press and commentators. Among those who promoted my favorable press coverage then was the man who is now my chief critic, Mr. Harry Ashmore, executive editor of the *Arkansas Gazette* in Little Rock.

There has been little, if any, change on my position on any of these questions of government from 1954 to the present time. My conviction and my stand, as an official and as a citizen, has always been, and is now, that the people are sovereign, that power is inherent with the people, and that it must continue to be so, if we have a democracy and are to continue to have a democracy. I contend that the people are the best judges of what is good for them or what is bad for them. I reject, as the founding fathers rejected, the theory of government that those in authority should hand down from above all the decisions on our problems, without any consultation with the people, and in complete disregard of the wishes of the majority.

Certainly, we all recognize that the people may make mistakes. But so long as they have the right to make a mistake, they also have the power to correct it. Unless we observe this fundamental precept of democracy, then liberty and freedom are on the wane. We must reaffirm the basic precepts of democracy, rule by the consent of the governed, or our nation will go the way so many others have gone.

Never, as an idealistic youth, reading of the goodness of our leaders, the greatness of our history, and the majestic principles of freedom, as embodied under our Constitution and in our precepts of democracy, did I ever dream of all the forms of pressure and inducements that could be brought to bear upon an individual—pressure and inducements to foresake the sentiments and ideas dearest to the American heart, by changing my policies in matters such as have faced me in the State of Arkansas. The harassment and the hammering is constant and never ceasing. They pose as friends in an effort to persuade, beguile, or deceive. They bring constant pressure in the form of never-ceasing criticism in the press and by other means. They attempt to cow and subdue by the threats of overwhelming force, which cannot be successfully resisted.

Then they offer, on the other hand, a period of security from the never-ending pressure and harassment—a period of peace for one's self, of tranquility for one's family. And, in addition, praise, which is sweet to the ears of any individual, and possible advancement, which beckons to most good men. There are few indeed who will not pause to consider these two alternatives, and, having paused to consider, there are fewer still who will not yield.

I am more than grateful for the privilege of speaking to you of the Illinois Press Association. The owners and editors of the small newspapers of America can constitute the greatest safeguard of Americanism among the nation's institutions. You are so close to the people that you do not choose to color, distort, and slant the news as is now being done by so many of the large newspapers and magazines. And you are so close to the people that you could not get away with it if you tried.

I leave you with these thoughts:

Can the republic long endure as a union of states, with the constant whittling away of the powers of the states and the people?

After the unwarranted invasion of the rights of the states to control their own schools, how long will it be until the school authorities are told what to teach, and what not to teach—what views the teacher must hold, or must not hold—who can teach and who cannot teach?

Look at the trend in the tax field. In 1932, federal tax was

22.7%, state and local 77.3%; in 1940, federal tax was 38.6%, state and local 61.4%; in 1957, federal tax was 73.0%, state and local 27.0%.

No wonder the states find it so difficult to finance the cost of state and local government.

We in Arkansas do not wish to tell you in Illinois, or any other state, how you should solve your problems. Is it too much to ask for ourselves the same consideration?

We have that right under the Constitution, if it can be restored to a sacred, living document, and does not become merely a scrap of paper.

Martin Luther King, Jr.

LETTER FROM BIRMINGHAM'S JAIL

MARTIN LUTHER KING, JR., catapulted into national and international prominence when, as president of the Montgomery (Ala.) Improvement Association, he helped sponsor the successful bus boycott in that city. He now serves as president of the Southern Christian Leadership Conference and has emerged during the last decade as the leader of the Negroes' nonviolent crusade against discrimination. Born in Atlanta, Georgia, in 1929, Dr. King obtained degrees from Morehouse College, Crozer Theological Seminary and Boston University. A former pastor of Montgomery's Dexter Avenue Baptist Church, he currently shares a co-pastorate with his father at Atlanta's Ebenezer Baptist Church. In 1956 he was selected one of ten outstanding personalities by Time *Magazine, which also named him, in 1963, "Man of the Year." He has been the recipient of several honorary degrees from leading American institutions of higher learning. Besides contributing to popular and religious periodicals, Dr. King is author of* Stride Toward Freedom *and other books.*

MARTIN LUTHER KING, JR.
Birmingham City Jail
April 16, 1963

Bishop C. C. J. CARPENTER
Bishop JOSEPH A. DURICK
Rabbi MILTON L. GRAFMAN
Bishop PAUL HARDIN
Bishop NOLAN B. HARMON
The Rev. GEORGE M. MURRAY

The Rev. EDWARD V. RAMAGE
The Rev. EARL STALLINGS

My dear Fellow Clergymen,

While confined here in the Birmingham City Jail, I came across your recent statement calling our present activities "unwise and untimely." Seldom, if ever, do I pause to answer criticism of my work and ideas. If I sought to answer all of the criticisms that cross my desk, my secretaries would be engaged in little else in the course of the day, and I would have no time for constructive work. But since I feel that you are men of genuine goodwill and your criticisms are sincerely set forth, I would like to answer your statement in what I hope will be patient and reasonable terms.

I think I should give the reason for my being in Birmingham, since you have been influenced by the argument of "outsiders coming in." I have the honor of serving as president of the Southern Christian Leadership Conference, an organization operating in every Southern state, with headquarters in Atlanta, Georgia. We have some eighty-five affiliate organizations all across the South—one being the Alabama Christian Movement for Human Rights. Whenever necessary and possible we share staff, educational, and financial resources with our affiliates. Several months ago our local affiliate here in Birmingham invited us to be on call to engage in a nonviolent direct action program if such were deemed necessary. We readily consented and when the hour came we lived up to our promises. So I am here, along with several members of my staff, because we were invited here. I am here because I have basic organizational ties here. Beyond this, I am in Birmingham because injustice is here. Just as the eighth century prophets left their little villages and carried their "thus saith the Lord" far beyond the boundaries of their home towns, and just as the Apostle Paul left his little village of Tarsus and carried the gospel of Jesus Christ to practically every hamlet and city of the Graeco-Roman world, I too am compelled to carry the gospel of freedom beyond my particular home town. Like Paul, I must constantly respond to the Macedonian call for aid.

Moreover, I am cognizant of the interrelatedness of all communities and states. I cannot sit idly by in Atlanta and not be concerned about what happens in Birmingham. Injustice anywhere is a threat to justice everywhere. We are caught in an inescapable network of mutuality, tied in a single garment of destiny. Whatever affects one directly affects all indirectly. Never again can we afford to live with the narrow, provincial "outside agitator" idea. Anyone who lives inside the United States can never be considered an outsider anywhere in this country.

You deplore the demonstrations that are presently taking place in Birmingham. But I am sorry that your statement did not express a similar concern for the conditions that brought the demonstrations into being. I am sure that each of you would want to go beyond the superficial social analyst who looks merely at effects, and does not grapple with underlying causes. I would not hesitate to say that it is unfortunate that so-called demonstrations are taking place in Birmingham at this time, but I would say in more emphatic terms that it is even more unfortunate that the white power structure of this city left the Negro community with no other alternative.

In any nonviolent campaign there are four basic steps: (1) collection of the facts to determine whether injustices are alive; (2) negotiation; (3) self-purification; and (4) direct action. We have gone through all of these steps in Birmingham. There can be no gainsaying of the fact that racial injustice engulfs this community. Birmingham is probably the most thoroughly segregated city in the United States. Its ugly record of police brutality is known in every section of this country. Its unjust treatment of Negroes in the courts is a notorious reality. There have been more unsolved bombings of Negro homes and churches in Birmingham than any city in this nation. These are the hard, brutal, and unbelievable facts. On the basis of these conditions Negro leaders sought to negotiate with the city fathers. But the political leaders consistently refused to engage in good faith negotiation.

Then came the opportunity last September to talk with some of the leaders of the economic community. In these negotiating sessions certain promises were made by the merchants—such as the promise to remove the humiliating racial signs from the stores. On the basis of these promises Rev. Shuttlesworth and the leaders of the Alabama Christian Movement for Human Rights agreed to call a moratorium on any type of demonstrations. As the weeks and months unfolded we realized that we were the victims of a broken promise. The signs remained. As in so many experiences of the past we were confronted with blasted hopes, and the dark shadow of a deep disappointment settled upon us. So we had no alternative except that of preparing for direct action, whereby we would present our very bodies as a means of laying our case before the conscience of the local and national community. We were not unmindful of the difficulties involved. So we decided to go through a process of self-purification. We started having workshops on nonviolence and repeatedly asked ourselves the questions, "Are you able to accept blows without retaliating?" "Are you able to endure the ordeals of jail?"

We decided to set our direct action program around the Easter season, realizing that with the exception of Christmas, this was the largest shopping period of the year. Knowing that a strong economic withdrawal program would be the by-product of direct action, we felt that this was the best time to bring pressure on the merchants for the needed changes. Then it occurred to us that the March election was ahead, and so we speedily decided to postpone action until after election day. When we discovered that Mr. Connor was in the run-off, we decided again to postpone action so that the demonstrations could not be used to cloud the issues. At this time we agreed to begin our nonviolent witness the day after the run-off.

This reveals that we did not move irresponsibly into direct action. We too wanted to see Mr. Connor defeated; so we went through postponement after postponement to aid in this community need. After this we felt that direct action could be delayed no longer.

You may well ask, "Why direct action? Why sit-ins, marches, etc.? Isn't negotiation a better path?" You are exactly right in your call for negotiation. Indeed, this is the purpose of direct action. Nonviolent direct action seeks to create such a crisis and establish such creative tension that a community that has constantly refused to negotiate is forced to confront the issue. It seeks so to dramatize the issue that it can no longer be ignored. I just referred to the creation of tension as a part of the work of the nonviolent resister. This may sound rather shocking. But I must confess that I am not afraid of the word tension. I have earnestly worked and preached against violent tension, but there is a type of constructive nonviolent tension that is necessary for growth. Just as Socrates felt that it was necessary to create a tension in the mind so that individuals could rise from the bondage of myths and half-truths to the unfettered realm of creative analysis and objective appraisal, we must see the need of having nonviolent gadflies to create the kind of tension in society that will help men rise from the dark depths of prejudice and racism to the majestic heights of understanding and brotherhood. So the purpose of the direct action is to create a situation so crisis-packed that it will inevitably open the door to negotiation. We, therefore, concur with you in your call for negotiation. Too long has our beloved Southland been bogged down in the tragic attempts to live in monologue rather than dialogue.

One of the basic points in your statement is that our acts are untimely. Some have asked, "Why didn't you give the new administration time to act?" The only answer that I can give to this inquiry is that the new administration must be prodded about as much as the outgoing one before it acts. We will be sadly mistaken if we feel that the election of Mr. Boutwell will bring the millennium to Birmingham. While Mr. Boutwell is much more articulate and gentle than Mr. Connor, they are both segregationists, dedicated to the task of maintaining the status quo. The hope I see in Mr. Boutwell is that he will be reasonable enough to see the futility of massive resistance to desegregation. But he will not see this without pressure from the devotees of civil rights. My friends, I must say to you that we have not made a single gain in civil rights without determined legal and nonviolent pressure. History is the long and tragic story of the fact that privileged groups seldom give up their privileges voluntarily. Individuals may see the moral light and voluntarily give up their unjust posture; but as Reinhold Niebuhr has reminded us, groups are more immoral than individuals.

We know through painful experience that freedom is never voluntarily given by the oppressor; it must be demanded by the oppressed. Frankly I have never yet engaged in a direct action movement that was "well timed," according to the timetable of those who have not suffered unduly from the disease of segregation. For years now I have heard the word "Wait!" It rings in the ear of every Negro with a piercing familiarity. This "wait" has almost always meant "never." It has been a tranquilizing thalidomide, relieving the emotional stress for a moment, only to give birth to an ill-formed infant of frustration. We must come to see with the distinguished jurist of yesterday that "justice too long delayed is justice denied." We have waited for more than three hundred and forty years for our constitutional and God-given rights. The nations of Asia and Africa are moving with jet-like speed toward the goal of political independence, and we still creep at horse and buggy pace toward the gaining of a cup of coffee at a lunch counter.

I guess it is easy for those who have never felt the stinging darts of segregation to say wait. But when you have seen vicious mobs lynch your mothers and fathers at will and drown your sisters and brothers at whim; when you have seen hate-filled policemen curse, kick, brutalize, and even kill your black brothers and sisters with impunity; when you see the vast majority of your twenty million Negro brothers smothering in an air-tight cage of poverty in the midst of an affluent society; when you suddenly find your tongue twisted and your speech stammering as you seek to explain to your six-year-old daughter why she can't go to the public amusement park that has just been advertised on television, and see tears welling up in her little eyes when she is told that Funtown is closed to colored children, and see the depressing clouds of inferiority begin to form in her little mental sky, and see her begin to distort her little personality by unconsciously developing a bitterness toward white people; when you have to concoct an answer for a five-year-old son asking in agonizing pathos: "Daddy, why do white people treat colored people so mean?"; when you take a cross country drive and find it necessary to sleep night after night in the uncomfortable corners of your automobile because no motel will accept you; when you are humiliated day in and day out by nagging signs reading "white" men and "colored"; when your first name becomes "nigger" and your middle name becomes "boy" (however old you are) and your last name becomes "John," and when your wife and mother are never given the respected title "Mrs."; when you are harried by day and haunted by night by the fact that you are a Negro, living constantly at tip-toe stance never quite knowing what to expect next, and plagued with inner fears and outer resentments; when you are forever fighting a degenerating sense of "nobodiness";—then you will understand why we find it difficult to wait. There comes a time when the cup of endurance runs over, and men are no longer willing to be plunged into an abyss of injustice where they experience the bleakness of corroding despair. I hope, sirs, you can understand our legitimate and unavoidable impatience.

You express a great deal of anxiety over our willingness to break laws. This is certainly a legitimate concern. Since we so diligently urge people to obey the Supreme Court's decision of 1954 outlawing segregation in the public schools, it is rather strange and paradoxical to find us consciously breaking laws. One may well ask, "How can you advocate breaking some laws and obeying others?" The answer is found in the fact that there are two types of laws: There are *just l*aws and there are *unjust* laws. I would be the first to advocate obeying just laws. One has not only a legal but moral responsibility to obey just laws. Conversely, one has a moral responsibility to disobey unjust laws. I would agree with Saint Augustine that "An unjust law is no law at all."

Now what is the difference between the two? How does one determine when a law is just or unjust? A just law is a man-made code that squares with the moral law or the law of God. An unjust law is a code that is out of harmony with the moral law. To put it in the terms of Saint Thomas Aquinas, an unjust law is a human law that is not rooted in eternal and natural law. Any law that uplifts human personality is just. Any law that degrades human personality is unjust. All segregation statutes are unjust because segregation distorts the soul and damages the personality. It gives the segregator a false sense of superiority and the segregated a false sense of inferiority. To use the words of Martin Buber, the great

Jewish philosopher, segregation substitutes an "I-it" relationship for the "I-thou" relationship, and ends up relegating persons to the status of things. So segregation is not only politically, economically, and sociologically unsound, but it is morally wrong and sinful. Paul Tillich has said that sin is separation. Isn't segregation an existential expression of man's tragic separation, an expression of his awful estrangement, his terrible sinfulness? So I can urge men to obey the 1954 decision of the Supreme Court because it is morally right, and I can urge them to disobey segregation ordinances because they are morally wrong.

Let us turn to a more concrete example of just and unjust laws. An unjust law is a code that a majority inflicts on a minority that is not binding on itself. This is *difference* made legal. On the other hand a just law is a code that a majority compels a minority to follow that it is willing to follow itself. This is *sameness* made legal. Let me give another explanation. An unjust law is a code inflicted upon a minority which that minority had no part in enacting or creating because they did not have the unhampered right to vote. Who can say the legislature of Alabama which set up the segregation laws was democratically elected? Throughout the state of Alabama all types of conniving methods are used to prevent Negroes from becoming registered voters and there are some counties without a single Negro registered to vote despite the fact that the Negro constitutes a majority of the population. Can any law set up in such a state be considered democratically structured?

These are just a few examples of unjust and just laws. There are some instances when a law is just on its face but unjust in its application. For instance, I was arrested Friday on a charge of parading without a permit. Now there is nothing wrong with an ordinance which requires a permit for a parade, but when the ordinance is used to preserve segregation and to deny citizens the First Amendment privilege of peaceful assembly and peaceful protest, then it becomes unjust.

I hope you can see the distinction I am trying to point out. In no sense do I advocate evading or defying the law as the rabid segregationist would do. This would lead to anarchy. One who breaks an unjust law must do it *openly, lovingly* (not hatefully as the white mothers did in New Orleans when they were seen on television screaming "nigger, nigger, nigger") and with a willingness to accept the penalty. I submit that an individual who breaks a law that conscience tells him is unjust, and willingly accepts the penalty by staying in jail to arouse the conscience of the community over its injustice, is in reality expressing the very highest respect for law.

Of course there is nothing new about this kind of civil disobedience. It was seen sublimely in the refusal of Shadrach, Meshach, and Abednego to obey the laws of Nebuchadnezzar because a higher moral law was involved. It was practiced superbly by the early Christians who were willing to face hungry lions and the excruciating pain of chopping blocks, before submitting to certain unjust laws of the Roman Empire. To a degree academic freedom is a reality today because Socrates practiced civil disobedience.

We can never forget that everything Hitler did in Germany was "legal" and everything the Hungarian freedom fighters did in Hungary was "illegal." It was "illegal" to aid and comfort a Jew in Hitler's Germany. But I am sure that, if I had lived in Germany during that time, I would have aided and comforted my Jewish brothers even though it was illegal. If I lived in a communist country today where certain principles dear to the Christian faith are suppressed, I believe I would openly advocate disobeying these anti-religious laws.

I must make two honest confessions to you, my Christian and Jewish brothers. First I must confess that over the last few years I have been gravely disappointed with the white moderate. I have almost reached the regrettable conclusion that the Negroes' great stumbling block in the stride toward freedom is not the White Citizens' "Counciler" or the Ku Klux Klanner, but the white moderate who is more devoted to "order" than to justice; who prefers a negative peace which is the absence of tension to a positive peace which is the presence of justice; who constantly says "I agree with you in the goal you seek, but I can't agree with your methods of direct action"; who paternalistically feels that he can set the time-table for another man's freedom; who lives by the myth of time and who constantly advises the Negro to wait until a "more convenient season." Shallow understanding from people of good will is more frustrating than absolute misunderstanding from people of ill will. Lukewarm acceptance is much more bewildering than outright rejection.

I had hoped that the white moderate would understand that law and order exist for the purpose of establishing justice, and that when they fail to do this they become the dangerously structured dams that block the flow of social progress. I had hoped that the white moderate would understand that the present tension in the South is merely a necessary phase of the transition from an obnoxious negative peace, where the Negro passively accepted his unjust plight, to a substance-filled positive peace, where all men will respect the dignity and worth of human personality. Actually, we who engage in nonviolent direct action are not the creators of tension. We merely bring to the surface the hidden tension that is already alive. We bring it out in the open where it can be seen and dealt with. Like a boil that can never be cured as long as it is covered up but must be opened with all its pus-flowing ugliness to the natural medicines of air and light, injustice must likewise be exposed, with all of the tension its exposing creates, to the light of human conscience and the air of national opinion before it can be cured.

In your statement you asserted that our actions, even though peaceful, must be condemned because they precipitate violence. But can this assertion be logically made? Isn't this like condemning the robbed man because his possession of money precipitated the evil act of robbery? Isn't this like condemning Socrates because his unswerving commitment to truth and his philosophical delvings precipitated the misguided popular mind to make him drink the hemlock? Isn't this like condemning Jesus because His unique God consciousness and never-ceasing devotion to His will precipitated the evil act of crucifixion? We must come to see, as federal courts have consistently affirmed, that it is immoral to urge an individual to withdraw his efforts to gain his basic constitutional rights because the quest precipitates violence. Society must protect the robbed and punish the robber.

I had also hoped that the white moderate would reject the myth of time. I received a letter this morning from a white brother in Texas which said: "All Christians know that the colored people will receive equal rights eventually, but is it possible that you are in too great of a religious hurry? It has taken Christianity almost 2000 years to accomplish what it has. The teachings of Christ take time to come to earth." All that is said here grows out of a tragic misconception of time. It is the strangely irrational notion that there is something in the very flow of time that will inevitably cure all ills. Actually time is neutral. It can be used either destructively or constructively. I am coming to feel that the people of ill will have used time much more effectively than the people of good will. We will have to repent in this generation not merely for the vitriolic words and actions of the bad people, but for the appalling silence of the good people. We must come to see that human progress never rolls in on wheels of inevitability. It comes through the tireless efforts and persistent work of men willing to be co-workers with God, and without this hard work time itself becomes an ally of the forces of social stagnation.

We must use time creatively, and forever realize that the time is always ripe to do right. Now is the time to make real the promise of democracy, and transform our pending national elegy into a creative psalm of brotherhood. Now is the time to lift our national policy from the quicksand of racial injustice to the solid rock of human dignity.

You spoke of our activity in Birmingham as extreme. At first I was rather disappointed that fellow clergymen would see my nonviolent efforts as those of the extremist. I started thinking about the fact that I stand in the middle of two opposing forces in the Negro community. One is a force of complacency made up of Negroes who, as a result of long years of oppression, have been so completely drained of self-respect and a sense of "somebodiness" that they have adjusted to segregation, and of a few Negroes in the middle class who, because of a degree of academic and economic security, and because at points they profit by segregation, have unconsciously become insensitive to the problems of the masses. The other force is one of bitterness and hatred and comes perilously close to advocating violence. It is expressed in the various black nationalist groups that are springing up over the nation, the largest and best known being Elijah Muhammad's Muslim movement. This movement is nourished by the contemporary frustration over the continued existence of racial discrimination. It is made up of people who have lost faith in America, who have absolutely repudiated Christianity, and who have concluded that the white man is an incurable "devil." I have tried to stand between these two forces saying that we need not follow the "do-nothing-ism" of the complacent or the hatred and despair of the black nationalist. There is the more excellent way of love and nonviolent protest. I'm grateful to God that, through the Negro church, the dimension of nonviolence entered our struggle. If this philosophy had not emerged I am convinced that by now many streets of the South would be flowing with floods of blood. And I am further convinced that if our white brothers dismiss us as "rabble rousers" and "outside agitators"—those of us who are working through the channels of nonviolent direct action—and refuse to support our nonviolent efforts, millions of Negroes, out of frustration and despair, will seek solace and security in black nationalist ideologies, a development that will lead inevitably to a frightening racial nightmare.

Oppressed people cannot remain oppressed forever. The urge for freedom will eventually come. This is what has happened to the American Negro. Something within has reminded him of his birthright of freedom; something without has reminded him that he can gain it. Consciously and unconsciously, he has been swept in by what the Germans call the *Zeitgeist,* and with his black brothers of Africa, and his brown and yellow brothers of Asia, South America, and the Caribbean, he is moving with a sense of cosmic urgency toward the promised land of racial justice. Recognizing this vital urge that has engulfed the Negro community, one should readily understand public demonstrations. The Negro has many pent-up resentments and latent frustrations. He has to get them out. So let him march sometime; let him have his prayer pilgrimages to the city hall; understand why he must have sit-ins and freedom rides. If his repressed emotions do not come out in these nonviolent ways, they will come out in ominous expressions of violence. This is not a threat; it is a fact of history. So I have not said to my people, "Get rid of your discontent." But I have tried to say that this normal and healthy discontent can be channeled through the creative outlet of nonviolent direct action. Now this approach is being dismissed as extremist. I must admit that I was initially disappointed in being so categorized.

But as I continued to think about the matter I gradually gained a bit of satisfaction from being considered an extremist. Was not Jesus an extremist in love? "Love your enemies, bless them that curse you, pray for them that despitefully use you." Was not Amos an extremist for justice? "Let justice roll down like waters and righteousness like a mighty stream." Was not Paul an extremist for the gospel of Jesus Christ? "I bear in my body the marks of the Lord Jesus." Was not Martin Luther an extremist? "Here I stand; I can do none other so help me God." Was not John Bunyan an extremist? "I will stay in jail to the end of my days before I make a butchery of my conscience." Was not Abraham Lincoln an extremist? "This nation cannot survive half slave and half free." Was not Thomas Jefferson an extremist? "We hold these truths to be self evident that all men are created equal." So the question is not whether we will be extremist but what kind of extremist will we be. Will we be extremists for hate or will we be extremists for love? Will we be extremists for the preservation of injustice—or will we be extremists for the cause of justice? In that dramatic scene on Calvary's hill three men were crucified. We must never forget that all three were crucified for the same crime—the crime of extremism. Two were extremists for immorality, and thus fell below their environment. The other, Jesus Christ, was an extremist for love, truth, and goodness, and thereby rose above His environment. So, after all, maybe the South, the nation, and the world are in dire need of creative extremists.

I had hoped that the white moderate would see this. Maybe I was too optimistic. Maybe I expected too much. I guess I should have realized that few members of a race that has oppressed another race can understand or appreciate the deep groans and passionate yearnings of those that have been oppressed, and still fewer have the vision to see that injustice must be rooted out by strong, persistent, and determined action. I am thankful, however, that some of our white brothers have grasped the meaning of this social revolution and committed themselves to it. They are still all too small in quantity, but they are big in quality. Some like Ralph McGill, Lillian Smith, Harry Golden, and James Dabbs have written about our struggle in eloquent, prophetic, and understanding terms. Others have marched with us down nameless streets of the South. They have languished in filthy, roach-infested jails, suffering the abuse and brutality of angry policemen who see them as "dirty nigger lovers." They, unlike so many of their moderate brothers and sisters, have recognized the urgency of the moment and sensed the need for powerful "action" antidotes to combat the disease of segregation.

Let me rush on to mention my other disappointment. I have been so greatly disappointed with the white Church and its leadership. Of course there are some notable exceptions. I am not unmindful of the fact that each of you has taken some significant stands on this issue. I commend you, Rev. Stallings, for your Christian stand on this past Sunday, in welcoming Negroes to your worship service on a non-segregated basis. I commend the Catholic leaders of this state for integrating Springhill College several years ago.

But despite these notable exceptions I must honestly reiterate that I have been disappointed with the Church. I do not say that as one of those negative critics who can always find something wrong with the Church. I say it as a minister of the gospel, who loves the Church; who was nurtured in its bosom; who has been sustained by its spiritual blessings and who will remain true to it as long as the cord of life shall lengthen.

I had the strange feeling when I was suddenly catapulted into the leadership of the bus protest in Montgomery several years ago that we would have the support of the white Church. I felt that the white ministers, priests, and rabbis of the South would be some of our strongest allies. Instead, some have been outright opponents, refusing to understand the freedom movement and misrepresenting its leaders; all too many others have been more cautious than courageous and have remained silent behind the anesthetizing security of stained-glass windows.

In spite of my shattered dreams of the past, I came to Birmingham with the hope that the white religious leadership of this community would see the justice of our cause and, with deep moral concern, serve as the channel through which our just grievances could get to the power structure. I had hoped that each of you would understand. But again I have been disappointed.

I have heard numerous religious leaders of the South call upon their worshippers to comply with a desegregation decision because it is the law, but I have longed to hear white ministers say follow this decree because integration is morally right and the Negro is your brother. In the midst of blatant injustices inflicted upon the Negro, I have watched white churches stand on the sideline and merely mouth pious irrelevancies and sanctimonious trivialities. In the midst of a mighty struggle to rid our nation of racial and economic injustice, I have heard so many ministers say, "Those are social issues with which the gospel has no real concern," and I have watched so many churches commit themselves to a completely other-worldly religion which made a strange distinction between body and soul, the sacred and the secular.

So here we are moving toward the exit of the twentieth century with a religious community largely adjusted to the status quo, standing as a tail light behind other community agencies rather than a headlight leading men to higher levels of justice.

I have travelled the length and breadth of Alabama, Mississippi, and all the other Southern states. On sweltering summer days and crisp autumn mornings I have looked at her beautiful churches with their spires pointing heavenward. I have beheld the impressive outlay of her massive religious education buildings. Over and over again I have found myself asking: "Who worships here? Who is their God? Where were their voices when the lips of Governor Barnett dripped with words of interposition and nullification? Where were they when Governor Wallace gave the clarion call for defiance and hatred? Where were their voices of support when tired, bruised, and weary Negro men and women decided to rise from the dark dungeons of complacency to the bright hills of creative protest?"

Yes, these questions are still in my mind. In deep disappointment, I have wept over the laxity of the Church. But be assured that my tears have been tears of love. There can be no deep disappointment where there is not deep love. Yes, I love the Church; I love her sacred walls. How could I do otherwise? I am in the rather unique position of being the son, the grandson, and the great-grandson of preachers. Yes, I see the Church as the body of Christ. But, oh! How we have blemished and scarred that body through social neglect and fear of being nonconformist.

There was a time when the Church was very powerful. It was during that period when the early Christians rejoiced when they were deemed worthy to suffer for what they believed. In those days the Church was not merely a thermometer that recorded the ideas and principles of popular opinion; it was a thermostat that transformed the mores of society. Wherever the early Christians entered a town the power structure got disturbed and immediately sought to convict them for being "disturbers of the peace" and "outside agitators." But they went on with the conviction that they were a "colony of heaven" and had to obey God rather than man. They were small in number but big in commitment. They were too God-intoxicated to be "astronomically intimidated." They brought an end to such ancient evils as infanticide and gladiatorial contest.

Things are different now. The contemporary Church is so often a weak, ineffectual voice with an uncertain sound. It is so often the arch-supporter of the status quo. Far from being disturbed by the presence of the Church, the power structure of the average community is consoled by the Church's silent and often vocal sanction of things as they are.

But the judgment of God is upon the Church as never before. If the Church of today does not recapture the sacrificial spirit of the early Church, it will lose its authentic ring, forfeit the loyalty of millions, and be dismissed as an irrelevant social club with no meaning for the twentieth century. I am meeting young people every day whose disappointment with the Church has risen to outright disgust.

Maybe again I have been too optimistic. Is organized religion too inextricably bound to the status quo to save our nation and the world? Maybe I must turn my faith to the inner spiritual Church, the church within the Church, as the true *ecclesia* and the hope of the world. But again I am thankful to God that some noble souls from the ranks of organized religion have broken loose from the paralyzing chains of conformity and joined us as active partners in the struggle for freedom. They have left their secure congregations and walked the streets of Albany, Georgia, with us. They have gone through the highways of the South on torturous rides for freedom. Yes, they have gone to jail with us. Some have been kicked out of their churches and lost the support of their bishops and fellow ministers. But they have gone with the faith that right defeated is stronger than evil triumphant. These men have been the leaven in the lump of the race. Their witness has been the spiritual salt that has preserved the true meaning of the Gospel in these troubled times. They have carved a tunnel of hope through the dark mountain of disappointment.

I hope the Church as a whole will meet the challenge of this decisive hour. But even if the Church does not come to the aid of justice, I have no despair about the future. I have no fear about the outcome of our struggle in Birmingham, even if our motives are presently misunderstood. We will reach the goal of freedom in Birmingham and all over the nation, because the goal of America is freedom. Abused and scorned though we may be, our destiny is tied up with the destiny of America. Before the pilgrims landed at Plymouth, we were here. Before the pen of Jefferson etched across the pages of history the majestic words of the Declaration of Independence, we were here. For more than two centuries our foreparents labored in this country without wages; they made cotton "king"; and they built the homes of their masters in the midst of brutal injustice and shameful humiliation—and yet out of a bottomless vitality they continued to thrive and develop. If the inexpressible cruelties of slavery could not stop us, the opposition we now face willl surely fail. We will win our freedom because the sacred heritage of our nation and the eternal will of God are embodied in our echoing demands.

I must close now. But before closing I am impelled to mention one other point in your statement that troubled me profoundly. You warmly commended the Birmingham police force for keeping "order" and "preventing violence." I don't believe you would have so warmly commended the police force if you had seen its angry violent dogs literally biting six unarmed, nonviolent Negroes. I don't believe you would so quickly commend the policemen if you would observe their ugly and inhuman treatment of Negroes here in the city jail; if you would watch them push and curse old Negro women and young Negro girls; if you would see them slap and kick old Negro men and young Negro boys; if you will observe them, as they did on two occasions, refuse to give us food because we wanted to sing our grace together. I'm sorry that I can't join you in your praise for the police department.

It is true that they have been rather disciplined in their public handling of the demonstrators. In this sense they have been rather publicly "nonviolent." But for what purpose? To preserve the evil system of segregation. Over the last few years I have consistently preached that nonviolence demands that the means we use must be as pure as the ends we seek. So I have tried to make it clear that it is wrong to use immoral means to attain moral ends. But now I must affirm that it is just as wrong, or even more so, to use moral means to preserve immoral ends. Maybe Mr. Connor and his policemen have been rather publicly nonviolent, as Chief Pritchett was in Albany, Georgia, but they have used the moral means of nonviolence to maintain the immoral end of flagrant racial injustice. T. S. Eliot has said that there is no greater treason than to do the right deed for the wrong reason.

I wish you had commended the Negro sit-inners and demonstrators of Birmingham for their sublime courage, their willingness to suffer, and their amazing discipline in the midst of the most inhuman provocation. One day the South will recognize its real heroes. They will be the James Merediths, courageously and with a majestic sense of purpose, facing jeering and hostile mobs and the agonizing loneliness that characterizes the life of the pioneer. They will be old, oppressed, battered Negro women, symbolized in a seventy-two-year-old woman of Montgomery, Alabama, who rose up with a sense of dignity and with her people decided not to ride the segregated buses, and responded to one who inquired about her tiredness with ungrammatical profundity: "My feets is tired, but my soul is rested." They will be young high school and college students, young ministers of the gospel and a host of the elders, courageously and nonviolently sitting-in at lunch counters and willingly going to jail for conscience's sake. One day the South will know that when these disinherited children of God sat down at lunch counters they were in reality standing up for the best in the American dream and the most sacred values in our Judeo-Christian heritage, and thus carrying our whole nation back to great wells of democracy which were dug deep by the founding fathers in the formulation of the Constitution and the Declaration of Independence.

Never before have I written a letter this long (or should I say a book?). I'm afraid that it is much too long to take your precious time. I can assure you that it would have been much shorter if I had been writing from a comfortable desk, but what else is there to do when you are alone for days in the dull monotony of a narrow jail cell other than write long letters, think strange thoughts, and pray long prayers?

If I have said anything in this letter that is an overstatement of the truth and is indicative of an unreasonable impatience, I beg you to forgive me. If I have said anything in this letter that is an understatement of the truth and is indicative of my having a patience that makes me patient with anything less than brotherhood, I beg God to forgive me.

I hope this letter finds you strong in the faith. I also hope that circumstances will soon make it possible for me to meet each of you, not as an integrationist or a civil rights leader, but as a fellow clergyman and a Christian brother. Let us all hope that the dark clouds of racial prejudice will soon pass away and the deep fog of misunderstanding will be lifted from our fear-drenched communities and in some not too distant tomorrow the radiant stars of love and brotherhood will shine over our great nation with all of their scintillating beauty.

Yours for the cause of
Peace and Brotherhood,
MARTIN LUTHER KING, JR.

Mississippi State Junior Chamber of Commerce

OXFORD: A WARNING FOR AMERICANS

THE MISSISSIPPI STATE JUNIOR CHAMBER OF COMMERCE, the Mississippi "Jaycees," with state offices in Jackson, prepared the following article which details their views on the integration battle at the University of Mississippi in September, 1962. Robin H. Mathis, of Houston, Mississippi, is state president of the organization.

OUR SENSE OF DUTY

THE WHOLE WORLD knows of the tragedy at Oxford, Mississippi, on the night of September 30, 1962, when Federal Marshals and U.S. Troops invaded the State of Mississippi. An almost infinite amount of national and international publicity has been devoted to it. However, the Mississippi State Junior Chamber of Commerce soon realized that much of the actual story remained untold. Imbued with a sense of duty to our beloved State and Nation and to Jaycees everywhere and realizing the desire of Jaycees and others to know the circumstances surrounding the invasion of the State of Mississippi, and dedicated to a sincere belief in the "Jaycee Creed," a portion of which states: "That government should be of laws rather than of men," the real story of Oxford will now be told.

BLUEPRINT FOR TRAGEDY

The tragedy at the University of Mississippi resulting in two deaths, injuries to many persons and heavy destruction of property was precipitated by the unwillingness of Attorney General Robert

F. Kennedy and President John F. Kennedy to await the completion of judicial processes which they had invoked, and which, if permitted to continue, would have resulted in a final determination of the James H. Meredith case and enforcement by regular judicial processes of whatever that determination might have been. The "blueprint for tragedy":

1. Neither Governor Ross R. Barnett nor Lieutenant Governor Paul B. Johnson were parties to the James Meredith case in the United States District Court. They were not parties to the appeal in the United States Court of Appeals nor parties to the petition for Writ of Certiorari (a request to be heard) before the Supreme Court of the United States. Neither they nor the State of Mississippi were joined until September 25, 1962, and then only as respondents to a restraining order issued without notice or hearing by the United States Court of Appeals. Their rights and duties under the Mississippi Constitution and statutes had not been adjudicated. At all times leading up to the tragedy the original Meredith case was before the Supreme Court on petition for Writ of Certiorari. From September 25, 1962, to the date of the tragedy, September 30, 1962, restraining orders obtained by the United States Attorney General were pending.

2. When Governor Barnett and Governor Johnson personally denied admission to Meredith at the University, this provided a legal test as to whether the Governor and the Lieutenant Governor were bound by a suit in which they had not been joined as parties. Additionally, it provided legal means to test the constitutional right of the Governor (under the Tenth Amendment to the Constitution of the United States) to enforce State statutes not before the Court in the suit between Meredith and the University of Mississippi officials and the Board of Trustees.

3. At the time Governor Barnett acted, the University of Mississippi officials and the Board of Trustees had found that Meredith was not qualified to become a student at the University; the United States District Judge had upheld the University's denial of admission after a full hearing and on the appeal one of the members of the three-judge panel of the United States Court of Appeals found that the United States District Judge was correct in holding that

Meredith was not qualified to become a student at the University and that "his entry therein may be nothing short of a catastrophe." In a two to one decision, the United States Court of Appeals reversed the United States District Court and held against the University. The University officials then petitioned the Supreme Court of the United States for a Writ of Certiorari (a request to be heard). The very nature of the case called for both the State of Mississippi and the Attorney General of the United States to pursue their legal remedies through the Courts to final completion.

4. Without awaiting a determination of these proceedings, the United States Attorney General and the President rushed in more than 400 armed Marshals and more than 25,000 troops on September 30th and October 1, 1962. Hasty action resulted in two deaths, injuries to many people, destruction of much property, and the most tragic situation which has occurred in the United States in many years. This was solely because of a refusal to await ordinary and proper judicial procedures to determine whether the United States District Court or the United States Court of Appeals would be upheld by the Supreme Court of the United States and, if the United States Court of Appeals was upheld, whether or not the judgment was effective as against the Governor and Lieutenant Governor and the State of Mississippi, who were not parties to the original suit. Attorney General Kennedy had invoked these procedures just five days before the use of armed forces, and a hearing on these procedures was set for only two days after the dispatch of the forces to Oxford. Just eight days later the United States Supreme Court considered the petition for Writ of Certiorari (a request to be heard).

5. There had not been any disturbances, property damage, injuries, or deaths while Governor Barnett was allowed to be responsible for law and order in Mississippi. Neither had there been a clash between law enforcement officers of Mississippi and armed officers of the Federal Government. Mississippi officers were unarmed until they were fired upon with tear gas. Governor Barnett (whose total force of State Highway Safety Patrolmen available for duty as traffic officers throughout the entire State numbers less than 225 officers) maintained peace and order at the University

of Mississippi so long as he was permitted. The tragedy was not precipitated by Mississippi or its public officials.

THE JUDICIAL SEQUENCE OF EVENTS

James Meredith had previously applied to the University of Mississippi for admission and his application was rejected for failure to comply with standard requirements for admission to the University.

February 5, 1962: The U.S. District Judge who heard the Meredith case ruled that Meredith failed to meet the requirements for admission to the University of Mississippi and further found as a matter of fact that he had not been denied admission because of his race. The case was then dismissed. The Governor of Mississippi was not a party to this suit.

June 25, 1962: The U.S. Court of Appeals for the Fifth Circuit reversed the District Judge's decision and ruled by a 2-to-1 vote that Meredith had been denied admission to the University because of his race.

The dissenting Judge in his written opinion stated that the District Judge "was correct in finding and holding that appellant (Meredith) bore all the characteristics of becoming a troublemaker if permitted to enter the University of Mississippi, and his entry therein may be nothing short of a catastrophe."

The Governor of Mississippi was not a party to this appeal.

July 17, 1962: The U.S. Court of Appeals ordered the District Judge to issue an injunction requiring University of Mississippi officials to admit Meredith. The Governor was not a party in this order.

July 18, 1962: A U.S. Court of Appeals Judge issued the first of three stays granted delaying enforcement of the injunction until the U.S. Supreme Court could decide the case. Such stays are not unusual.

August 31, 1962: After the U.S. Court of Appeals twice overruled the Court of Appeals Judge who had issued the stays, the case reached the U.S. Supreme Court for the first time. The U.S. Attorney General and the Justice Department intervened in the

Meredith case by requesting that Justice Hugo Black of the United States Supreme Court set aside the stays.

September 10, 1962: Justice Black vacated the stays and ordered the Court of Appeals' ruling put into effect. Such actions are very unusual. Justice Black signed the ruling alone but said he had polled the other Justices. There was no hearing before the Supreme Court.

GOVERNOR ROSS BARNETT INTRODUCES DECLARATION OF STATE SOVEREIGNTY

On September 13 in a television address, Mississippi Governor Ross Barnett introduced his declaration of State Sovereignty, quoting the Tenth Amendment of the Constitution of the United States, as follows:

> The powers not delegated to the United States by the Constitution, nor prohibited by it to the States, are reserved to the States respectively, or to the people.

Here are additional quotations from Governor Barnett's address:

> I speak to you as your Governor in a solemn hour in the history of our great State—in a solemn hour, indeed, in our nation's history. . . .
>
> In the absence of Constitutional authority and without legislative action, an ambitious Federal Government, employing naked and arbitrary power, has decided to deny us the right of self-determination in the conduct of the affairs of our sovereign State. . . .
>
> As your Governor and Chief Executive of the Sovereign State of Mississippi, I now call on every public official and every private citizen of our great State to join with me in refusing, in every legal and constitutional manner available, to submit to illegal usurpation of power by the Kennedy Administration.
>
> I especially call upon all public officials, both elected and appointed in the State of Mississippi, to join hands with the people and resist by every legal and constitutional means the tyrannical edicts which have been and will be directed against the patriotic citizens of our state. . . .
>
> The last hope of our Constitutional form of Government rests in the conscientious enforcement of our State laws; and the perpetuation of

the sovereignty of the States. Without this, there can be no government of, by and for the people. If our nation is to survive, we must maintain strong State Governments and unity in matters of national security.

Therefore, in obedience to legislative and constitutional sanction, I interpose the rights of the Sovereign State of Mississippi to enforce its laws and to regulate its own internal affairs without interference on the part of the Federal Government or its officers, and in my official capacity as Governor of the State of Mississippi, I do hereby make this proclamation:

WHEREAS, the United States of America consists of fifty (50) Sovereign States bound together basically for their common welfare; and,

WHEREAS, the Constitution of the United States of America provides that each State is sovereign with respect to certain rights and powers; and,

WHEREAS, pursuant to the Tenth Amendment to the Constitution of the United States, the powers not specifically delegated to the Federal Government are reserved to the several States; and,

WHEREAS, the operation of the public school system is one of the powers which was not delegated to the Federal Government but which was reserved to the respective States pursuant to the terms of the Tenth Amendment; and,

WHEREAS, we are now face to face with the direct usurpation of this power by the Federal Government through the illegal use of judicial decree;

NOW, THEREFORE, I, Ross R. Barnett, as Governor of the Sovereign State of Mississippi by authority vested in me, do hereby proclaim that the operation of the public schools, universities and colleges of the State of Mississippi is vested in the duly elected and appointed officials of the State; and I hereby direct each said official to uphold and enforce the laws duly and legally enacted by the Legislature of the State of Mississippi, regardless of this unwarranted, illegal and arbitrary usurpation of power; and to interpose the State sovereignty and themselves between the people of the State and any body politic seeking to usurp such power. . . .

Let us invoke the blessings of Divine Providence as we struggle to maintain our liberties. With the help of Almighty God, and with the unbounding determination of our people to remain free, we shall be invincible and we shall keep the faith.

ATTEMPTS MADE TO ENROLL MEREDITH; GOVERNOR BARNETT "TRIED IN ABSENTIA"

September 13: U.S. District Court entered an injunction ordering University of Mississippi officials to enter Meredith as required by the U.S. Court of Appeals. Governor Barnett was not a party to this injunction.

September 20: While case was still pending before the U.S. Supreme Court, Meredith attempted to enroll at the University and Governor Barnett personally denied him admission at Oxford.

September 25: Governor Barnett refused admission to Meredith at Jackson. On request of the U.S. Attorney General, the U.S. Court of Appeals made the Governor a defendant to a restraining order granted without notice and without a hearing. The Court cited the Governor to appear at New Orleans on September 28th to face a charge of contempt of court.

September 26: Lieutenant Governor Paul B. Johnson, Jr., refused admission to Meredith at Oxford. U.S. Court of Appeals ordered Governor Johnson to appear in Court on September 29th to face contempt charges. On that date he did not appear in New Orleans. He was tried in absentia and was found guilty of contempt and given until October 2nd to absolve himself of contempt or be fined $5,000 for each day of delay.

September 28: Governor Barnett did not appear in New Orleans. The U.S. Court of Appeals tried him in absentia, found him guilty of civil contempt and ordered him to admit Meredith by October 2nd or face arrest and be fined $10,000 for each day of delay.

September 29: Meredith's case for admission was before the U.S. Supreme Court awaiting action. A hearing was set in the U.S. Court of Appeals for October 2nd on the enforcement of the contempt orders. Without waiting on normal judicial processes, U.S. Attorney General Kennedy and President Kennedy ordered hundreds of U.S. Marshals to Oxford, where the University of Mississippi is located. Thousands of Federal troops were ordered into action. At midnight, President Kennedy federalized Mississippi's National Guard.

ON A QUIET SABBATH EVENING MISSISSIPPI INVADED—VIOLENCE RESULTS

September 30: Meredith, protected by over 400 Federal Marshals, arrived on the University campus. The Marshals encircled the Lyceum Building—the main Administration Building—fully armed with night sticks, gas masks, tear gas guns, revolvers and wearing protective vests and riot helmets. A crowd of University students and outsiders, many from other states, gathered in the vicinity of the Marshals. The unarmed Mississippi Highway Safety Patrolmen stood between the Marshals and the crowd. Some of the crowd began to taunt and jeer the Marshals. Several articles were thrown in the direction of the Marshals. Without warning, on orders of James P. McShane, the chief Federal Marshal, the Marshals fired tear gas projectiles at close range directly into the crowd. This incensed the crowd and the riot began.

October 1: U.S. troops poured into Oxford. By dawn on Monday, order was restored on the campus, but rioting continued in downtown Oxford. Meredith was then enrolled by armed force as a student and started attending classes escorted by Federal Marshals. In Mississippi, the force of federal troops was built up to more than 25,000 men. (U.S. has only 6,000 men in Berlin.) The entire town of Oxford was under strict military control.

October 8: The petition for Writ of Certiorari (a request to be heard) was denied by the U.S. Supreme Court eight days after the U.S. Attorney General Kennedy and the President resorted to armed forces.

THE CONDUCT OF THE FEDERAL MARSHALS

Despite reports to the contrary, the conduct of the Federal Marshals during the tragic events at Oxford was not something of which Americans can be proud. In fact, their conduct was reprehensible! Their inexperience was confirmed by President Kennedy at a meeting of Democratic Congressional leaders, as reported by the nationally syndicated "Allen-Scott Report," when the President was said to have stated, . . . "the U.S. Marshals were inexperienced and blundered in their use of tear gas. It was a very sad day."

After the battle began the night of September 30th the marshals went on a rampage firing tear gas projectiles at close range into students and even into the back of the head of a Mississippi Highway Safety Patrolman knocking him unconscious. The marshals actually invaded the dormitories, firing tear gas projectiles. Because of the unnecessary use of tear gas by the marshals, the campus was thick with gas for several days. Some of the classrooms could not be used for days.

The treatment of "prisoners," many of whom did not participate in the battle, was shocking. Many of the "prisoners" were fifteen- and sixteen-year-old boys; several were students; many were outsiders; and a few were elderly men.

The night of September 30th and the next day were hours of unbelievable terror for those prisoners, some of whom had nothing to do with the riot. The marshals administered beatings with nightsticks, knocking a few almost into a state of unconsciousness. A storeroom with no windows located in the Lyceum Building was converted into a virtual dungeon. Ordinarily, about fifteen persons could have gotten into that room, and the marshals had packed it with almost one hundred "prisoners." The "prisoners" were neither fed nor given water for many long hours. With tear gas still in the air, the area was hardly bearable. Many of the boys had dried blood on their clothes and faces. A television newsman told at a press conference of the cruel treatment the "prisoners" received from the marshals in the Lyceum Building.

The events of the night of September 30th and the morning of October 1st were a long nightmare to many University students, townspeople, and particularly so for the "prisoners." Beatings, unlawful searches and seizures, and harassments were not isolated instances at the University and in Oxford. One student, testifying under oath before a legislative investigating committee, told of his "capture" about nine o'clock A.M. on the campus while driving to his girl's house (the daughter of a professor) on the morning of October 1st. He was ordered out of his automobile and it was searched. An unloaded shotgun kept in the trunk for a planned hunt later, and which had not been fired in two or three weeks, was seized. The shells were in his hunting jacket in his dormitory room. He was taken under guard to the Lyceum Building, where the marshals blurted, "make room for the shotgun boys," and he was handcuffed to another boy. The marshals, while using filthy language, also, screamed at him "killer," "murderer." His personal belongings were taken from him and he was lined up against a wall. Later, in a national news service photo taken of him and some other prisoners, the caption said, "These prisoners were taken in rioting disturbances at the University of Mississippi at a place outside of a building in downtown Oxford." Of course, it was false. The picture was taken in the Lyceum Building on the campus and he and some of the others in the picture were not captured in any rioting. A marshal hit him in his ribs and back with a nightstick. He was not allowed to call his girl friend, his parents or an attorney; they held him incommunicado. He told of beatings by the marshals of other prisoners and their refusal to obtain medical aid for the injured. Finally, after being told to sign a release of his shotgun, and through the intervention of a faculty member, he was released. Many other innocent people were arrested without cause and subjected to inhuman treatment. This boy can still not believe that it all happened in America.

PRESS CONFERENCE . . . HEARD BY FEW

In a press conference on October 2 in Jackson, Mississippi, members of the national press gathered together and heard certain details and reports that had failed to reach the American people. Part of this news conference is presented:

Lt. Governor Paul B. Johnson: "Ladies and gentlemen, I have a panel of gentlemen here with me who are willing to answer questions pertaining to the trouble at the University of Mississippi on Sunday (September 30) and Monday (October 1). I'll be glad to answer any questions if you have them."

Newsman: "First, I would like to know if the Mississippi Highway Patrol was withdrawn from the campus in a critical moment in the demonstrating as Attorney General Robert Kennedy has charged."

Gov. Johnson: "The Highway Patrol has never been withdrawn at any time since they went there Sunday night (September 30) until late yesterday (October 1) afternoon after the Army had come in and completely taken charge with 6,000 or 7,000 troops."

Newsman: "A newsman, who was up there, and others in our crew reported at various times during the demonstrating that highway patrol cars were being brought out or had moved off the campus. At one time, they reported only a few officers of the highway patrol, I believe at the Alumni Building—and what is the cause of that maneuvering back and forth?"

Gov. Johnson: "Many of the cars were leaving—some of them hauling different people who had been hurt. In addition to that—trying to get out of the gassed area because of the heavy concentrations of gas. They were not equipped to operate in such a melee as that. That is the reason that many of them had pulled off back from the scene of the rioting—because they were overcome by gas the same as the students and others who were present."

Newsman: "Governor, were you there on the campus when the disturbances began?"

Gov. Johnson: "No, I was not present . . . Officer (Gwin) Cole, the investigator from the Mississippi Highway Patrol, was present at the time. I'd like for Mr. Cole . . . to tell you what happened."

Officer Gwin Cole: "I was standing in the street in front of the Lyceum Building. There were about 200 marshals, I would say, surrounding this building and Army trucks sitting in front of the building that brought the marshals in. Highway patrolmen, sheriffs and deputy sheriffs and other officers were engaged in getting these students back out of the street, on the curb—they were heckling the marshals and some of them were heckling us and throwing cigarette butts and what have you. And all at once I saw a Chief Deputy Marshal, Mr. James P. McShane—he shouted, 'Let 'em have it—gas.' And I dropped to my knees—the gas was coming by me and over my head fired from these guns and I dropped down to my knees—and I saw him run back in the Lyceum Building. I followed him with my eyes full of gas and I got inside the building and I told him, I said, 'That's the dirtiest trick that I have ever seen done.' And he dropped his head and walked off and Mr. (Deputy U.S. Attorney General) Katzenbach of the Justice Department walked up to me and told me he was sorry but somebody jumped the gun. And that's when the riot started."

Newsman to Governor: "What did you find when you reached the campus?"

Gov. Johnson: "When I reached the campus, I found the entire area covered with gas—there had evidently been tons of it that had been released—I found that a lot of it had been shot into the dormitories and they had driven the students from their dormitories out onto the campus. I found that it was so heavy that you couldn't stay in there unless you did have gas masks and when I got there I contacted Colonel (T. B.) Birdsong (Director, Mississippi Highway Patrol) and Officer Cole and had them go with me to the Lyceum Building to see Mr. John Doar of the Justice Department and Mr. Katzenbach. And I told them at that time the Highway Patrol wanted to help and cooperate in any way that they could, but that they could not operate on the campus in that gas—that if they would stop shooting the gas we felt that it would die down where we could come in and help them, but that the other proposition was that we could set up road blocks and prevent others from coming onto the campus. Mr. Doar said he thought that was the thing that needed to be done—set up the road blocks, and we set the road blocks up and kept people out all night and until the following morning when our *Highway Patrolmen were relieved at the point of bayonets by the troops.* They walked around to their backs and ordered them to move and used curse words and ran them off after we had helped them all night long."

Newsman: "What about the report from the Attorney General last night that at one point the Highway Patrol, I think he mentioned possibly 150 of them in some 80 cars, parked a half mile from the campus?"

Gov. Johnson: "They gave orders for them to come down there so that they would all be available for further orders. They had left there in the Lyceum Building—the Highway Patrol had left a walkie-talkie radio in order that we might have connection between the Justice Department officials there and the Highway Patrol—so that we could help them in the ways in which it was possible for us to help them. We had to call the men to these concentrations so we could talk to them and give them the orders and have the road blocks set up."

Newsman: "In other words, those 150 were waiting for instructions on road blocks in accordance with John Doar's wishes?"

Gov. Johnson: "A large part of our patrolmen were there—a good many of them were still around the edges of the campus where they could operate effectively."

Newsman: "How long do you think the situation can continue up there as it is now?"

Gov. Johnson: "That would be a very difficult thing to say—strictly because of this use of the troops as an excuse to come in there and to have a tremendous buildup. I think actually what was trying to be done, they were trying to keep from doing the same thing that Eisenhower did at Little Rock. They provoked this incident in order that these troops could have an excuse to come in there. As a matter of fact, a good many of the troops were already on the way to the Oxford campus when I left Jackson to go to Ole Miss."

Newsman: "You think it was a deliberate provocation, sir?"

Gov. Johnson: "This is the only thing that I can see because evidently those orders had been given a long time previous to this incident for the MP's to have been able to get in there as quickly as they did and then the crowd from Georgia being called in at the same time when I was headed for Oxford—the Kosciusko (Mississippi) unit of the National Guard. . . . I'd say this—since there is a question about who started it—I do feel that for the benefit of the American people, in order that this sort of thing may never happen again in this country—I do think that the truth ought to come to light through a Congressional investigation and it ought to be done quickly before any changes are made."

THE USE OF TROOPS WAS ILLEGAL

Literally thousands of the Armed Forces of the United States, including units of the 101st and 82nd Airborne Division, moved onto the University campus and into the small town of Oxford. Citizens were arrested and searched without proper warrant, shoved around at bayonet point, detained for long periods without cause, and many were deprived of personal property by force. And yet "martial law" was never declared.

The invasion of the State of Mississippi by armed troops of the Federal Government was in direct violation of Article IV of the United States Constitution, which states:

> The United States shall guarantee to every State in this Union a Republican form of Government, and shall protect each of them against invasion, and on *application of the Legislature, or of the Executive* (when the Legislature cannot be convened) against domestic violence.

There was no such application made by thc Legislature or Executive of the State of Mississippi. The United States did not protect the State of Mississippi against invasion as guaranteed under Article IV of the United States Constitution, but rather the Federal Government, through President Kennedy and the U.S. Attorney General, did, without legal authority, cause Oxford, Mississippi and the University of Mississippi to be invaded and occupied by armed forces of the Federal Government. There is no express grant of power in the Constitution that authorized the President of the United States to use Federal troops as he did in Oxford and at the University of Mississippi.

The federalization of the Mississippi National Guard by the President of the United States under the circumstances in this case was in direct violation of the Second Amendment to the United States Constitution, which states:

> A well regulated Militia, being necessary to the security of a free state, the right of the people to keep and bear arms, shall not be infringed.

The calling of the Mississippi National Guard into Federal Service deprived the State of Mississippi of the security of the militia as guaranteed by the Constitution of the United States. Therefore, the state had withdrawn from it by the Federal Government the very source of its state power to enforce law and order in Oxford, Mississippi.

Prior to the use of troops at the University, Senator John Stennis of Mississippi stated: ". . . It is shocking, to me, that consideration would be given, even for a moment, to the use of troops. The Meredith case, now pending . . . in the Federal Courts, is strictly a civil matter, and all the proceedings in connection with it should be confined to the civil authorities."

Senator Stennis pointed out that the Attorney General of the United States intervened "so he said" as *amicus curiae* (friend of the court). The Senator then stated: "I bring up this point expressly at this time, because it relates to the Civil Rights Bill of 1957, which then contained what was called Title III.

"Title 3 proposed that the Department of Justice have exactly the same authority that the Department of Justice is exercising today in this case. Title 3 was debated for a long time on this floor; and when the vote was taken, the Senate—by a vote of 52 to 38—struck that provision from the bill.

"But that is not all. The vote I have mentioned was taken in 1957. But in 1960 another vote was taken in the Senate on the same provision, in substance; perhaps a few words were changed, but the substance was the same. Again, part 3 was stricken from the bill, that time by a vote of 55 to 38.

"That is not all. In 1961, Title 3 or its substance, was offered as an amendment to an appropriation bill. The Senate again rejected Title 3—this time by a vote of 47 to 42.

"In the brief span of less than five years, on three separate occasions, this identical proposal or proposed authority has had its day in this legislative chamber, and every time it has been voted down.

"The use of Federal troops in Mississippi or in any other state is an exercise of a power of a police state at its worst. I believe such action is illegal.

"So, I think, at all levels of the Federal Government, among all authorities, this is a time to stop, look, and listen, with calmness, and to have a prayerful consideration of the major points involved . . . not just for my state, but for all states and all the people of our great United States. We should calmly weigh the consequences. How many red lights are we running by?"

A BROKEN PROMISE

Governor John Patterson of Alabama, formerly one of President Kennedy's strongest supporters in the South, on September 29, 1962, wired the President's brother, Robert Kennedy, U.S. Attorney General, "I wish to remind you of your pledge at the Democratic National Convention in 1960 that federal troops would never be used against the Southern states." Governor Patterson received his answer on September 30 when the federal troops were sent into Oxford, Mississippi.

DESIRE FOR EDUCATION

There are two important facts which cause one to doubt that James Meredith's enrollment at the University was a sincere desire to obtain an education. On October 9, 1962, it was revealed by Aaron Henry, Mississippi's president of the National Association for the Advancement of Colored People, in an interview with the Associated Press, that the James H. Meredith case has "already cost it upwards of $30,000." That same day James H. Meredith, in an interview with the Associated Press, criticized the U.S. Army for segregating the Army troops at Oxford. Is he a sincere student or is he a spokesman for the NAACP?

NOT "THE LAW OF THE LAND," BUT RATHER "THE LAW OF THE CASE"

When the Constitution of the United States became a living document, the world was given for the first time a government upon the premise that people as individuals are endowed with the rights of life, liberty and property, and with the right of local self-government. The people and their local governments formed a central government and conferred upon it certain stated and limited powers and those necessarily implied therefrom. All other powers were reserved to the states and to the people.

The tragedy which has occurred at the University of Mississippi arose from a difference between one of the sovereign states and our central government. It is the right of every citizen, however humble he may be, to stand courageously against whatever he conscientiously believes to be the exercise of power beyond the constitutional rights conferred upon our federal government. This is also true of any one of the sovereign states whenever it acts to protect the powers reserved to it and the other states by the Constitution of the United States. Mississippi acted through its governor, lieutenant governor, attorney general, legislature and its other public officials. Such action is not defiance of the law or defiance of the President of the United States or the Attorney General. Such action is an exercise of the heritage of freedom and liberty under the law.

The courts of our land, and particularly the Supreme Court of the United States, are entitled to and receive our deference and respect. Yet, their decisions are not now and never have been "the law of the land." Such decisions are "the law of the case."

Article VI, Paragraph 2, of the Constitution of the United States provides that:

> This Constitution, and the laws of the United States which shall be made in pursuance thereof; and all treaties made, or which shall be made, under the authority of the United States, shall be the supreme law of the land. . . .

In 1922, the eminent historian of the U.S. Supreme Court, Charles Warren, in Volume 2, Warren, *The Supreme Court in the United States History,* on page 748, stated:

> However the Court may interpret the provisions of the Constitution, it is still the Constitution which is the law and not the decision of the Court.

Alfred J. Schweppe, one of the outstanding constitutional lawyers in the United States, formerly Dean of the University of Washington School of Law, said in an article appearing in the *American Bar Association Journal* in February, 1958:

Thus, the law-making power is in Congress alone. Only Congress makes the law of the United States. Supreme Court decisions and district court decisions are not "law of the United States" in the constitutional and statutory sense, . . . suffice it to say at this point that they are merely decisions between parties to a case or controversy which declare what law is binding between those parties. They do not bind any person anywhere. On the other hand, "laws of the United States" passed by Congress bind everybody everywhere within the jurisdiction of the United States.

If there is one thing clear from the history of our nation and from the plain words of the Constitution, it is the proposition that a decision of the Supreme Court is not "the law of the land."

LAW IGNORED

(From *Congressional Record*)
Extension of Remarks
of Hon. W. J. Bryan Dorn of South Carolina

IN THE HOUSE OF REPRESENTATIVES, Tuesday, October 2, 1962.

MR. DORN: Mr. Speaker, the following article by David Lawrence appeared in the *Washington Evening Star,* Monday, October 1.

Most of the members of the American Bar agree with the thinking advanced by Mr. Lawrence.

I commend this article to the attention of each member of the Congress and the Justice Department.

DUE PROCESS OF LAW IGNORED—
ROOT OF MISSISSIPPI CONFLICT SEEN
IN ILLEGALLY ADOPTED 14TH AMENDMENT

(By David Lawrence)

There is nothing in the Constitution of the United States or in the laws passed by Congress which authorizes the use of Federal troops to compel any public educational institution to admit a certain student just because he demands that he be enrolled.

There is nothing in the Constitution which denies the governor of a state an opportunity to be heard by the full membership of the Supreme Court of the United States in a dispute between State and Federal authority.

There is nothing in the Constitution which even mentions education as one of the subjects coming within the powers of the Federal Government.

Whatever authority the Department of Justice or the Federal courts claim today in this field is derived from a decision of the Supreme Court of the United States in 1954 which gave no legal reason but only sociological consideration as an argument for reversing an 1896 decision that permitted separate but equal facilities in dealing with segregation.

The 1954 decision cited the 14th amendment as the basis for its ruling, but the amendment was never legally adopted by the necessary number of States. In fact, the legislatures of some of the Southern States were compelled at the point of the bayonet by Federal troops to ratify it. Since this happened in 1868—three years after the War Between the States was over—the Supreme Court has never been willing to rule on the validity of the process by which the 14th amendment was allegedly ratified.

Yet one of the ten original amendments—known as the Bill of Rights and duly ratified in 1791—does say that no person shall be "deprived of life, liberty or property, without due process of law."

Governor Barnett nevertheless has been threatened with jail—without due process of law.

Last Saturday Attorney General Robert F. Kennedy, in a telephoned address to the American Bar Association's Convention at San Francisco, said that the distinguished lawyers of Mississippi had not spoken out in the battle over integration. Apparently Mr. Kennedy didn't note the speech made in the Senate just two days before by Senator John C. Stennis of Mississippi, one of the ablest lawyers in the country. He has sat on the bench. He is one of the fairest minded men in the Senate. He told of the origin of the case of James Meredith, the Negro applicant, as a private suit against the board of trustees of Mississippi's State University and how a learned judge of the U.S. district court ruled that the Mississippi college authorities were justified in denying admission to Meredith. Mr. Stennis described the subsequent legal battles in the U.S. circuit court of appeals. He referred to the fact that in the circuit court of appeals one judge said he thought Meredith would be a troublemaker and should be denied admission.

But the main point of criticism made by Senator Stennis was that the State of Mississippi was being denied a hearing by the Supreme Court of the United States. The Constitution specifically provides that the Supreme Court must hear as a matter of original jurisdiction all cases involving a conflict between a State and the Federal Government and that the lower courts have no right to decide such a question. But only one member of the highest court —Justice Black—ruled on it, though he claims he consulted the other judges individually, since the Court was not in session. He doesn't say whether he did this by telephone or by personal visits, as the case arose recently during the time the Supreme Court members were on vacation. Certainly no opportunity was afforded the defendants for oral argument by their attorneys before the entire Court.

"This," says Senator Stennis, "is certainly not judicial consideration of the case on its merits. This is not the type of searching thought and application of legal principles which should be given such a serious case. Is it really true that a Governor might be held in contempt of court, or sent to jail, or a sovereign State might be invaded by Federal troops and its citizens terrorized at the point of bayonets, on this fragmentary attention by one judge?"

Senator Stennis also pointed out that on three separate occasions the Senate had "soundly defeated proposals to give the Attorney General the very authority to exercise the powers which he has assumed." Senator Stennis referred to the substitution of the Attorney General as a plaintiff in court for a private citizen.

Senator James O. Eastland, of Mississippi—who has been for many years chairman on the all-important Judiciary Committee of the U.S. Senate—said to the Senate:

"If the day has come when not only a citizen of Mississippi, but also the Governor of that great State, can be dragged across a State line by Federal marshals or troops and subjected to the dictates of appellate judges appointed to their cushy jobs for life, then judicial tyranny is a reality and not a fiction."

There is serious doubt from a legal standpoint whether a President has the right to send troops into a State under the circumstances existing in Mississippi. This correspondent made the same criticism five years ago when President Eisenhower ordered Federal troops to Little Rock, Arkansas.

Whatever one's individual feelings may be about segregation or desegregation, it seems only fair to express agreement with Senator Stennis that the whole case should be "heard on its merits by the Supreme Court." It seems fair also to suggest that the fraudulent method of "ratifying" the 14th amendment—on which the whole series of court rulings and new executive orders mobilizing Federal military forces are based today—should be opened up for trial after 94 years of tragic silence by the Supreme Court of the United States.

—*Congressional Record,* Vol. 108, No. 179.

THE TRAGIC LESSONS

Certainly, nearly all of mankind would agree that the Oxford saga is a sad one. Americans have witnessed one of the most tragic events in the history of their beloved country—federal force against a sovereign state, brother against brother, education at bayonet point, violence at its worst, the loss of two lives, injuries to many persons, extreme property destruction, damage to the reputation of a great university, and deep wounds that will be long in passing.

At a time in the history of our country when the need for national unity has never been greater, all Americans should pause and reflect on the tragic situation at Oxford. Was it all really worth it? Is the forced education of one man, regardless of his race, worth millions of dollars in expense, the interruption of an education for 5500 other students, denial of the Constitutional rights of many, violence, and death and destruction? We do not believe so!

Tyranny is tyranny—whatever the form. It is the duty of every American citizen to be alert when his freedom is endangered. Our forefathers were not without courage—now the same responsibility to defend freedom is ours.

Let us not be unmindful of the right of dissent and our freedoms under the U.S. Constitution. In a recent speech, John C. Satterfield, a former president of the American Bar Association, stated:

> We must realize that a person or state which tests whether or not he is or it is bound by the decree of any court to which he or it was not a party, or attempts to persuade a court to overrule any one or more of its decisions, is exercising a heritage of freedom which is ours under our form of government and is not a violation of the laws or a defier of the Constitution of the United States. In this time of peril, these truths should be recognized by all citizens of our great country, whether they be liberal, moderate or conservative, radical, middle of the road or reactionary. There must be forbearance and there must be understanding.

Every citizen of this great country must recognize that our nation of liberty under the law, of freedom of speech and action, is a nation in which men may honestly differ and yet respect each other. This will never be attained until we learn to disagree without being disagreeable, that might does not make right, that liberty under the law means the freedom of dissent, and that those with whom we disagree may nevertheless be honest, law-abiding and patriotic American citizens.

Charles Butts

MISSISSIPPI: THE VACUUM AND THE SYSTEM

CHARLES BUTTS was born in Hartford, Connecticut, reared in northern Ohio and attended Oberlin College. Recently married, he now lives in Jackson, Mississippi, where he is associated with the Mississippi Free Press, *a liberal statewide weekly. Beginning as editor when the publication was small and struggling, he has helped to build it into the largest weekly in Mississippi. Its circulation now ranks with most of the state's dailies. He presently serves as general manager and a member of the Board of Directors of Hico Publishing Company, the firm which publishes the* Free Press. *Prior to coming to Jackson, he traveled extensively in the Deep South, usually while doing research. He lived and worked in Tennessee and Florida. He spent part of 1961 in Colombia, South America, studying social conditions. His father, W. Marlin Butts, is a professor at Oberlin College.*

"Having been somewhat amazed by the distorted picture of Birmingham flashed to the nation with false pictures of male agitators getting squirted with fire hoses while dressed up as women, we view with apprehension what cute little tidings will be evolved out of Jackson."
—From an editorial, *Jackson Daily News,* May 30, 1963.

"It was a refreshing experience for picture editors in America to see the President of the United States posing with swarms of Germans and Irish. This was, for the first time since he took office, the longest period of time Mr. Kennedy has gone without posing with some tribal chief from Africa or our own home-grown savage agitators. Of scores of pictures we have seen from Europe, in no case did the President hug a Negro—a record of some sort."

—From a column, *Jackson Daily News-Clarion-Ledger* (combined edition) June 30, 1963.

"Mississippi Negroes know that our progress for both races is sound and solid. They know the white man and the Negro together have brought this state in one hundred years from the brink of desolate and piteous poverty to a living, breathing, growing state, and that together we have shared the hours of sorrow and together we are sharing hours of harmony, industrial, agricultural and educational growth."

—From a column, *Jackson Clarion-Ledger,* June, 1963

The above quotes are from a campaign speech by Lieutenant Governor Paul B. Johnson when running for Governor. (The *Daily News* and the *Clarion-Ledger* are far and away the two largest Mississippi dailies.)

EVEN IN MISSISSIPPI, freedom of the press exists. In fact, probably only in Mississippi, where laws do not shackle newspapers in the printing of the news, does the press take such freedom with the disbursement of the truth. By carefully selecting what it will print, and then molding even this scanty material to suit its ends, the state's press has drugged its readers into a deep sleep.

The percentage of the population that reads the news in Mississippi, such as it is, is the lowest in the nation. The minds of the people are like pale, stunted plants which are not given proper water, fertilizer and exposure to the sun. Because Mississippians do not get enough information to be able to see events in perspective, to make comparisons between themselves and the way people live in other parts of the country, it is even difficult for them to comprehend that something is really wrong.

Mississippi newspapers tremendously distort some stories, particularly if they involve race. But a close look at Mississippi reporting, however, shows that the greatest fault lies not in what is distorted, but rather in what is left out. The state's press lacks any interest in exposing and dealing with the serious social, economic, and political problems which are constantly corroding the governmental structure and the well-being of the people.

Hand in hand with the politicians, Mississippi newspapers make every effort to avoid exposing those areas in which the state fails to provide for its population. Although it is expected that a newspaper should chronicle the virtues and pleasantries of the community, it clearly should also be the role of the editor and his journalists to record the community's shortcomings and the deficiencies of its public officials.

At the heart of the issue is economics. The white oligarchy, composed of a numerically small, but economically and politically significant group of men, knows that to maintain their power they must preserve the state's agricultural character—and in Mississippi, agriculture requires plenty of cheap labor. Any progress towards better education, widespread unionization, or the like, would mean the end of cheap labor, and the weakening of the oligarchy's control. At the same time, these men know that they must have the support of the rural whites—among the very people they are exploiting—to remain in political control; and the key to the rural white vote is the race issue. Here is the common ground where traditional enemies, the affluent and the impoverished, can embrace each other. By magnifying and warping the race issue and then painting themselves as the protectors of the rural whites, the oligarchy is able to keep these people divided, uneducated, and poor—and at the same time win their votes. In reality, the system of the old South is not as interested in color as it is in exploitation.

It is no surprise, for example, that a list of the most important men of economic power and the molders of public opinion in the state would be almost identical with a roster of White Citizen's Council members. In Jackson, particularly, the morning-afternoon newspaper combination, the primary source of newspaper information in the city, is published by a family which is, according to Hodding Carter in a recent *New York Times Magazine* article: "a family whose animation can only be described as an admixture of fundamentalism, furious racism, and greed."

In these papers, and in most other Mississippi dailies, segregation is discussed in a way which makes it appear to be of great value to the poor white. It is a means by which he is able to maintain a superior attitude over other human beings, even though he has very little of his own that can give him security.

By forcing the poor to fight among themselves, the holders of political and economic power who wish to maintain the status quo, and who have much to lose by any kind of enlightenment and progress, are relieved of the threat of being forced into change.

The very politician who was elected to office by yelling "nigger, nigger, nigger," is also the one that is so vigorously fighting to keep the Federal government out of civil rights, and in the process, reducing the possibility of much-needed Federal aid coming into the state. He knows that any kind of progress will jeopardize his position, because any kind of progress will bring with it enlightenment that will reveal to the people how the oligarchy has used, rather than served them. And so it becomes clearer why the mass media, with the blessings of the state leadership, would create an atmosphere which would allow a major tragedy like the Ole Miss crisis to take place.

The resultant national and international black eye means nothing. These leaders have no interest in improving the view of Mississippi that the rest of the world holds. In fact, the worse this image gets, the more cut off the state will be, and the firmer will be their grip.

Although Governor Ross Barnett claims that the bringing of new industry to Mississippi is one of his important activities, his interest appears hollow when one realizes that he was elected mainly on his strong support in rural areas. It is clear to those in control that new industry will bring higher living standards, and the subsequent greater security and improved conditions would threaten the established system.

The fact that out of 82 counties in Mississippi, only a handful can be considered urban in any sense of the word (Jackson, the state capital, is the only city over 50,000), and that these urban counties are disproportionately represented in the legislature, means that farm interests have control and can successfully block legislation conducive to bringing progressive industry into Mississippi.

A recent move to expand the underdeveloped industrial potential in the state resulted in a Balance Agriculture with Industry program. In attempting to industrialize the state while still maintaining the cheap labor necessary to support the power structure, the BAWI has only brought light exploitive industries, such as garment making. Such industries are difficult to organize and are traditionally low-paying. They do not threaten the low wage scale which makes the system work.

The average Southern white is not shown and does not understand how he is being economically abused. The only threat he sees is social and manifests itself in the field of civil rights.

While covering a story in a town in the impoverished Mississippi delta, I met this head on. On my way out of town, I stopped beside a police car to ask directions. We engaged in a short conversation, and I asked the policeman what he thought of the voter registration drive that was going on at the time.

"There is going to be a big change here," he said.

I nodded my agreement.

"Do you think you are going to be around to see it?"

"Yes, I hope so," I replied.

"Well, they're going to take over," he said, "and they outnumber us two to one, and I don't want to be around when they do."

Here was the policeman with his uniform and badge, a revolver at his side—the spokesman for the white Delta community—and he was afraid, afraid because he stood to lose about the only thing that gave him much prestige in the world: his slight superiority over the Negro. This thought terrified him; and so to maintain his present social position he was willing to give up any chance of forcing economic progress, the one thing that would give him true security in place of the fear which is his present lot. The fact of the existence of this paradox, and its cruel alliance of opposites, is proof enough of the fear and frustration of the poor white, and of the effectiveness of the plan of the white establishment.

The same blackout and misunderstanding exists in many other crucial areas in addition to race. Although a Mississippian myself, with a great deal of hope for the future of the state, it is difficult to believe that the Magnolia State is one of the happiest and most prosperous in the nation because it has a large football stadium, the world's longest man-made beach, and two Miss Americas.

The two most crucial non-racial problems are the state's frightful poverty and its grossly inadequate educational system. Seventy-five percent of Mississippi families earn less than $2,500 per year. In Copiah County, records show that in 1959, 21.7 percent of the white families and 49.2 percent of non-white families were existing on $500 per year or less. On such issues the press remains silent. Consequently, Mississippians do not know how far behind the rest of the nation they are. They have no conception of how the well-being of the citizenry is being short-changed.

About all the public reads about Mississippi's tax structure is that it is the white people who pay and therefore the Negroes do not have a real right to use the public facilities. But this is only part of the story. What is not revealed is that the four percent state sales tax on all purchases, including food, is one of the highest in the nation. Here the low-income Negro is paying a much higher percentage of his total earnings in taxes than the richer white. Forty-eight percent of the state's revenue in 1962 was raised through the sales tax.

Farmers are also favored by not having to pay taxes on all gasoline used on their farms. Further, under the administration of Governor Barnett, those in the upper income brackets received substantial income tax reductions. The tax situation is made even worse by the fact that the money the state might garner from a tax on alcohol ends up in the pockets of politicians—put there by dry Mississippi's numerous bootleggers. (Mississippi does have a state tax on bootlegging.)

The whole matter of education in Mississippi is so blasphemous that it is unpleasant even to think about. For example, four times as much is spent per capita on white students in public schools as on non-white students. Teachers, particularly in Negro schools, are hired on the basis of their attitudes—their "proper attitudes" towards the status quo. They must give the right answers to questions about politics and the position of the Negro. There are also other questions that are asked of the young Negro women who apply for teaching positions, questions about what favors they are willing to offer the local superintendent in order to get the job. Since teaching is the only profession of any size now open to the Negro in Mississippi, many yield to these demands, thereby sacrificing their own integrity, and any possible effectiveness as teachers.

But it is in the field of human relations that the ignorance is most calamitous. Although most of the white population would claim to be in a position to speak knowingly about race relations in the South, the upshot of their contacts with "many good colored people in the community" is the conception that the "nigras" are very "happy folks." Rarely is the white man's communication with the Negro based on a relationship that allows it to be honest. Most frequently, the contact takes place on the job, where the white man is the Negro's immediate and overpowering superior. Under these circumstances, many Negroes do try to give the impression that they are happy with their job, and happy with their way of life. This notion is daily re-enforced by the mass media, which explain any discontent as the result of agitation by outsiders and the Federal government. To make any charge stick, the press utilizes statements of a few Uncle Tom Negro leaders.

Although the white man conceives of the Negro as satisfied, at no point is this true. On the part of many Negroes, there is an acceptance that they may be, in some ways, different. On all sides, this is the only information to which the Southern Negro is exposed. Because of the constant pressure, acceptance becomes an easy alternative.

Both races are guilty of believing something simply because it appears in print. "It said so in the newspaper." One of the leading dailies offers separate editions for whites and Negroes, further widening the misunderstanding between the races. The white community never sees a Negro face in a newspaper and has no way of knowing of any church, civic, and social groups existing within the Negro community.

The lens of the state's press serves then as a filter—removing truth from the picture of each other and of the state that both races have. Fact is replaced by fiction, knowledge by fear, and motion gives way to stagnation. Paralysis sets in on all sides, and the preservation of the status quo, inequitable though it is, holds in the eyes of the people fewer horrors than change. The racial issue thwarts all attempts at progress, and prevents the voters from seeing that it is this very lack of progress that gives the oligarchy its power, and the racial issue its urgency. As time has passed, the myths have begun to be believed, and the fable has become fact. Men are now acting against their own interests in sincere conviction that their actions are necessary and correct.

The problem in Mississippi can no longer be solved by the reasoned thought of the average citizen—for his ideas are warped by deceptive biasses. Progress can only come through education, which again and again will present the people with the true information and sensible analysis so that the cycle of false facts and false action can be entered and broken.

Two years ago a group of Jackson Negro business and professional men conceived an idea of a weekly newspaper which would tell the other side of the news to the people of Mississippi—the *Mississippi Free Press.* One of the group, and the man who first suggested the paper's name, was Medgar Evers. Because the promoters of the plan were Negro, and since they were particularly concerned with covering the news relating to civil rights, they knew that circulation would be limited principally to the Negro community.

At first, their plan was rather unsuccessful. Though the men who inaugurated the project were dedicated, they themselves had neither the time nor the means to promote the circulation or advertising that would make the newspaper a stable institution.

About a year and a half ago, the paper had a scanty circulation of 240. The potential was there, but the *Free Press* lacked a full-time person who could, as editor and manager, set about the task of building. Intrigued with the possibility of making a working reality of the paper, I accepted the job. The circulation now totals nearly 14,000, but, considering the vacuum of the South, it can still only be considered a beginning.

Although developing the business side of the small tabloid was crucial to its continued existence, building a philosophy of a newspaper in the context of the existing mass media was also essential. Since its inception, a major aim of the *Free Press* has been to seek out the faults in the area in which it circulates and then push and prod until these faults are brought into the open. It has tried to expose and deal with the serious social, economic, and political problems which are constantly corroding the governmental structure and threatening the well-being of the people—in terms the people themselves can understand.

It is difficult to conceive of the tightly sealed-off world of the poor in Mississippi. If white, he does not have too much, but he has a feeling of slight superiority over the Negro, and since he has so little this is of great importance. He will resort to any tactic to keep the Negro in his place. Not until the grinding pressure of his own poverty is lifted can the poor white be expected to ease the corresponding pressure that he places on the Negro.

And if a Negro? When a third-grader comes on the stage to do his part in a play and is not at all certain of his lines, be pretty sure that he is afraid. A Negro in Mississippi is born into and grows up in a world that is a continuing lie about his potential. He is told by everyone that he is inferior—including, in many cases, his own parents. He is told there are certain boundaries he must not cross. In the rural areas he has no exposure to anyone except those who share the equally poor environment, where such a thing as school is an exercise in attendance. Many Negroes use overt signs to express their own inferiority in conversation with a white man: they hide behind the safety of complete agreement, or feign ignorance. This can be explained, in many cases accurately, as techniques to gain favor. But some stereotypes are maintained by Negroes themselves.

The Negro has always been told that it is well for the white man to take care of the money because he cannot handle it wisely himself. One of the organizers of the *Free Press* owns and operates an attractive supermarket which is steadily increasing in size and trade. He has mentioned that on several occasions Negroes have come to him and asked who it is that backs him, that puts up the finances. When he answers that he owns the store himself, they say, "No, no, go ahead, that's all right. You can tell me," not believing that some white man is not responsible for his thriving business.

The poor white and the poor Negro are so carefully and completely cut off that the fear they feel is almost omnipotent. It is difficult to describe how frightful the fear of not knowing can be. Here in Mississippi, most particularly in the rural areas, schooling seems to lack the essence of education: learning how to hang ideas together so that this knowledge forms a basic skill which will see one through life, and provide a measure of assurance besides.

The *Free Press* is attempting to talk about the issues which directly affect the life of the people, and then is trying to explain how something as radical as the democratic process can be used to make some necessary changes. But this process cannot begin without a certain basic understanding about how life is right now, so that the concepts of change can be fitted into the facts somewhere, and not hang in the limbo of words, meaningless and isolated in the vacuum that is Mississippi. This is a mountainous task.

A man's fear will be inversely proportional to the amount of understanding he has about the situation in which he exists. At present the very poor in Mississippi understand little more than that things are wrong. Even though it may appear that life might be more unbearable once one understands how things are wrong and how life might be, at least then a man has a working knowledge of how to proceed. The *Free Press* is struggling to learn how to best convey this working knowledge, and the background which must precede it.

The language must be simple because most of the state, though literate, does not read and comprehend easily. A grocery store owner, and friend, recently remarked that a customer said as he picked up the four-page *Free Press*, "Tonight I am going to do me some reading." It probably would indeed be a full evening of reading—and more likely be his reading for the week.

But there is much more than just the small vocabulary and poor reading skills to be overcome. In Mississippi it is not possible to begin to talk right off about a current problem since the background information necessary to make the article meaningful is not present in the reader's mind. First it is necessary to explain why the article is being published. For instance, when talking about the advantages of trade unions, the newspaper had to take up and explain job security, better working conditions, higher wages, and so forth. For people who have never had a voice on the job and have never known justice or protection when attempting to mount a protest, the advantages of a union seem difficult to believe.

In the whole critical area of voter registration, time and again the *Free Press* has run articles trying to point out how almost every part of a citizen's life is affected by the kind of leadership that he chooses, or fails to choose, to run his government. We explain how pressure can be applied even to the men in office, by threatening to deny them your vote at the next election. The idea that voting is a right guaranteed by the U.S. Constitution has aroused many people, but often it does not strike close enough to home to spur a Negro to make the kind of possible sacrifices that he must face if he wishes to attempt to register in Mississippi. To close the gap, we attempt to make clear the connection between the power of the ballot and the responsibility of better schools, better jobs, and a better future.

While the fear bred by ignorance is real, so is the fear that arises from facing the possibility of irrational physical violence. The Southern Negro must walk with this fear every day. And it is not just the fear of being beaten, of being shot, but the fear of not knowing when, or by whom, or for what. A white man can do things that will put him in a very frightening position, but in his case, he knows for what, how, and by whom, at least in most cases. But the Southern Negro cannot, because in many instances he is wrong simply by virtue of his color.

A young Negro woman, a student at a prominent Eastern law school, who had never been in Mississippi before, tried to express to me the way in which she had come to know this fear after she had visited Greenwood during the height of the recent voter registration campaign. She described her fear when she realized how isolated she was from any foundation of reason which could serve to protect her from the ugliness of the white crowd. As a student of law she was shattered by the realization that there were policemen who had no respect for the law; that the whole concept of law and justice, which most people rather take for granted, simply did not exist. This intelligent young woman, who had a background with which she could expect to handle almost any situation, knew the naked fear of being a Negro in a Southern town. Forty-three percent of Mississippians, the Negro population, live their entire lives with this naked fear.

The people of Mississippi have vast pride in their past, a pride so deep that it can lead to serious neuroses. The man accused of killing Medgar Evers is a fallen scion of a proud old family, somewhat reminiscent of Faulkner's *The Sound and the Fury,* an extreme case of the tendency to hark back to the glories of the past, and to rebel at the realities of the present. Nevertheless, even with almost no contact with the rest of the world, many are becoming aware that something is wrong. With some hope and determination and given the faintest glimmer of the link between what they are and what they might be, the determination and excitement building throughout the South could yield significant results.

It is in this context that the *Free Press* must try to operate. It recognizes that it is not in a position to affect directly the attitudes of the police toward justice; it can do little to bring Federal pressure to bear to keep the law. But the newspaper can provide the information which will point out how things are, and how they might be changed. It can penetrate the darkness, and the fear which darkness breeds. It can explain how the system is really working.

Informing the people of Mississippi is an arduous task, but it is an essential prerequisite to progress. The larger problems are complicated and in themselves fearful; only in theory and in talk do they even seem to come close to relating to concrete improvement and change. Yet they do underlie all the other issues, and they do relate. Until the relationship is explained in the language and manner of the people, democracy cannot be expected to serve them. But when the connection is made, and the men who run Mississippi know this, the people will become a powerful force. The *Free Press* hopes to mold a cogent force for progress and dignity.

Ross R. Barnett

ADDRESS TO THE HARVARD LAW SCHOOL FORUM

ROSS R. BARNETT was Governor of the State of Mississippi from 1960 to 1964. A native Mississippian and the son of John William Barnett, a Confederate veteran, Governor Barnett attended the public schools of Leake County, where, at the age of sixteen, he operated a barbershop to help pay his expenses. After graduation from Mississippi College in 1922, he taught school and coached athletics at Pontotoc High School for two years. He graduated from the University of Mississippi Law School with honors in 1926. At the University he was president of his law class. After June, 1926, he began the practice of law in Jackson, Mississippi. He served as president of the Jackson and Hinds County Bar Association six different terms. He is now the senior member of a law firm composed of seven members, one of Mississippi's largest and most distinguished law firms.

IT IS A PLEASURE to be with you tonight. I would like to tell you a little about Mississippi, our opportunities, our economic development and our progress.

I hope all of you will visit our great state. I would like for you to see our beautiful new football stadium seating 46,000; our coliseum which will seat 10,000; I wish you could see the 35,000 acres of water known as the Great Pearl River Reservoir, which will be completed within the next year, and see the beautiful, scenic, historic Gulf Coast where we have the longest man-made beach in the world—a twenty-eight-mile sand beach.

Our tourist business is at an all-time high as thousands of

people from every state in the nation come and enjoy our wide assortment of outdoor sports, our recreation facilities, visit our historic shrines and ante-bellum homes, fish, boat and ski on our many lakes and rivers, play year 'round golf in the warm sunshine throughout various sections of our state.

In 1960, the Mississippi Legislature passed thirty-nine separate acts to make Mississippi more than competitive in our fight to secure industry and payrolls. We voted a right-to-work law into our state constitution by more than 2½ to 1. We reduced our state income taxes in 1960. We created a climate highly favorable to business and industry. Ninety-eight per cent of our people voted to give industry a ten-year ad valorem tax exemption.

Mississippi has secured over 400 substantial new industries and expansions in the last two and a half years. When these new industries and expansions get into full production, they will provide over 31,000 new industrial jobs for our people.

The United States Department of Commerce, in a December, 1962, report, showed that Mississippi's rate of progress was 25 per cent greater than the national average in manufacturing gains, 105 per cent greater in expenditures for new plants and equipment, and 13 per cent greater in new wholesale establishments.

Mississippi, in the last two years, has staged a reversal in population. Instead of losing, Mississippi has gained more than 73,000 since the 1960 census—a rate exceeding that of 22 other states. Every economic indicator points to the fact that Mississippi is moving forward at a record pace, and indications are that 1963 will surpass all previous records in economic gains.

The Standard Oil Company of Kentucky will complete a 125 million dollar oil refinery in Mississippi this year which will refine 100,000 barrels of crude oil per day and which will open the way for a great petro-chemical complex on the Mississippi Gulf Coast. In discussing the location of this major refinery in Mississippi, Mr. W. C. Smith, president of Standard of Kentucky, said:

> There is little room left on the old frontier. Mississippi is one of the last resorts for industry. Look at the other states that are broke or nearly broke as the result of the New Deal and the Fair Deal and you

will see why we are glad to be in Mississippi where there is a friendly and healthy industrial and political climate.

The president of the great W. W. Sly Manufacturing Company said, in October, 1961:

We, like you, still believe in the dignity of man, in a state's sovereign rights, that the Christian principles should be put ahead of material ones, that people have the right to work, that private property should be protected and that the Constitution of the United States should be interpreted in the same spirit in which it was written and not altered to suit expediency. Many people have asked why we built this plant in Mississippi. I'll tell you why. The attitudes, the spirit of the people of this state and this town came closer to our own beliefs than any other spot we could find.

Another industrialist said:

We chose Mississippi because we felt that it possessed the healthiest political and industrial climate in the nation—the best potential for production workers, as well as all other necessary requisites for sound logical plant location.

Another said:

Mississippi's understanding of industry problems in creating and maintaining a favorable climate for business is outstanding.

This is conclusive evidence that all areas of this nation are aware of the peace, harmony and opportunities that exist in Mississippi.

Another yardstick is the fact that, educationally, there is not a city in this nation that equals Mississippi's capital city of some 150,000 population. The citizens of Jackson have covered an average of 12.1 grades, unsurpassed in the nation. I would like to ask—what are the best-educated cities in the United States? What cities have the largest proportion of college graduates among their citizenry? You would be right if you answered Cambridge, Massachusetts . . . Madison, Wisconsin . . . Pasadena and Berkeley, California . . . and Jackson, Mississippi.

Mississippi is the greatest states' rights state in the nation. Mississippians, as far back as 1944, took a firm stand against the socialistic platforms that were then shaping up. For twenty years, we have stood upon the sound foundation of constitutional government and states' rights. In the last presidential election, our people voted unpledged and we gave our electoral votes to that great conservative, Senator Harry Byrd of Virginia.

Massachusetts was the Queen Mother of states' rights and constitutional government. For almost one hundred years of the history of the states under the Constitution, her statesmen were the most conservative and pronounced proponents and sticklers for preserving the faith embodied in her Declaration of Rights and in resisting the encroachments, potential or actual, of the federal government. These included many of your famous men such as Samuel and John Adams, John Hancock, George Cabot, and many, many others, equally as great.

The political ideas and principles of these men found eloquent expression in the Declaration of Rights prefacing the first Constitution of Massachusetts and in all future constitutions of this state, including the present one. Some of those political ideas merit repeating on this occasion. A few of them are:

(1) The people inhabiting the territory formerly called the Province of Massachusetts Bay, do hereby solemnly and mutually agree with each other to form themselves into a free, sovereign and independent body politic, or state, by the name of the Commonwealth of Massachusetts. (Paragraph 32, present Constitution.)

(2) The people of this commonwealth have the sole and exclusive right of governing themselves as a free, sovereign and independent state; and do and forever hereafter shall exercise and enjoy every power, jurisdiction and right, which is not, or may not hereafter be, by them expressly delegated to the United States of America and Congress assessed. (Paragraph 5, Article 4, present Constitution.)

(3) All power residing originally in the people, and being derived from them, the several magistrates and officers of the

government vested with authority, either Legislative, Executive or Judicial, are their substitutes and agents, and are at all times accountable to them. (Paragraph 6, Article 5, present Constitution.)

In 1809, during the controversy over Jefferson's Embargo, the Legislature of Massachusetts resolved as follows: "That the people of this state as one of the parties to the federal compact, have a right to express their sense of any violation of its provisions, and that it is the duty of this General Assembly to interfere for the purpose of protecting them from the ruinous infliction usurped by an unconstitutional power."

Later, the General Court of Massachusetts resolved again respecting the Embargo, that "We spurn the idea that the free, sovereign and independent state of Massachusetts is reduced to a mere municipal corporation, without power to protect its people and defend them from oppression, from whatever quarter it comes. Whenever the national compact is violated, this Legislature is bound to interpose its power." (February 22, 1814.)

We have heard much here of late with reference to the rights of the states being sacrificed and ruthlessly destroyed by an all-consuming federal government. The federal government is constantly making a whipping boy of the states and is overstepping its constitutional powers. The federal government is assuming to exercise powers it does not have under the Constitution and that, by the Constitution, were expressly reserved in the states and the people thereof by the Tenth Amendment.

Today, more than at any time in this century, men and women, North and South, East and West, are rallying in defense of fundamental principles. In recent months, I have had thousands of letters and telegrams from people in every state in the nation calling for a return to constitutional government.

These Americans hold, with me, that the preservation or maintenance of state sovereignty is indispensable to the preservation of human rights. We are convinced that once the right of a state to exercise exclusive jurisdiction over a local problem is lost, human rights, liberty and freedom will perish.

A year ago, in February of 1962, Mississippi had the pleasure of having an official visit from Senator John E. Powers, president of the Massachusetts State Senate, accompanied by several leaders of the Massachusetts Senate and other state officials. In his address before a joint session of the Mississippi Legislature, Senator Powers told Mississippians that the time had come to reverse trends and put the legislative branch of government in first place, because it is closest to the people. He said that usurpation of authority by the executive and subsequently the judiciary is a lamentable trend that must be halted. He said that the state level government is lulled to impotency and that he, in his capacity as president of the Senate, "Will not in my state preside over the liquidation of legislative powers or a legislative body."

I recently received a letter from the president of a bar association in Florida, from which I quote:

> We in this area are greatly interested in the position of your sovereign state . . . some of our association feel that our states are presently being reduced to the position of a province, much along the lines of some other countries. This is a matter of wide general interest.

In September, 1962, the National Legislative Conference, at its fifteenth annual meeting in Phoenix, Arizona, adopted a resolution in an effort to strengthen and uphold the Tenth Amendment to the United States Constitution. The Council of State Governments at its biennial general assembly of the states, held in Chicago, Illinois, in December, 1962, endorsed the resolution and recommended its adoption by all the states.

The people of the states are extremely conscious of this usurpation of the constitutional rights of the states, but much needs to be done to awaken the states to their perilous condition. There is a crying need for the states to organize into a compact, expressing the feeling of the states with reference to these usurpations, the consequent destruction of our constitutional form of government, and presenting a common front against such unconstitutional encroachment by the federal government.

Not only the Southern states, but all of the states in the union must be and are conscious of the present peril to state sovereignty.

All of the states have a common interest in their own survival and the restoration of their respective constitutional powers.

Surely, the states are conscious of their peril and of the peril to their people. We must no longer remain idle or complacent. The clarion call must be sounded for the states to come to their own defense and obtain a restoration of constitutional government.

States' rights and constitutional government are inseparable. The Tenth Amendment to the Constitution of the United States very clearly states the position of the states as related to the federal government, and here is what it says:

> The powers not delegated to the United States by the Constitution nor prohibited by it to the states are reserved to the states respectively, or to the people.

Any high school student can understand what those twenty-eight words mean. It is indeed regrettable that many decrees, orders and edicts have been issued wholly contrary to the meaning of the Tenth Amendment.

The courts adhered to the meaning and fundamental principles of the Tenth Amendment for nearly a hundred years, and further held that state sovereignty could not be bartered away or surrendered by legislative action. Then suddenly, they reversed decisions handed down by such great and eminent scholars and jurists as Oliver Wendell Holmes, Chief Justice Taft, Chief Justice Hughes, McReynolds, Stone, Cardozo and other eminent jurists and began to enter orders, decrees and edicts based on sociological ideas as advanced and advocated by Gunnar Myrdal and others, thereby whittling away, year by year, the rights that are reserved to the states by the Tenth Amendment. These decisions are in conformity with the wishes of left-wing and communist front organizations.

We must not fall into the trap of world-wide communism. The basic tactics of world-wide communism is to divide and to conquer. It is to set free nation against free nation, and within the nation, to set brother against brother. Its objective in the United States is to promote tension, turmoil, strife, and to bring about misunderstanding and mistrust.

States' rights and local self-government are older than the Constitution. They existed before the nation was formed and were recognized and protected by Thomas Jefferson and the other founding fathers when they wrote the Constitution itself.

The preservation of the prerogatives of people of a sovereign state, their right to deal exclusively with domestic problems and the absolute and unqualified denial of a totalitarian state in the United States—these principles are just as vital as, and more intimately affect, the welfare of every man, woman and child in America than even such important questions as foreign policy and all other serious questions which we face today, important as those issues are. May God forbid that your respective states and mine, our counties, our cities, our farms and our businesses shall ever be subjected to Washington bureaucratic police rule.

If we lose states' rights which safeguard the most precious of all human rights—the right to control and govern ourselves at home—the right of life, liberty and the pursuit of happiness—then may we ask, "For what is a man profiteth if he shall gain the whole world and lose his own soul?"

A state that loses the right to exercise exclusive jurisdiction over its own local affairs loses its political soul and its citizens have lost their most valuable freedom.

I wish to emphasize that the term "States' Rights" means much more to the people of this nation than simple theory. It means the preservation of democracy and freedom itself.

The oldest form of government in the world is the highly centralized one, with all power concentrated. It is only with the founding of this country that democracy developed, and it came, and this country grew great, because the centralization of power was curtailed.

Every section of this nation favors human rights. Everybody favors human rights. But it is a fraud upon the American people to pretend that human rights can long endure without constitutional restrictions on the power of government. Many people living today have seen this truth written in blood in recent human history.

Hitler offered the people of Germany a short cut to human progress. He gained power by advocating human rights for minority groups. Under his plan, the constitutional rights of the people were destroyed. The proposal to take from you the right to deal with your local problems in a way that is satisfactory to you and to invest the right to deal with those problems in Washington in a way that is wholly unsatisfactory to you is so antagonistic to our form of government and so contrary to everything that we have stood for since 1776 that it is obliged to be un-American in principle and undemocratic in execution.

The moment that government becomes remote, distant, mysterious and beyond the comprehension of the people themselves, danger arises and we subject ourselves to the possibility of abuse of power and ultimate dictatorship. When the United States of America was formed and the Constitution was written, the people were insistent in demanding that local government be forever preserved in all of its dignity and all of its safeguards. In the drafting of the Constitution, it was specifically provided that the right and authority of the states to conduct their own affairs should be preserved inviolate and there was conferred upon the federal government only so much power and authority as was necessary to control and regulate the relationships of the states one with another and the conduct of this nation's foreign affairs and unified defense.

Ratification of the Constitution by the original states—of which Massachusetts was one—was obtained only after the citizens in each state received definite and positive assurances that this fundamental concept of government was recognized by the Constitution. Is this principle of states' rights an archaic doctrine, as insisted by those who seek the concentration of power in Washington? I say to you that it is a living principle, as vital and essential today as it was in the foundation days of the Republic—the doctrine of free society and free men, as opposed to regimentation of thought and action.

Democracy is not a thing of Washington. Democracy is a thing of the crossroads. It is at the crossroads of America that the children of this nation live. It is at the crossroads that their children are born—that they go to church on Sunday—that the schools are placed—that the average American citizen lives his life and is finally taken to his reward. It is at the crossroads that the life of America takes place—not in Washington.

That is where I stand tonight. I am convinced that our schools are local affairs, as is the police, the fire department, the city and county governments, the habits of the people, the conduct of local business and all the hundreds of affairs of daily life. The right to work, loaf or play, to choose our vocation and to change our job, to guide the education of our children, to attend the church of our choice, to work with whom we please, to go where we choose, are not inherent and divine rights. These rights are ours solely because the federal government, by the Constitution, was denied the power to interfere with them. Also, the fields of education, housing, employment, apportionment of state legislatures, voting qualifications, police powers, tidelands oil rights, and other sundry situations, are reserve powers under the Tenth Amendment.

Government, if not properly restricted, is essentially a dangerous thing. There is no truth more fundamental than that power seeks always to increase. I believe that the maintenance of states' rights is indispensable to the preservation of human rights—that once the right of a sovereign state to exercise exclusive jurisdiction over a local problem is lost, human rights, liberty and freedom will perish in the catastrophe. The people of all communities, cities, counties and states must either rule or they will be ruled.

There is no such thing as a vacuum in politics or government. If the rights of a sovereign state and local units of government are taken away, they will be replaced by a totalitarian government—a police state. Only our Constitution stands between the people and a dictatorship. If politicians are allowed to circumvent, misconstrue, cripple or disobey the Constitution, then constitutional government is in jeopardy and the liberty and freedom and right of every American citizen to the pursuit of happiness are menaced.

This republic is an indestructible union of indestructible states. But a historical fact that many seem to have forgotten is that the states of this union are the fundamental sources of all sovereignty and all power. The Constitution merely states, in the form of a written contract, the degree of sovereignty that the states transfer to the federal government. This sovereignty was principally in the field of defense and operating highways and post offices. The sovereignty of the states flows both upward and downward—upward to the federal government and downward to the counties and municipalities. Some theorists try to reduce the principle of states' rights to an absurdity by saying that if states have a right to disagree with matters of national policy affecting their interest, then counties and municipalities likewise have a right to disagree with policies of the state affecting their interests. These people are simply not familiar with the facts of history.

Counties and municipalities are creatures of the state, even as the federal government is the creature of the states. The Constitution was not ratified by the people of the United States or by the people of the thirteen colonies voting in a mass referendum. It was ratified by the legislatures of the thirteen states, acting as the duly constituted officers of the people. In other words, the states ratified the Constitution in their capacities as sovereign political communities.

This dual sovereignty feature of our government is what sets it apart as an economic creation of the political genius of man. It sets it apart from all other governments in that it puts the powers which matter most to the people—namely, the police powers and the administration of local affairs—it places these close to the people where they can exercise vigilance on their adopted servants.

Not a single word of the Constitution can be changed by judicial decree or Congressional act. Any change is the prerogative of the legislatures of the states. They are the only ones who can change the wording—either by adding to or taking from—this is clearly stated in the Constitution.

A lot of people outside the South have the impression that states' rights is only concerned with segregation. This is far from the truth. Just to mention a couple of examples—the states of the West are deeply concerned about the federal government's encroachments of their water rights and I have heard a distinguished Republican senator say that if the federal government did not stay out of this field, they were going to find out what a scrap really was. (Water rights there have always gone with the land—it is an established principle in the West that when you buy a piece of land, whatever stream goes through it, you own the water rights, and the federal government is now trying to establish a principle that this is not true—that it belongs to the federal government and they have no right to use it.)

Other examples to illustrate the point are Nevada and Indiana. Nevada has legalized gambling on a large scale. Very few people in Mississippi believe in this, but we just don't think it is our place to try to tell the State of Nevada what to do about its internal affairs.

You might recall that a few years ago, the State of Indiana flatly refused to permit the federal government to inspect its old-age assistance rolls. The officials were very successful in preserving the right of their state to handle this matter as it saw fit.

Mississippians know we do not have the right to say what the people in Ohio or in any other state should do towards solving their problems. We certainly would not want to be discourteous in projecting our ignorance of conditions in other states because we could not contribute anything worthwhile to their solution—this is the American way—and all the South asks is the same simple courtesy from those who are not familiar with our problems.

Daniel Webster said in his *Eulogy of George Washington:*

> If disastrous war should sweep our commerce from the ocean, another generation may renew it; if it exhausts our treasury, future industry may replenish it; if it desolates and lays waste all our fields, still, under a new cultivation, they will grow green and ripen to future harvests.
>
> It were but a trifle even if the walls of yonder capitol were to crumble, if its lofty pillars should fall and its gorgeous decorations be all covered by the dust of the valley. All these may be rebuilt.
>
> But who shall reconstruct the fabric of demolished government? Who shall rear again the well-proportioned columns of constitutional liberty? Who shall frame together the skillful architecture which unites national sovereignty with states' rights, individual security and public prosperity?
>
> No, if these columns fall, they will be raised not again. Like the Colosseum and the Parthenon, they will be destined to mournful im-

mortality. Bitterer tears, however, will flow over them than were ever shed over the monuments of Roman or Grecian art; and they will be the monuments of a more glorious edifice than Greece or Rome ever saw—the edifice of constitutional liberty.

It is time to identify the traitors throughout America. It is time to take the cowards out of the front lines. It is time for true Americans to become awakened.

P. D. East

NOTES FROM A SOUTHERN EDITOR

P. D. EAST was born in Columbia, Mississippi, in 1921, and has lived most of his life in his native state. He attended Pearl River Junior College and the University of Southern Mississippi. Since 1953, he has been Editor and Publisher of The Petal Paper, *a weekly originating in Petal, Mississippi, near Hattiesburg, where he now lives and continues to publish the paper. He became nationally known (and somewhat less appreciated locally) when* The Petal Paper *came out in support of the U.S. Supreme Court ruling regarding the desegregation of schools. As a result of his stand on this and other issues, he has been much in demand for lectures and discussions in leading universities across the nation. He has appeared in interviews with Mike Wallace and Paul Coates, and has made additional television appearances on numerous programs. He is the author of* The Magnolia Jungle *(an autobiography), and the forthcoming novel,* A Cock For Asclepius. *Harrison Salisbury, of the* New York Times, *wrote of East: "He is in the great tradition of editors and satirists that produced Mark Twain and Bret Harte." Mr. East received the Lasker Civil Liberties Award in 1962. Of the four selections that follow, the first three clearly illustrate Mr. East's satirical wit; the fourth, "The Death of Medgar Evers," shows him as a serious crusader against the evils of the South.*

THE MISSISSIPPI METHODIST MISFITS

IN THE EARLY PART OF 1958—March or April—some of the Methodist Misfits in the Magnolia Jungle—or Mississippi—had a stern, a severe, lesson taught them; it had to do with an integrationist being invited to Millsaps College in Jackson to speak. Some of the home-grown Christians—and they're the best kind, too—demanded of Dr. Ellis Finger, the Board of Trustees, the Bishop of Mississippi and, I think, of God himself, to state the college's position on the terrible question of integration. The only defense Millsaps, the president, the board, any and all of them, had was the poor excuse about "Academic Freedom." Now, let's face it, that's a typical commie line—Academic Freedom, indeed!

The local, home-grown Christians gave the Mississippi Methodist Misfits a second chance, and that was mighty good of them, something like Christian Charity, I'd venture to say. But, alas, did the Methodists learn from that lesson? Perhaps some of them did; still there were others who didn't.

"The purpose of a college is not to tell people what to think, but teach them to think. Our purpose at Millsaps College is to create an atmosphere in which Christian convictions may grow and mature," so stated Bishop Marvin Franklin in defense of academic freedom at that time in 1958.

Obviously, some of the fellows took the Bishop seriously: they matured and their convictions grew. So then what did they do? But before I report what twenty-eight of them did, let me tell you that on the second day of January, 1963, all was well here in this state. God was in his heaven, the governor in his mansion, and James Meredith was enjoying his stay at Ole Miss. Everyone hereabouts knew his place; moreover, he kept in it. In fact, we were one big, happy family, until the second of January—that's when twenty-eight young Methodist Misfits set off the fuse from which sparks still fly.

Let me clear up one thing right now. I may have left the impression that all of the twenty-eight were graduates of Millsaps. Some of them are, but among the group are graduates of schools far worse than Millsaps. Some are from Emory; others are graduates of Southern Methodist University, and, heaven help us, there were some from Yale!

And now that you know the schools from which they come, you won't be too surprised by what they did. Those radical Methodist Misfits got together and wrote a statement, the most subversive thing I've ever seen, and had the nerve to entitle it: *Born of Conviction.*

Well, now, that statement set the sparks flying, believe me. One young minister had two of the tires on his car slashed; word was spread that he'd probably get clobbered if he remained in his community. This time his wisdom was greater than when he signed that "Conviction" thing; he was forced to leave, so he left. And that's wisdom in these parts. Some forty to fifty per cent of the churches which have (in some cases, had) these young Misfits for pastors held emergency meetings. I think, by and large, they had to decide just how to administer Christian Charity best—by lynching, or just withdrawing their pastor's salary. At one time in January there were three young preachers off the payroll. And during all this turbulence Mississippi Methodists all over the state waited to hear the word of the Bishop. Almost two weeks passed before Bishop Marvin Franklin spoke, and when he did, man, was it powerful. It was one of those rare, earth-shaking things, the likes of which happens no more than once in a generation. Said the Bishop:

> In a cabinet meeting we have been going over the program and work of our church in the Mississippi Conference. We rejoice in the great progress made during the year that is past. Multitudes have been added to the church, and the Conference has received the largest financial support in her history.
>
> We each declare anew our support of the doctrines and historic positions of the Methodist Church.
>
> Tensions of many kinds are in the world today, among them is that of race relations. The ninth amendment to the Constitution of the Methodist Church places racial relationships on a voluntary basis. By the provisions of this amendment, integration is not forced upon any part of our church.
>
> Our Conference has a great program in evangelism, education, missions, and other areas. Let us move on to do the work of the church, loving mercy, doing justly, and walking humbly with our Lord, pressing towards the mark of the prize of high calling of God in Christ Jesus.

While the Bishop didn't say so, the Mississippi Conference is held in late May. Could be that some young preachers may decide they went into the wrong business . . . at undetermined dates during the year following the Conference . . . but only time will tell.

And do you know what some of the Methodist Misfits actually called that terribly subversive statement? "A Plea for Freedom of the Pulpit." Now, in the name of heaven, how misguided can anyone get?

Well, there followed letters, and more letters, some by lay members, others by uncorrupted ministers in the Methodist Church. For example, one is presented here, written to Dr. Sam E. Ashmore, editor of the *Mississippi Methodist Advocate:*

Dear Brother Ashmore,

In the January 2, 1963, issue of the *Mississippi Methodist Advocate,* I read the article entitled "Born of Conviction," in which twenty-eight ministers of the Mississippi Conference have boldly endorsed integration. As a minister of the Gospel of Jesus Christ, I feel that I too am "Born of Conviction," that integration is "unalterably opposed" and contrary to the teaching of the Bible, especially the Old Testament (Deut. 7, 1–3, Joshua 23, 12–13, and Ezra 9, 12). Jesus was a champion of the Old Testament scriptures and He did not come to change, but to fulfill.

I do not know who wrote the introduction to the article, but I readily question the statement that "They represent some of our best trained and most promising ministers." What do we judge a preacher's training by? Do we say they are well trained because they have had seminary training? One of the last things Jesus told His disciples was to tarry until they had received the best training God could offer, the baptism of the Holy Ghost. I really wonder if they are "our best trained . . . ministers." Men led by the Holy Spirit are in accordance with God's will.

We cannot have much more conformity and "blind leaders of the blind." We need men of vision, or the Methodist Church will "fall into the ditch" like the mixed races of the past. (What happened to the Edomites?)

Brother Ashmore, I believe that you are also a man "Born of Conviction," and ask that you print this comment from an approved supply pastor who some day wants to be a member of a Conference that stands on a solid foundation—"If the foundations be destroyed, what can the righteous do?" (Psalms 11:3).

Yours in His Service,

Bertist C. Rouse, Pastor
Dixie Methodist Church
Route 3,
Hattiesburg, Mississippi

And that, my friends, is the way a good, solid Mississippi preacher ought to sound—whether he can read or not.

Have you any idea of the evil done by those twenty-eight Methodist Misfits? Well, the day following the publication of the statement, twenty-three misguided souls, all Methodist Misfits, too, in the northern part of the state said they endorsed the thing. That was bad enough, to corrupt that many young men of the cloth; however, the evil spread, and to probably the largest Methodist Church in the state, the Galloway Church in Jackson, to the pastor there, Dr. W. B. Selah, who made a wild and completely reckless statement. You don't believe it? Read this:

Jesus said, "One is your Father and you are all brothers." The doctrine of the Fatherhood of God and the Brotherhood of Man is fundamental in Christ's teaching. For seventeen years I have preached the law of Christian love from the pulpit of Galloway Methodist Church. This law means that we must seek for all men, black and white, the same justice, the same rights, and the same opportunities that we seek for ourselves. Nothing less than this is Christian love. To discriminate against a man because of his color or his creed is contrary to the will of God. Forced segregation is wrong. We should voluntarily desegregate all public facilities. We should treat men not on the basis of color, but on the basis of conduct.

In the light of Christian principle, there can be no color bar in a Christian church. It is not sinful for white people to prefer to worship with white people or for colored people to prefer to worship with colored people. The sin comes when a church seeks to erect a color bar before the Cross of Christ. As Christians, we cannot say to anyone, "You cannot come into the house of God." No Conference, no preacher, no official board can put up a color bar in the church. That matter is determined by the nature of Christianity, which is an inclusive fellowship of those who seek the Lord. The house of God is a house of prayer for all people—black and white.

When a person seeks membership in the church he is not asked about the color of his skin. He is asked about his faith in God as revealed in Christ. Salvation is not by color, but by faith. There can be no color bar in a Christian institution.

Race prejudice is a denial of Christian brotherhood. Any kind of prejudice—racial or religious—weakens the nation by dividing it into hostile groups. It sets race against race, church against church. This plays into the hands of the communists and makes it easier for them to do their diabolical work.

Every American citizen, black or white, is entitled to the best educational opportunity the state affords. In our struggle with communism we need to offer all our people the best possible training, for in the long run the fight for freedom will be won by that nation which produces the finest brains and the best character. The public schools must be kept open.

No doubt there are some places where laymen expect the preacher to echo their opinions. The freedom of the pulpit must be maintained. The preacher must get his message not from the community but from Christ. He must state his convictions and allow others to disagree. I'm sure that many of my people disagree with things I say. But they want me to declare my convictions. "Think and let think" is the genius of the Methodist Church. Thoughtful laymen will demand a free pulpit. Only a free pulpit inspires people to think.

All these things I have stated to my people many times before.

You may think that wasn't an evil and subversive statement, but it's apparent God thought otherwise. A day or two after making the statement, Dr. Selah was hospitalized with a hemorrhaging ulcer. And in these parts we call that "Divine Retribution," and at supersonic speed, too.

Personally, I long for that old-time religion. It was good for Paul and Silas, without benefit of twenty-eight upstarts who do *really, sincerely believe* what they said they did.

One final note on all this, and it's to show how bad things in Mississippi are, at least in the Methodist Church. One of the ministers who signed the—the awful thing—told me that letters they'd received had been about ten to one in their favor.

Mercy! That's about all I can think to say—and it's kind of a little prayer at that.

QUO VADIS, RED NECK?

There has been much palaver of recent date concerning the passing of the "Mississippi Red Neck." We confess that until a short time ago we were unfamiliar with the term in any form, and as a result had to inquire as to its meaning.

From what we have been told, the "Mississippi Red Neck" is, generally speaking, a farmer of a few acres, who wears blue denim shirts, overalls, long drawers summer and winter, chews tobacco, and comes to town every Saturday afternoon.

Too, he is described as being generally narrow-minded and quite ignorant.

From all accounts that is the famed "Mississippi Red Neck."

Numerous press accounts reveal his departure from the Mississippi scene. Well, so be it. We really don't know.

What with the above described characteristics, it would seem a safe conclusion that the "Red Neck" was ignorant and was unaware of it totally.

Now, from observation, and we haven't had to ask anyone about this, there has appeared on the scene a substitution for the "Red Neck." The substitute wears white shirts, clean, pressed pants, shines his shoes, smokes cigarettes, drinks beer, and stays around town all the time.

Like the "Red Neck," for whom he has substituted, he is also ignorant. But the tragic part of it is this: He doesn't know it! Generally, he considers himself quite brilliant, having been to college. Thus, his arrogance and conceit are capable of nauseating the strongest of men.

There are many places to find the substitute, but for a close look, in abundance, check the Citizens' Councils of Mississippi.

A LETTER TO RALPH MCGILL

P.O. Box 1486
Hattiesburg, Mississippi

Mr. Ralph McGill, Publisher
The Atlanta Constitution
Atlanta, Georgia

Dear Ralph:

For a few years now we've been friends, and I'm sure I needn't tell you of my affection and regard for you as a man, nor do I think it necessary to tell you of my admiration and respect for you as a writer.

Ralph, it is because of my friendship that I write you this brief letter. I hope, I trust you'll accept my comment in the spirit in which it's written. I assure you that were you a lesser person in my evaluation, I'd ignore the matter. However, as I said, because of my regard and respect for you, I must call a certain matter to your attention.

Not too long ago you appeared on a television report on NBC, having to do with the situation here in Mississippi. On that program you said, "Mississippi is not a sovereign state. It hasn't been a sovereign state since the Constitution was adopted in 1789." (This is the essence of what you said, if not a direct quote.)

I do hesitate to say this, Ralph, but I must assume you chose the wrong dictionary when you sought a definition of the word sovereign. "SOVEREIGN—(1) Chief or highest; for example, Webster says: supreme. (2) Supreme in power; superior in position to all others. (3) Independent of, and unlimited by, any other; possessing, or entitled to, original and independent authority or jurisdiction."

Well, *Webster's Dictionary* is published north of the Mason-Dixon line; therefore, no one can rely on anything it says, especially when it comes to important, life-or-death words, like sovereign.

I know, of course, your city of Atlanta was overrun by the Yankees a few years ago. It's entirely possible that you don't have access to the proper, the correct, the only dictionary to be used by Southerners, what with it probably having been burned or in some way destroyed by Yankees. The dictionary to which I refer is the *Dixiecrat Dictionary,* published by the Confederate Publishing Company in Richmond and-or Montgomery. (You'll recall, they also printed our money.) The *Dixiecrat Dictionary* was edited and compiled by John C. Calhoun and Jefferson Davis, with footnotes by Uncle Tom. Anyway, this is where we in Mississippi get our definition of all words. For example:

SOV'REN, STATE: (1) The most. Means what any state governor wants it to mean, when he wants it to mean it, and for whatever reason he may have.

So, Ralph, you can see that our own dictionary goes further than the one published up north. I trust you'll be guided by our own when next you choose a word that has to do with a Sov'ren State.

Ralph, believe me as a friend, it's so much better to be informed correctly.

Warm regards,

P. D. East, Associate Editor,
Confederate Publishing Co.

THE DEATH OF MEDGAR EVERS

At 11:30 A.M., Tuesday, June 11, 1963, the first human lung transplant in this country was achieved by a group of surgeons at the University of Mississippi Medical School in Jackson. The experiments had been underway for seven years, and more than five hundred small animals were used before the successful transplant was made on a human.

This represents a feat truly remarkable; it is a breakthrough which may well save many thousands of lives in the years to come.

And it happened in Jackson, Mississippi.

Thirteen hours later, at 12:30 A.M., June 12th, the life of a human being was taken by a murderer, for no reason other than he had dedicated himself to the attainment of his rights, and the rights of members of his race, as guaranteed under the Constitution of these United States. I speak of Medgar Evers, and I have no doubt you've read all the news stories relating to his murder.

The success of the lung transplant and the murder of Medgar, to me, constitute another of the paradoxes of which Mississippi and the South are filled.

As you would expect from civilized people there were words of protest, words of regret, words of sympathy. The mayor of Jackson, Allen Thompson, said he and "all the citizens of Jackson were shocked, humiliated and sick at heart." And the city posted a five thousand dollar reward.

And the paradox in all this?

For weeks the Negro citizens of Jackson had pleaded with the mayor to appoint a bi-racial committee, the purpose of which was to simply discuss the differences in citizenship which exist between the first-class citizens (white) and the second-class citizen, the Negro. Mr. Thompson refused repeatedly to even consider such a committee and, at last reports, continued to refuse the request. Mayor Thompson did not murder Medgar Evers, but his very attitude did its part in helping load the rifle that did murder him.

Senator John Stennis, in Washington, said, "Along with all Mississippians I deplore the violence and loss of life within our state." Frankly, I do not doubt the words spoken by Senator Stennis, nor do I doubt the words of Mayor Thompson.

Also in Washington, Senator James O. Eastland said, "The murder was very regrettable and deplored by everyone. . . . I know I speak for everybody in the state in expressing the hope that justice will be meted out to the guilty party or parties."

I have no reason to doubt his words, either.

However, on that same day, a group of eighteen Southern senators met—and this included the two from Mississippi—and issued an angry denunciation of the President's proposal for civil rights legislation. A paradox? To my mind it is, yes. No, our two senators didn't murder Medgar—but they certainly seem to have added their bit to the loading of the rifle that did.

On the day of Medgar's murder, the two newspapers in Jackson added one thousand dollars to the reward being offered for the apprehension of the murderer; *The Clarion-Ledger* stated: "Such lawlessness must not go unpunished." And the paradox here?

Frankly, you'd have to read both the *Clarion-Ledger* and *Daily News* to see it. Neither of them, insofar as I know, has helped toward the attainment of social justice or legal equality. But more specifically, on the day before Medgar was murdered, one of the daily columnists in *The Clarion-Ledger* wrote a piece—well, in part, herewith:

> A leftist group, the American Veterans Committee, passed the hat at the final session of its recent twentieth annual convention in Washington and raised $477 for a Mississippi leader of the NAACP.
>
> The fund was raised for Medgar W. Evers, Jackson Negro who is "Gulf States Field Secretary" for the NAACP, arrested here during downtown picketing activity. AVC has been loud for "civil rights" but silent on the menace of Red Cuba.
>
> Evers, who was also elected to the board of the American Veterans Committee, was to have received the group's Meritorious Achievement Award but was unable to be in Washington because of desegregation agitations here.
>
> A telegram accompanying the impromptu floor collection said the $477 was "to be used to help provide whatever aid is necessary to keep Jackson's courageous children safe and well." Evers was not asked to give an accounting of how the money is spent.

No, not for one second do I think the newspapers in Jackson murdered Medgar but, again, I believe firmly they helped load the rifle.

And did anyone else help? Well, the authentic reports of police brutality seem to help just a little—the beating of a white professor—the beating of a fifteen-year-old Negro girl—both on the day after the murder—this, along with the mayor's comment that "There has been no sanction of police brutality. As far as I know there has been no police brutality." Yet, according to news stories, there were several newsmen who actually saw the two incidents mentioned above.

This kind of blindness has loaded, does, and will load guns. The last one was aimed at Medgar Evers, that's true, but who can say where the next one will be aimed? At you? At me?

I don't want to preach; I'm much too angry and sad and hurt

by what happened to want to get into a sermon. However, let me say, and very simply, that so long as we feel that the Negro is demanding "special rights," there's going to be trouble—with our present attitude, believe me, there'll be more blood spilled in Mississippi—or in any Southern state, for that matter—and never think for one moment that it can't possibly be yours, or mine—it can be, and easily.

Before God, I cannot see that the Negro wants anything more than equal rights—his rights under the law—his dignity as a human being, created in the image of his Maker.

Is that too much for any man to ask? I think not; moreover, I think so long as we continue as we are—and that's you and it's me—we, too, are helping to load guns—all of us have done it in the past. In a very real sense it doesn't matter who pulled the trigger that took a human life on June 12th in Jackson—all of us share the blame, the guilt is that of us all.

So help me God, I believe this with all my heart.

Franklin H. Littell

THE CHURCHES AND THE RULE OF LAW

FRANKLIN H. LITTELL is a Professor of Church History at the Chicago Theological Seminary and has formerly held teaching positions at the Candler School of Theology at Emory University and the Perkins School of Theology at Southern Methodist University. Born in Syracuse, New York, Dr. Littell holds degrees from Cornell College, Union Theological Seminary and Yale University. In 1957, he received his Doctor of Theology degree from the University of Marburg. A noted lecturer and organizer of church projects, especially in the field of youth education, he is the author of the award-winning The Anabaptist View of the Church, *which received the Brewer Award of the American Society of Church History in 1952. His other books include* The Free Church *and* The German Phoenix. *He has been decorated* Grosse Verdienstkreuz *by the Federal Republic of Germany.*

IN HIS NOW FAMOUS "Letter from Birmingham's Jail,"[1] Dr. Martin Luther King, Jr., replied to a group of clergymen who had criticized the demonstrations as poorly timed and ill-conceived. In a message remarkably ironic throughout he nevertheless expressed his disappointment in the white churches.

You deplore the demonstrations that are presently taking place in Birmingham. But I am sorry that your statement did not express a similar concern for the conditions that brought the demonstrations into being.
We know through painful experience that freedom is never voluntarily given by the oppressor; it must be demanded by the oppressed.

1 See pp. 62–80.

> Frankly, I have never yet engaged in a direct action movement that was "well timed," according to the timetable of those who have not suffered unduly from the disease of segregation.

After stating simply his disappointment in the white moderate, long in verbalization but short on action, he concluded:

> Let me rush on to mention my other disappointment. I have been so greatly disappointed with the white Church and its leadership. . . . All too many . . . have been more cautious than courageous and have remained silent behind the anesthetizing security of stained-glass windows.

Dr. King's disappointment is soundly grounded, even though there have been some encouraging exceptions to the general rule of failure. As a distinguished leader of the Reformed Church in America recently put it,

> Birmingham is a tragic story for us because it represents a Christian failure, a Protestant failure, and its tragedy is only a dramatic illustration of the same failure which goes on in the community in which you and I live. But it is time we Anglo-Saxon Protestants ask ourselves some serious questions. If differences in race and culture are really more important to us than unity in Christ, then what have we become in the light of the gospel? I make bold to suggest that a church which is simply white supremacy at prayer is one which our Lord will spew out of his mouth.[2]

The onus is rightly placed, for the Deep South is the largest bloc of intact Protestant culture left in the world, and the question must be faced whether the failure of the white churches to provide a clean-cut and disciplined witness is not related to the fact that a certain type of Protestant ethos is there dominant.

PROTESTANT INDISCIPLINE

At the level of verbalization, the stand of the leading churches of the area is clear enough, as can be seen by reference to the Ap-

[2] Howard G. Hageman, as reported in *Presbyterian Outlook* 145 (7/8/63), 26:8.

pendix of the Campbell and Pettigrew study of Little Rock.[3] Words which never become incarnate, resolutions which have no binding quality, are less honest, however, than outright racism. Ignorance may be overcome, wickedness may be purged, but hypocrisy awaits the Judgment. "I learned just one fundamental thing during the Third Reich," said one leader of the Christian resistance to Hitler. "The Christian should never verbalize a position which he is not willing to make a matter of witness."

The lack of integrity of the white churches can be seen at two levels: (1) in the failure to maintain a decent practice of Christian brotherhood; (2) in the failure to maintain a decent standard of discipline against mob violence and anarchy. Although these two areas blend together when the discussion is carried on at the level of principles, in actual practice two different situations are involved. The first issue is the integrity of the church as a universal community, within which men and women of all races and peoples and tongues have become One Body. The second issue is a civic one in impact, in which the Christians are supposed to be better than the laws—as one early Father of the Church could proudly claim for his people. Today, the behavior of many so-called "Christians" is much worse than the laws, and the church leadership has so far been unwilling to enforce classical standards of discipline in the face of it.

If the church be truly the Church, then ". . . the cross of Christ has created a new nation of men. This new nation, this sturdy race is unique in the history of mankind. It is a race created not by blood, but by grace."[4] This point was made most poignantly by a Mississippi editor, winner of a Pulitzer prize:

Well, certainly, the Governor's cousin is correct when she complains that the racial attitudes of her native State's leaders make more difficult her job as a missionary in Nigeria.

3 Ernest G. Campbell, and Thomas F. Pettigrew, *Christians in Racial Crisis: A Study of Little Rock's Ministry* (Washington, D.C.: Public Affairs Press, 1959), pp. 137–70.

4 Quotation in John LaFarge, *The Catholic Viewpoint on Race Relations* (New York: Hanover House, 1956), p. 111.

"You send us out here to preach that Christ died for all men," wrote Antonina Canzoneri in a Mississippi Baptist newspaper. "Then you make a travesty of our message by refusing to associate with them because of the color of their skin. . . ."

In Mississippi, a person who attempts to carry Christianity out the church door, who dares to practice the Christian virtue of tolerance outside the church, is branded as a liberal, a leftist, a Communist, a nigger-lover.

Christ was the greatest champion of the underdog the world has ever known. If He were to visit us here, now, by whose side would He stand—beside the brick-throwing, foul-mouthed, destroying, profaning, slavering members of the mob and their "nice-folk" eggers-on, or beside the trembling victim of their hate?

There cannot be one answer for Sunday between 11 A.M. and noon and another for the rest of the week. And there cannot be one brand of Christianity for Mississippi and another for Nigeria and the rest of the world.[5]

A church is either loyal to the Universal Church and Her Lord or it is not a "church" at all. The various congregations which have turned away Negro worshippers have in that same act cut themselves off from the Church of Jesus Christ. In spite of their professed commitments, however, those who have vowed to maintain the form of sound words and sustain the discipline of the Covenant have been unwilling to deal with apostasy as required by Scripture and by the various denominational disciplines.

Moreover, many of the church leaders have preferred to defer to individuals of status who have defied Christian standards (as well as the law of the land) rather than maintain the bonds of peace and brotherhood with Negro Christians of highest integrity. America has been very fortunate to date that the key leaders in the Negro initiative have been Christians, and that the churches have a far greater influence so far in the life of the Negro community than among the whites. Nothing else can account for the astonishing patience and long-sufferingness of the Negroes in the face of brutality and mob violence to try a saint. But where is the loyalty of

5 Ira B. Harkey, Editor of the Pascagoula (Miss.) *Chronicle,* as interviewed and reported in the *San Francisco Chronicle* (July 10, 1963), p. 8.

the white Christians to men like Martin Luther King, Jr., President of the Southern Christian Leadership Conference, or James L. Farmer, Executive Secretary of the Congress of Racial Equality?

Dr. King is the son of a Baptist minister, himself a distinguished Baptist minister. He was educated at Crozer Theological Seminary and took his Ph.D. at Boston University. A great preacher and a great-hearted Christian, he has to watch many white ministers cultivating their association with figures like Ellender and Eastland and Barnett and Wallace in preference to the practice of Christian brotherhood.

Mr. Farmer is the son of a Methodist professor of theology and —like Dr. King—was educated in church colleges (Wiley and Howard). He was for several years an officer in the National Council of Methodist Youth, the official Methodist youth movement. A man of culture, a writer, a long-time leader in the NAACP and CORE, he has to face dogs and beastly men while many who should stand beside him as his peers watch from afar off and perhaps criticize the action of free men as "untimely." "Untimely," indeed! When Gabriel blows his horn, it is later than we think.

THE PROBLEM OF LAW

Perhaps the source of difficulty is the fact that the particular type of Protestantism strongest in the Deep South—Baptist and Methodist—is that which was traditionally long on grace and short on law. Sectarian Protestantism has always, in contrast to Lutheranism and Anglicanism and Calvinism, had an unusually strong sense of loyalty to the small fellowship of brethren. But it has had increasing difficulty in maintaining a responsible relationship to the claims of the Universal Church. And it has never had a very fruitful understanding of the importance of the law. Certainly the life of fellowship, sustained by the loving use of the means of grace, is a dimension of the Christian life. But fundamental to it is respect for order against anarchy, for the law as against the jungle. And a religious ethos which gives too little attention to the significance of law and structures may very well be insensitive to the sufferings of those who are deprived of protection from marauders and beasts of prey.

Initially, the weakness was not so apparent. In the 16th century the movements which stressed the voluntary fellowship were savagely persecuted and had no possible relationship to government and law. In the 17th century, when the radical Puritans came to have some role in the Commonwealth, they learned to use the Old Testament as the rule of law and the New Testament as the rule of grace. If their descendants still had the Ten Commandments written on their hearts, as it were; if they still remembered the God who purposes justice and mercy and the redemption of the oppressed—then there would be clear and objective reference for dealing with corrupt administrations enforcing immoral local laws. But as it is we have only the infantile remark of the Governor of Alabama: "How can they make us obey a law we don't like?" As though the God of the Bible, the God of nations and generations before whom the peoples rise and fall, were suddenly reduced to the status of one of the Penates, to the level of a household god! As though law and justice and righteousness were nothing but matters of opinion!

On the edge of the jungle, the law is a hard-won and wonderful thing. It is especially significant that when the spirit of the jungle is incarnate in a mob, anti-Semitism is almost always present. For the Jew, whether believer or not, symbolizes the law to the spiritual underworld. In the press toward totalitarianism, the churches can take on protective coloration and accommodate to the spirit that rages through the streets. The Jew cannot: by his very existence he serves to remind men of the God who is the Author of law, who wills order. Even if the dominant Protestantism of the area were not weak in the concerns of the Old Testament, the latent anti-Semitism of the natural man (Gentile) would come to the fore. It is frighteningly significant that Jewish temples were bombed and defaced in considerable number following the announcements of Byrnes and Thurmond and Talmadge and Russell and Faubus an Davis and the rest that they would call out the mob to defy the l The churches would have suffered too had they remained fai

And where they did, ministers and church college presidents have suffered indignity and even buildings have been despoiled.

There is another level too at which disrespect for the law and the structures which guarantee orderly process expresses itself: in tolerating city and state administrations which have become demonic. At the present time several of the state administrations of the Deep South are semi-totalitarian in style of operation, and four —South Carolina, Alabama, Mississippi and Louisiana—are virtually indistinguishable from the finished product commonly seen in Nazism or Communism.[6] They are governed by tiny cliques which have never won an honest election, which survive by disfranchising a majority of the population, which manipulate one party systems, which vote "rotten boroughs" when all else fails. Admittedly, democratic political theory and action have not yet caught up with the realities of the totalitarian methodology and system. When is the citizen obligated to resist a government which is no longer representative, which perpetuates itself by fraud and force, which intimidates and brutalizes whole sections of the population, which calls up the denizens of the jungle to bolster its shaky power?

As Roscoe Drummond pointed out in his report from Washington, voter registration is higher than the population in 115 counties of seven states (Alabama, Florida, Georgia, Louisiana, North Carolina, Tennessee and Virginia), ranging from 101 per cent to 165 per cent of the white voting-age population.[7] This is but the beginning of the story which ends in the most cruel fraud and defiance of the law in treatment of Negro citizens. What is truly at stake in these areas is not, therefore, racial justice: what is at stake whether that section of the Federal Constitution which guaran- these states a republican form of government will continue red. It is worth remembering that no totalitarian system en overthrown without outside intervention. Doubly therefore, is the fact that the major churches which area are churches with an inadequate understanding

"From Germany to Georgia," *Christian Century* LXXVI this article Georgia has held an open primary and part of sentative clique has begun to fall.

ılian Sentinel (Mont.) June 29, 1963, p. 4.

of the law and the liberties which are only available under due process of law.

WHAT IS TO BE DONE?

The first problem of the large Protestant churches is to recover internal integrity and discipline. They are the products of a century and a half of extraordinarily successful mass evangelism, in the course of which internal discipline—both in the instruction of catechumens and in maintaining the standards of full membership—has been virtually eliminated. Until there is a renewal of the life of these churches they will continue to function as private clubs rather than members of the Universal Church.

As they are renewed, as they slough off the comfortable status of social establishments (culture-religion), their style of life will begin to reflect their commitments rather than the spirit of the times. When this happens, they will face again the problem of reclaiming or dis-fellowshipping those who by blatant and stubborn defiance of the church and the honor of her name bring shame and discredit upon her work and mission.

Then the question of the missionary in Nigeria will be answered, and the question of Martin Luther King, Jr., to the white churches will be answered too. For then the tune of the churches' music will be set by the absolute pitch of God's law and will for His people, and not oscillate with the wild cries and tumult of sound of the uncreated and disordered—chaotic as it was before He laid His hand upon the waste and void, and made it good.

August Thompson and John Howard Griffin

DIALOGUE WITH FATHER THOMPSON

FATHER AUGUST THOMPSON, born July 7, 1926, was the second of Eunice and Louis Thompson's nine children. Both parents descended from generations of Catholics. As a child, he worked in rice fields, earning from 25¢ to 50¢ for "a long half-day's work." His parents maintained a devout home atmosphere and they insisted that all of the children receive an education. Father Thompson attended local grade schools, and entered the seminary at the age of fifteen. After ordination in 1957 at New Orleans' historic St. Louis Cathedral, Father Thompson served as assistant at St. Anthony's in Cottonport, Alexandria Diocese. In 1962 he was transferred to St. Charles Church, Ferriday, Louisiana, as administrator.

JOHN HOWARD GRIFFIN joined the front ranks of contemporary American novelists in 1952 with the publication of his best-selling first novel, The Devil Rides Outside. *A native Southerner, he is much sought after as a lecturer, both in the fields of music (he is a recognized authority on Gregorian Chant) and race relations, his wide knowledge of which led to the writing of the incredible personal documentation of race hatred in the South,* Black Like Me. *The film version of that book is scheduled for release in 1964. A forthcoming book,* Scattered Shadows, *chronicles his years of blindness—he was blinded during World War II, but later, almost miraculously, recovered his sight on his farm in Mansfield, Texas. In addition to contributing to major periodicals in this country and abroad, Mr. Griffin is the author of two other books,* Nuni *and* The Land of the High Sky.

FATHER THOMPSON, *since you are a priest who happens also to be a Negro, we might begin talking of the effects of racism on religion in the U.S. The Church has, of course, been strongly outspoken on this subject.*

Yes, I have in my hand *Pacem in Terris,* which means so much to me because here is the Pope speaking, and we can't evade the fact that once the Holy Father speaks, we must listen. Pope John XXIII's death was a grievous loss to us, but I am happy to see that Pope Paul VI is moving ahead in the same spirit.

There is one part here in *Pacem in Terris* where His Holiness speaks specifically about racism. "But truth requires the elimination of every trace of racism," Pope John says in paragraph 86. Racism is our major problem in the world today. If we face this truth, we must get rid of racism. I'd like to concentrate on this—to air some of these truths even where they hurt, even where they are likely to cause strong disagreement.

We needn't beat around the bush, Father. We are going to discuss one of the greatest incongruities in our times—the racism that exists quite openly in some areas of the South and other areas of the country as practiced by Catholics. Didn't your own sister have to leave the South in order to become a registered nurse?

Yes, my sister Margarette. She had to leave the South for her studies because no Catholic hospital in the South would take her for training. This was about 1951, I believe, but even today in the so-called Deep South I do not think that any Negro girl could get into a Catholic hospital for her nurse's training. This story can be found in the September 1955 issue of *Jubilee* Magazine. Now, with Archbishop Hallinan's courageous stand, it might be possible in Atlanta.

Father, to clear the air, let's talk about racists' claims that Negroes are morally inferior by nature; that there are more Negro crimes, a looser sexual morality . . .

I'd like to make two points here. Much of this kind of talk comes from the need to justify injustices. Only by believing that Negroes are intrinsically inferior can non-Negroes tolerate in conscience the system that defrauds us of our civil and human rights. We hear talk about "Negro crime," but do Negroes commit any crimes that men of other complexions do not commit? No, these are not Negro crimes, but the crimes of men. If statistically Negroes commit more crimes in America than non-Negroes, the cause lies not in our "Negro-ness" but in the very ghetto life that we are forced to lead under a system of rigid segregation, in the formation we receive. This system, with all its injustices, deprives men of any sense of dignity or personal value—and no man can live without that. If you kept a significant number of white men in such a degrading environment, systematically deprived them of dignity and hope, closed most doors to self-fulfillment and left open only the door to despair, the white crime rate would soar. Also, since Negroes see that law-enforcement generally means abuse for us, we grow up with less respect for the law than we should have. In the South, where so many of the police belong to the Klans or other racist groups, no example is set that might give Negroes any true respect for the law.

Here again, I would like to refer to the Holy Father's *Pacem in Terris.* He says: "It is not true that some human beings are by nature superior and others inferior. All men are equal in their natural dignity."

Another thing—statistics can be most misleading. Every time a Negro youth snatches a purse, this goes on the books—as it should. But a white group of racists can burn down a Negro's home because he attempts to register to vote—they can bomb, beat, intimidate and otherwise deprive Negroes of rights which we guarantee to every citizen, but these criminal acts, committed under the cloak of anonymity, do not get into the statistics.

The second point I would like to make is that "morality" has come to mean only one thing in our society—sex. Yet morality has to do with the right and wrong in human behavior. The deliberate distortion of statistics, as used by racist propagandists, to prove that we are morally "inferior" is in itself immoral: "Thou shalt not bear false witness. . . ." Negroes see clearly the contradiction involved where men know all the nuances of the Sixth and Ninth Commandments, but are seemingly unaware of the others, particularly the Eighth. We know that we, as American citizens, are *born* with certain inalienable rights and that to be denied those rights without just cause constitutes a gigantic fraud. This kind of crime does not get into the statistics either.

And yet, Father, we hear constantly the cant that Negroes must change, *must earn the rights we unhesitatingly accord even the most degraded non-Negro. We hear it also among Catholics, don't we?*

Yes, and here the truth is going to be painful. I realize that white Catholic Southerners are the products of their environment—the prisoners of their southern segregated culture just as we Negroes are. From their point of view, changes in their attitudes are difficult—and in fact they are not even aware that such changes might be indicated. I sympathize deeply with the agony that comes when the need for such changes of attitude is perceived—and more and more are perceiving it.

But let me speak from the Negro's point of view. We have our own dilemmas. They expect us to "change" and yet they give little help to bring about change. This is particularly true and troublesome in the area of religion. In some southern dioceses for example Negroes cannot attend retreats or days of recollection. I have had parishioners come up and ask me what a retreat is. They have only heard about them. But we cannot attend retreats—

Except as a group?

Not even as a group. They just don't want us. In some places our young people cannot attend camps. Too often we cannot join church societies. Yes, it is true that we could form our own little segregated Negro versions of these same societies, but you lose the whole spirit—the very Catholicity—of it when you do that. In such areas, Negro couples cannot attend Cana Conferences. Do you know that I, as a priest, have never attended a Cana Conference? Do you know that white non-Catholics are welcomed into Catholic churches and can attend church functions where I, as a Negro priest, would not be permitted?

But look at the problem. Here we constantly call on Negroes to be patient, humble, virtuous—and this is right, of course. But Negroes are expected to learn these things with the one little sermon we hear on Sundays. And if the priest who serves us is not fervent—or if he unknowingly treats us in a way to deprive us of our dignity, paternalistically, calling us "boy" or "girl"—then we have little opportunity of developing into anything but poor Catholics indeed.

Didn't St. Thomas Aquinas say that no man can live without love, and that if he is denied the love of the things of the spirit he will surely fall into the love of the things of the world? Here is the crux of the problem. I think it is almost impossible for non-Negroes, even in the Deep South where they think they know all about us, to realize how many doors that lead one to a love of the things of the spirit—education and religion particularly—are effectively closed to Negroes. Or how deeply we are scandalized to see Catholics helping to hold those doors closed to us by cooperating with the kind of segregation that Holy Mother Church has declared abominable.

Negro writers in particular have spoken out with a kind of slashing bitterness that often shocks the white community. Do these writers mirror resentments felt by most members of the Negro community? What they say certainly disagrees with the often-heard contention of Southern whites that Negroes were a happy, contented people until outside agitators and the U.S. Supreme Court began stirring them up.

Yes, one doesn't know whether to laugh or cry when our discontent is blamed on outside instigators and the 1954 Supreme Court decision. How false. How false to think that our discontent is anything other than the discontent of men who are not allowed to be whole.

Professor Dwight L. Dumond, in his recent great work which is now the definitive study in its field, "Antislavery," *explodes many of these southern myths and demonstrates how old this discontent is, what desperate attempts Negroes made to escape, how many others committed suicide.*

Yes, our discontent is as old as our history in this country. But for a long time we had to hide it. If we did not smile and act happy, we were considered arrogant, soreheads and we were taught a lesson. Do you remember Paul Laurence Dunbar's outcry, written around the turn of the century:

We wear the mask that grins and lies . . .
We smile, but, O great Christ, our cries
To Thee from tortured souls arise . . .

That was written fifty years ago. We had to accommodate, as we used to call it—but what the whites never realized is what went on in our homes at night. I can remember back some thirty years myself, to what I heard when I was a little boy. Of course, we went out and worked every day. We worked in the fields, we worked in the houses. But when we went home, the times we wept, the resentments we spilled out to one another—well, if the whites had heard them, none of us would have had a livelihood the next day. This has gone on a long, long time. These resentments have grown and have finally reached a stage where we simply cannot hide our discontent any longer. This is especially true since World War II, in which Negroes fought to protect and defend rights and liberties which they have not found when they returned home.

What about claims frequently made by whites that Negroes, never having known anything else in the South, become inured to all of these undignifying things—that they do not really suffer from the lack of rights they have never known?

How can any man ever become accustomed to getting cheated? When the body is never fully fed, it never stops being hungry. It is the same with man's spirit—it hungers, hungers after dignity, freedom and love; and it never stops hungering after these things until it is finally crushed. We Negroes have often referred to our treatment as being like a bone thrown to a dog. You don't ask the dog if it wants this bone, or if it wants another or if it wants a piece of meat. You just throw the bone and tell the dog it must take that. And that's what happens too often to our citizens of color. Negroes are thrown a bone and told: "This is what you want. This is how you want it." The Negro just cannot understand why it is that some persons never think we can grow up enough to know exactly what we want and always have to have others tell us what we want and how we want it. In the past, Negroes who said: "I want more than a bone. I need something more than that for myself and my children," were called "bad niggers" and silenced.

This one point should be emphasized. The Negro has never become accustomed and he will never become accustomed to being treated as less than fully a human being. The American Negro will never become accustomed to being treated as less than fully an American. The Catholic Negro will never become accustomed to being treated as less than fully a Catholic.

What about the role of religion in solving this problem of racism? In your youth and even now, how have religious leaders solved this problem? I do not mean Catholics exclusively, but all religious leaders.

In my youth, it simply wasn't solved. It wasn't solved because everyone was silent. Everyone was afraid.

Afraid of what, Father?

Afraid of the truth. Afraid to face facts. Negroes and some percipient whites have for a long time tried to make these truths known—but they are too painful for most to face. And finally, you get tired of trying to bring forth the truth when no one listens. You are talking to the wall. You are talking to the wind.

Father, this truth about which we speak—this truth as you know it and as I have known it as a Negro Catholic—in many of its aspects, this truth is deeply scandalizing. Many of us have held back telling these things out of our love of the Church. Do you think we were right?

We are never right in suppressing any truth that could help to bring about right.

Let's pursue this. We very often hold back for fear of offering scandal, particularly to non-Catholics; for fear that anti-Catholics might build their case against Catholicism even stronger through over-emphasis on this scandal of truth. And yet I wonder if by doing this—and you can answer this better than I—we have not deepened and in effect perpetuated the scandal. Have we hidden our problems rather than solved them?

This has been a source of the deepest trouble with me. Many believe that we should keep our skeletons in the closet; but I am convinced that we simply cannot afford to have any skeletons—especially skeletons that disillusion souls and drive them from God.

Imagine what happens to a new Negro convert who has been taught only what the Church is, what the Church stands for, and who then encounters the kind of segregation-within-the-Faith one finds in many areas of the South. I know that I, in my convert classes, have been guilty of hiding many of these things, not telling the converts what they are likely to find: that in some "non-segregated" but still segregated churches they must sit to one side; that in some Catholic churches they will not even be permitted to worship. And then I have seen them suffer the terrible shock of discovery. In taking account of our silence here, we must not forget these souls that have been sickened and alienated—souls of Negroes, yes, but precious in God's sight. The fault—the ramifications of segregation within some southern churches—becomes monstrous when seen in this light. How can any Christian soul ever be justified in acting in any way to deprive any other Christian soul of full and unhampered participation in Christian life and worship?

Do you, as a priest, feel any direct effects of prejudice within the Church?

Yes, some Catholics will not even call me Father—they dodge around such an endearing term by calling me Reverend or Padre or something like that. Of course, there are many churches and functions which I do not attend. We'll talk about that later.

In other areas of activity, prejudice complicates the priestly life at the personal level. I am rarely invited, for example, to do anything with other priests—to go fishing, for example, or make a trip. But this is simply the way things are, and does not indicate prejudice on their part necessarily. In general, priests enjoy such recreation and indeed many non-recreational pastimes with one another. I am not directly excluded from such activities, I am just never *included* in them. Of course there are really very few places where a Negro and a Caucasian priest can go together in the South. Everything is segregated. In the early days of my priesthood, this isolation was very difficult for me. It is hard to be young and to be alone and to try to live the priestly life without the companionship of fellow priests. The grace of God makes it possible, of course.

Father, when I lived for a time as a Negro in the Deep South, my greatest shock came with the discovery that if there was a Negro Catholic church in the area, I had better attend that one and that I was not free to go to Mass, for example, in the "white" church, even if that happened to be much nearer. Most Catholics are under the illusion that the Catholic Church has no taint of this kind of segregation—that any Catholic can attend any Catholic church anywhere in the world. I recall that when a Negro companion first mentioned the "Negro Catholic church," I told him there was no such thing. But in practice, there is this kind of distinction, isn't there?

I'm afraid there is. When we refer to the Negro church, it means two things: first, it means the church that is located in the Negro neighborhood, where Negroes are expected to attend, as people within any given parish are expected to attend their parish church; second, it means also that all Negroes in the vicinity, even if they happen to live miles away and are located in an area served only by a "white" church, are expected to come to the Negro church. Or, if the distance is inordinate, then Negroes can receive the sacraments at the local "white" church, but usually with a special protocol—they sit in a section reserved for them and they do not go to the communion table until all whites have received and returned to their places.

Let me tell you something else. In an area where there is a Negro church, if we have one Mass or two Masses at the Negro church and a Negro cannot attend either of them for some legitimate reason; then, even though there might be two or three other Masses that he could attend in some "white" church, he has no obligation to attend any of them. I must say here that some churches *have* opened their doors to Negro Catholics. But in many areas this has not happened yet—and so the Negro who has missed Mass in the Negro church is under no obligation to attend Mass if that means going into a white church. I can't see this double standard of morality at all.

How does this happen? I mean by what authority does a Negro feel that if he has missed Mass in his home church he has no obligation to attend Mass elsewhere?

It's tradition and it's also practice. If he went to some white churches, he would simply be put out. This doesn't seem possible, but in practice it's true enough. He would not be accepted. I know of an instance where there was only one Negro Catholic in a town and the parish there paid someone to drive this person every Sunday to the nearest town where there was a Negro Catholic church—this rather than let the person worship with them. I have people come to my church from as far as seventeen miles away, and some from towns ten or eight miles away.

How do these people react, Father?

They often talk with me about it. It is very hard—not that they mind the hardship of coming such distances—but it is hard for them to accept the fact that we Catholics preach one thing and then practice another.

Do they often protest?

Some do. Most often, though, they love their faith too much to do anything that might cause scandal. They try to "keep the peace" and offer up any sacrifice this causes. They keep silent.

Do you think silence in the face of such a gross religious injustice is wise, Father?

I doubt its wisdom when the silence serves to prolong the injustice. The longer we have this sort of scandal among Catholics, the more harm it does the Church. It alienates potential converts, both Negro and white.

Father, you received much of your seminary training in the South. Were you aware of any discrimination as a seminarian—either within or outside the seminary? Did the fact that you were a seminarian nullify any of the prevailing prejudices?

The fact that I am a priest has not nullified them, so they were certainly not nullified by the fact that I was a seminarian. There were certain churches I could not enter then just as there are churches and church activities—first communions, confirmations, Cana Conferences—where I am not allowed now, where I cannot say a scheduled Mass.

How are you made aware that you should not attend these things, Father? Does someone actually tell you that you should not—?

I have been told, yes. I have been told that I should not attend these functions or say a scheduled Mass.

So you are segregated as a priest also. Is this the same for all Negro priests in the South?

Well, let's say that in some areas, we Negro priests might be called second-class Christs, if that's possible.

We know that we do have the profound scandal of second-class Catholics—I mean this is a thing that is too well known to hide any longer, but when it is the scandal of a "second-class Christ" it becomes inconceivable. You are really a Negro first and a priest second, then?

The priesthood should take primacy over everything else, of course, but with us it's "a Negro first, a Negro second and finally a priest."

How do you react to this? This must burn you very, very deeply —not as August Thompson, but as a priest of the Catholic Church, does it not?

As a priest it does, because it degrades the priesthood. And that's why I try to do everything possible to right it. It's not just me—it's others—it's the scandal of it as it affects other Catholics that hurts the deepest.

Have you spoken this frankly to others—to priests and members of the hierarchy?

I think I have done my share of speaking frankly.

How has this been received?

I don't think I succeed in making myself clear. The simplest facts in this sort of problem tend to sound like complaining. It is suggested that I do not appreciate the complexities of the problem. But still, this does not answer the questions, nor, much more importantly, does it give me answers to the questions that others are asking.

Yes, now, you as a priest obviously cannot keep this completely from your parishioners. And eventually the whole Negro community knows about it. How do your parishioners and the potential converts in your community feel about this? Or do you hide it from them?

I do not think such things should be hidden, but I guess I do hide it as much as possible. I hide it because I know this is *not* the Church, but only the sinful acts of other Catholics—we have to make that clear. But nothing can really be hidden. Let me give you an example of how this affects new converts. Last year we went to a Christ the King rally where every parish was supposed to be represented. We went there to give honor to Christ the King of the whole world. At this rally, I was the only Negro in the procession. The Negro families who accompanied me—all of them converts of recent years—watched from the sidelines. They saw that we had only white altar boys and flower girls—no Negro children in that procession. Well, things like that stand up and cry to be seen, and you can be sure that the full impact of it hit every one of my parishioners. And they wanted to know *why*. "Why, Father, why?" They ask this all the time, and I have no answers. What can I tell them? How can I explain this sort of thing?

Father, what is being done by groups like Caritas, *the* Grail *and so forth?*

These groups, and a number of others, have done a tremendous amount of work—and still do a tremendous amount of work among Negroes. They are sometimes frowned upon by white Catholics and discriminated against.

Do you see any perceptible change for the better? What about Bishop Gerow's recent statement after the murder of Medgar Evers in Mississippi?

I was heartened to see this statement. I have it right here. I was particularly heartened by this. He said: "I am ashamed when I review the events of recent days and weeks. As a loyal son of Mississippi and a man of God, I feel in conscience compelled to speak out in the face of the grave racial situation in which we now find ourselves. This problem is unmistakably a moral one. We need frankly to admit that the guilt for the murder of Mr. Evers and the other instances of violence in our community tragically must be shared by all of us. Responsible leadership in some instances has been singularly lacking." Certainly, he is including himself as part of that leadership and is accepting his part of the guilt. It took a humble man to make such a statement.

Many people seemed to feel that it was very late in the day for Bishop Gerow to speak—that he should have spoken up a long time ago.

I can only say that I am very glad and edified to see that he spoke so well when he did speak.

Father, I would like to get down to this question of religious leadership in the Deep South as it concerns specifically human and civil rights. We have two striking examples of action on the part of Catholic leaders—the work of Archbishop Rummel in New Orleans and of Archbishop Hallinan in Atlanta. What about other bishops? Are we moving ahead, stagnating or falling back?

There have been many other moves, certainly, made with no fanfare. I myself do not believe in a lot of fanfare in connection with good actions. Out of the twenty-five dioceses in the South, twenty have desegregated schools. But even five dioceses represent a sufficiently large area to cause us grief. Yes, we are moving ahead, but of course in many cases, Negroes think it is a little too slow and that we are perhaps a little too cautious. Many Negroes still use the old "bone" symbol. They feel that white Catholics are throwing us the bone and telling us this is what we want and this is what we should have.

I'm not saying either that Negro Catholics want any kind of special treatment. They feel they are getting special treatment right now, and that is the trouble. All they want is to be treated exactly the same as any other Catholic. It cannot be repeated too often that Negroes are intensely aware of second-class citizenship in the Church; and this is the one place where it is absolutely devastating, no matter how some southern white Catholics might rationalize or try to justify it.

Father, on research trips through the Deep South, I have often encountered non-Negro Catholics who are deeply concerned. Almost invariably these people—and these are not Negroes—will ask me: "Why doesn't the Church speak now?" *The Church has been "speaking" for a long time, of course. What they mean is why do not the local prelates speak up now. This was particularly true in Mississippi before Bishop Gerow issued his recent statement. Do you, as a Negro priest, feel that the silence of some of the bishops is as loud as we Catholics sometimes seem to hear it?*

I fear that the silence in some areas is quite loud. Many people think that this silence is a sign that those in authority agree with the situation as it exists. Whether they do or not, that is not for me to say. It does seem that the splendid statement of the American

Bishops on racial justice has not always been implemented—or at least the Negro Catholic in the South can not always see evidence of its having been implemented. I feel that something must be done, and done fast, or the misunderstanding will grow. I mean the misunderstanding that grows with the illusion that local prelates condone second-class Christianity by their silence. This allows for a permissive climate of suppression. The whole tenor that is created by racists, political demagogues and so forth is not rebutted by this silence and, as Bishop Gerow states, was certainly in part responsible for the murder of Medgar Evers. Now we cannot, must not, have an Evers in every diocese to awaken us to the need to shout from the housetops the teachings of the Church on justice and human dignity.

My impression, and I would like to see if it corresponds with yours, is that in the past few years Negroes—both Catholic and non-Catholic—have become progressively disillusioned with the Catholic Church, and this because of this tacit segregation and all it implies and our slowness to correct it.

That appears to be true, and it is an agonizing admission for me to make. But it is only by practicing what we preach that we can hope to undo this disillusion. I am not exaggerating when I say that this is a deeply disturbing and widespread feeling among Negroes. The apparent gains very often show up to Negroes as merely other aspects of tokenism. Even many of the authentic gains appear in a suspicious light.

Have we lost ground in this area?

We have. There are many Catholics who do not go to church because the pain of this kind of humiliation is simply unbearable. Think of going to church, going to communion, and in order to receive Christ you must wait until every white Catholic has gone to the communion table and returned to his seat—knowing that you might well be skipped if you approached the altar while some white person was still there. Think of that encouraging people to receive communion. Many do, of course, but with a deep sense of sickness, and then resentment that even this great sacrament should be clouded in indignity for them. Many are so affronted by this that they fall away or simply do not enter the Church—and think of this tremendous harvest of souls we lose by simply disgusting them away from the Church. Believe me, this is known by Negroes all over America, by Negroes who have never been in the South at all. Once disillusioned, it is most difficult to rekindle illusions—so the resonances of our fault here spread outward and outward to disgust souls everywhere.

Prejudiced Catholics, even the really bigoted ones, are surely unaware of all of this, aren't they, Father?

Oh, yes, they are unaware of most of it. And the difficulty lies in the fact that Southerners always think they know everything about "their Negroes." So the tragedy, as Gerald Vann once remarked, lies not in the fact that they are largely unaware of all this, but in the fact that they are unaware of their unawareness. I know this is the truth, and this is why I have spoken so frankly. Our intergroup conflicts have now become critical. We can see clearly to what horrors racism leads even when it walks in a benign guise, a religious guise. It dehumanizes all of us. Every soul that is disillusioned with Christianity is a soul for which we have some responsibility. Each day we see more Negroes disillusioned with what they call "the white man's Christianity." And each day we see more whites disillusioned by the same scandal; let's not forget that. Men are talking about the failure of Christianity and turning away—not because Christianity is a failure, God knows—but because it appears so through the bad actions of Christians.

What are the answers, Father?

The answers are not simple but the Church has given them. The Church has told us what Man is, a *res sacra* or sacred reality . . . a *res sacra* regardless of color. She has told us that strict justice admits of no modification, and that anything less than strict justice is simply injustice, regardless of what you choose to name it. Let every Catholic, no matter what his color, become a real Catholic, a true Catholic. To prevent a man from being fully Catholic and to expect him to be satisfied—these are both against the very nature of the Faith. Pope John XXIII crystallized it in his statement that truth requires the elimination of every trace of racism.

Illtud Evans, O.P.

THE SELECTIVE CONSCIENCE

ILLTUD EVANS, O.P., is a priest of the English Province of the Order of Preachers, with residence at Cambridge. He is author of One and Many *and* The Voice of Lourdes, *and was editor of* Blackfriars, *a monthly review, from 1950 to 1962. He is a frequent contributor to the* London Times Literary Supplement, Tablet, Listener, Commonweal, *and other publications. Especially interested in questions of criminology, Father Evans lectured to the American Correctional Association's Convention in 1961. He is a regular speaker on the B.B.C.*

WHEN HAMLET SAYS that conscience makes cowards of us all, he is hardly thinking of the conscience which the moral philosopher discusses: the judgment a man makes that this is right, the practical application of a principle he holds to be true. He is thinking rather of the insight that must come at some moment to every man, when he sees—perhaps for the first time—the remote places of motive and desire within himself, and he is appalled at what he sees.

But conscience is more than that, and cowardice can be no part of it. For conscience means choice, the inexorable decision that must follow the awareness that this situation here and now demands a response of me: this I must do, for this in terms of decision is the consequence of being human, of being able to choose; of being able to seek what I believe to be good, of being able to turn away from what I believe to be evil.

The appeal to conscience is, then, simply an appeal to what it means to be human. The insane can have no conscience, for they can have no free choice, no knowledge of the moral quality of what they do. And in many others conscience can be clouded: the principles they apply have no place in right reason. For conscience is concerned with human acts, with the rights and duties of man as man. That is why the appeal to conscience, absolute and inalienable as it is, must always relate to what a true conscience is designed to serve: it is always *for* man and not against him, for life and not for life's denial.

The emergence in our time of a new realization of the dignity of the human person—reflected in such declarations as the Human Rights Charter of the United Nations—has undoubtedly arisen from the universal reaction against such cosmic iniquities as the Nazi persecution and destruction of the Jews. And yet the empire of cruelty grows stronger every day, so that high-sounding declarations can seem but cynical platitudes. The truth is that conscience is always invoked, but its absolute demands are rarely accepted. One man's—or one nation's, or one section of a nation's—conscience can too easily be invoked simply to justify their own right to choose and speak and act. "My conscience is inviolable," they say in effect, "and let others look after their own."

But if we appeal to conscience at all, we must take the consequences—and they can reach very far. For as soon as we use the word we are saying something essential about man: his integrity as a person, rights and duties that belong to him because of what he is, the freedom that uniquely marks him out from all creation. What we demand for ourselves we must concede to others. And yet the moral indignation that is aroused by some outrage or injustice that touches us, when our own "side" is involved, is a hypocrisy if we remain silent when what is in question is not immediately our affair. A selective conscience is no conscience at all.

It is of course true that the individual cannot be personally involved in every appeal to conscience that is made. But he must recognize the universal nature of conscience: it is commensurate with the nature and the needs of man, and the rights and duties it implies flow from the natural law itself and depend on no legislation or arbitrary authority. He must, in other words, see the rights that he claims for himself as always involving the rights of others who share his humanity and all that must imply. That is why Pope John XXIII, in his Encyclical Letter, *Pacem in Terris,* having summarized the consequences that follow from the recognition of every human being as a person, endowed with intelligence and free will, with "rights and duties of his own, flowing directly and simultaneously from his very nature, which are therefore universal, inviolable and inalienable" (Part 1, 9), goes on to emphasize that "he who possesses certain rights has likewise the duty to claim those rights as marks of his dignity, while all others have the obligation to acknowledge those rights and respect them" (Part 1, 44).

This may perhaps seem an academic argument, irrelevant when the need for action is urgent. But any human action that is worthy of the name must be faithful to all that the word "human" implies. And that must always mean an awareness of the communality of the human situation. Whether I think of it or not, another man's sufferings for conscience's sake touch me: something of human dignity as such is diminished when a man is discriminated against because of his color or race, when economic excuses are invented to deprive him of the opportunity to work, when social necessities are appealed to in order to keep him in a ghetto that reduces him to a servitude of the spirit.

It is important that every appeal to conscience should be seen against this large landscape of absolute rights and duties. The very structure of the world in which we live has made it imperative, for what happens in Alabama or Mississippi is in a very few moments known the whole world over. It is no longer possible to conceal an incident which involves issues of human rights and keep it local. There are so many others in so many parts of the world who feel identified with that local victim: they share his color, and until the other day they shared his servitude, but now they are free. And there are others again who may share no overt common features of race or class but who have come to realize that there can be no end to injustice and cruelty in the world unless men everywhere affirm their unity in face of oppression. And so it is that one man's conscience can become the world's affair.

It was this realization that led an Englishman, Peter Benenson, to found a movement called *Amnesty* in May, 1961. While traveling to his office in London one day, he happened to see a paragraph in the newspaper which reported the arrest of two Portuguese friends of his. They had been sitting in a café, discussing the government and its refusal to allow political liberty to its opponents. They were overheard, arrested and held without trial. Mr. Benenson, a lawyer who had been prominent in *Justice*, an international organization of eminent jurists concerned to implement the rule of law, decided that the time had come to do more than deplore the spread of oppression and the denial of basic human rights. In a letter to the *London Observer* he proposed the formation of a society to be called *Amnesty*, which would work for the release and support of all men and women everywhere who were imprisoned or victimized because they had taken their stand on conscience—a conscience whose rights had been denied by governments that could not tolerate the right to differ.

The response was immediate—and remarkable. Thousands of people felt that here at last was the appeal that mattered: an appeal to conscience as such, to human rights as such. Basing itself on Articles 18 and 19 of the United Nations Declaration of Human Rights, *Amnesty* set out to defend all those who, without resorting to violence, were prisoners of conscience. It has sent lawyer-observers to political "trials," it has brought pressure to bear on governments through publicity, it has helped to support the families of the victims. Above all, it has set up "Groups of Three," which now exist in many parts of the world, consisting of local groups of some twelve people who undertake to work for the release of three prisoners of conscience—whose names are provided by the central organization—drawn from the three main ideological groupings. This gives a personal emphasis to the pursuit of justice: it is persons, and not abstractions, that suffer. Moreover, the choice of three victims, whose specific beliefs may not necessarily commend themselves to every member of the group, means that the disinterestedness of the appeal to conscience is preserved. The rights of conscience are not merely the beliefs that I happen to share: they are rights that spring from human freedom itself, and, in defending the individual's freedom to hold them, I defend not this or that opinion or belief but the whole concept of human liberty.

The example of *Amnesty* is relevant to the particular issue of racial discrimination in America, because the truth is that the issue is not particular at all. Its specific features certainly reflect a particular history and the legacies it has left in a whole host of social and economic problems. But what is at stake is not simply a local adjustment, a matter of legislation or decree. For those who appeal to conscience in this matter—in whatever sense—are appealing to a truth that goes far beyond the difficulties that have arisen in a special social and cultural context. They have to ask themselves whether what they propose or defend is in accord with what the human conscience can endorse. And in doing this, whether they recognize it or not, they are at once allying themselves with men and women of good will everywhere who have taken their stand in defense of human rights and of the duties which those rights imply. As soon as they utter the word "human" they have stated the case for equality, for human equality is the complement of human dignity. What makes a man a person and not a thing is his essential freedom: he can never be used as though he were a mere pawn in another man's power. He may be externally compelled, but the citadel of his essential freedom, and hence his dignity, can never be destroyed. So whatever is being said about the American Negro is being said about humanity itself, and the way he is treated is an exact indication of the way in which it is thought that man as such should be treated.

The paradox is that men of good will, who in all else can seem just and considerate and kind, who abhor the cruelty they read of in other countries or at other times, can, with an apparently good conscience, continue to deprive their immediate neighbors of elementary rights that belong to them as persons. They would deny that this is what they intend: their conscience is clear, they say. But their conscience is in fact selective, for they fail to apply principles whose validity they recognize in other spheres. This moral schizophrenia is perhaps the gravest aspect of the situation in

America today. And as the pressures of opinion grow, to say nothing of the development of violence as a policy to end injustice, the moral reasons that a selective conscience must seek in order to justify the continuation of discrimination against minorities will necessarily become more and more divorced from reality. A *moral* cover must be provided for reasons that are rooted in a very different soil: the legacy of old prejudices and social attitudes, economic fears, and—worst of all—pseudo-scientific theories that postulate inherent racial inferiorities and so give the appearance of objectivity to injustice.

Here one might instance a single example among many of the temptations to give a moral cover to arguments that proceed from fallacious evidence. It is that of the alleged criminality of Negroes. How, it is asked, can you accord equal rights to people who are three times—or whatever the figure is said to be—as criminal as their white neighbors, for that is what the prison statistics show? The conscience of the law-abiding white is outraged: he could not "in conscience" allow his children to mingle with those who have such a record—or at least the likelihood of following its pattern. The cold truth is that exactly the same sort of figures, the identical pattern, will be found among any minority—and in the past such a minority has been as white as any Southern senator could wish—that has been deprived of equal opportunities for housing and employment and a free life in society. What the criminologist calls a syndrome of significant factors can more than adequately account for the alleged criminality of the Negro, uneducated, brought up in a ghetto, unemployed, perhaps the victim of police discrimination, poorly defended at his trial, and, often enough, sentenced in circumstances, which, if he were not a Negro, might have produced a very different result.

The example is legitimate, for it is the sort of argument that is given a moral color, a reason in conscience, that is invalid. One need not apologize, then, for what may seem an abstract argument, a reference to the moral quality of human judgments and the nature of conscience itself, since what is involved is much more than a matter of local custom, "the way that things are done down South."

It was once said of a senator that, when asked what his policy was, his answer would be, "Hands off McCloskie Boulevard." The trouble about boulevards is that, however rough and obscure they may seem to be, they lead to larger roads, to highways that encompass the earth.

Benjamin E. Mays

THE MORAL ASPECTS OF SEGREGATION

BENJAMIN E. MAYS is one of America's leading educators. He has been President of Morehouse College in Atlanta, Georgia, since 1940; prior to that time he served six years as Dean of the School of Religion at Howard University, and has taught at various schools. Born in Epworth, South Carolina, Dr. Mays holds degrees from Bates College and the University of Chicago, plus numerous honorary degrees. He represented the U.S. at the Oxford Conference on Churches at Oxford University in 1937. He is a former pastor of the Shiloh Baptist Church in Atlanta. In 1952, he initiated the Henry B. Wright lecture series at the Yale Divinity School. He has authored several books in the fields of religion and race relations, including The Christian in Race Relations, The Negro's Church, *and* The Negro's God. *He has been a frequent contributor to such magazines as* Crisis, Christian Century, *the* Journal of Negro Education, Religion in Life, Christendom, The Pulpit, Sepia *and* Ebony.

WHENEVER A STRONG DOMINANT GROUP possesses all the power, political, educational, economic; and wields all the power; makes all the laws, municipal, state and federal, and administers all the laws; writes all constitutions, municipal, state and federal, and interprets these constitutions; collects and holds all the money, municipal, state and federal, and distributes all the money; determines all policies—governmental, business, political and educational; when that group plans and places heavy burdens, grievous to be borne, upon the backs of the weak, that act is immoral. If the strong group is a Christian group or a follower of Judaism, both of which contend that God is creator, judge, impartial, just, universal, love, and that man was created in God's image, the act is against God and man—thus immoral. If the strong group is atheistic, the act is against humanity—still immoral.

No group is wise enough, good enough, strong enough, to assume an omnipotent and omniscient role; no group is good enough, wise enough, to restrict the mind, circumscribe the soul, and to limit the physical movements of another group. To do that is blasphemy. It is an usurpation of the role of God.

If the strong handicaps the weak on the grounds of race or color, it is all the more immoral, because to penalize the group for conditions over which it has no control, for being what nature or nature's God made it, is tantamount to saying to God, "You made a mistake, God, when you didn't make all races white." If there were a law which said that an illiterate group had to be segregated, the segregated group could go to school and become literate. If there were a law which said that all people with incomes below $5,000 a year had to be segregated, the people under $5,000 a year could strive to rise above the $5,000 bracket. If there were a law which said that men and women who did not bathe had to be segregated, they could develop the habit of daily baths and remove the stigma. If there were a law which said that all groups had to be Catholics, the Jews and Protestants could do something about joining the Catholic Church. But to segregate a man because his skin is brown or black, red or yellow, is to segregate a man for circumstances over which he has no control. And of all immoral acts, this is the most immoral.

So the May 17, 1954, decision of the Supreme Court and all the decisions against segregation are attempts on the part of the judges involved to abolish a great wrong which the strong has deliberately placed upon the backs of the weak. It is an attempt on the part of federal and state judges to remove this stigma, this wrong, through constitutional means, which is the democratic, American way.

I said a moment ago that if the strong deliberately picks out a weak racial group and places upon it heavy burdens, that act is immoral. Let me try to analyze this burden, segregation, which has been imposed upon millions of Americans of color. There are at least three main reasons for legal segregation in the United States.

1. The first objective of segregation is to place a legal badge of inferiority upon the segregated, to brand him as unfit to move freely among human beings. This badge says the segregated is mentally, morally, and socially unfit to move around as a free man.

2. The second objective of segregation is to set the segregated apart so that he can be treated as an inferior: in the courts, in recreation, in transportation, in politics, in government, in employment, in religion, in education, in hotels, in motels, in restaurants, and in every other area of American life. And all of this has been done without the consent of the segregated.

3. The third objective of legalized segregation follows from the first two. It is designed to make the segregated believe that he is inferior, that he is nobody, and to make him accept willingly his inferior status in society. It is these conditions which the May 17, 1954, decision of the Supreme Court and other federal decisions against segregation are designed to correct—to remove this immoral stigma that has been placed upon twenty million Negro Americans, and these are the reasons why every thinking Negro wants the legal badge of segregation removed, so that he might be able to walk the earth with dignity, as a man, and not cringe and kowtow as a slave. He believes that this is his God-given right on the earth.

Segregation is immoral because it has inflicted a wound upon the soul of the segregated and so restricted his mind that millions of Negroes now alive will never be cured of the disease of inferiority. Many of them have come to feel and believe that they are inferior or that the cards are so stacked against them that it is useless for them to strive for the highest and the best. Segregate a race for a hundred years, tell that race in books, in law, in courts, in education, in church and school, in employment, in transportation, in hotels and motels, in the government, that it is inferior—and it is bound to leave its damaging mark upon the souls and minds of the segregated. It is these conditions that the federal courts seek to change.

Any country that restricts the full development of any segment of society retards its own growth and development. The segregated produce less, and even the minds of the strong are circumscribed because they are often afraid to pursue the whole truth and they spend too much time seeking ways and means of how to keep the segregated group in "its place." Segregation is immoral because it leads to injustice, brutality, and lynching on the part of the group that segregate. The segregated is somebody that can be pushed around as desired by the segregator. As a rule, equal justice in the courts is almost impossible for a member of the segregated group if it involves a member of the group imposing segregation. The segregated has no rights that the segregator is bound to respect.

The chief sin of segregation is the distortion of human personality. It damages the soul of both the segregator and the segregated. It gives the segregated a feeling of inherent inferiority which is not based on facts, and it gives the segregator a feeling of superiority which is not based on facts. It is difficult to know who is damaged more—the segregated or the segregator.

It is false accusation to say that Negroes hail the May 17, 1954, decision of the Supreme Court because they want to mingle socially with white people. Negroes want segregation abolished because they want the legal stigma of inferiority removed and because they do not believe that equality of educational opportunities can be completely achieved in a society where the law brands a group inferior. When a Negro rides in a Pullman unsegregated he does it not because he wants to ride with white people. He may or may not engage in conversations with a white person. He wants good accommodations. When he eats in an unsegregated diner on the train, he goes because he is hungry and not because he wants to eat with white people.

He goes to the diner not even to mingle with Negroes, but to get something to eat. But as he eats and rides, he wants no badge of inferiority pinned on his back. He wants to eat and ride with dignity. No Negro clothed in his right mind believes that his social status will be enhanced just because he associates with white people.

The Supreme Court is the highest law of the land and we should respect that law.

Negro leaders believe that each local community should bring together the racial groups in that community, calmly sit down and plan ways and means not how they can circumvent the decision, but how they can implement it and plan together when and where they will start. They will be able to start sooner in some places than in others and move faster in some places than in others, but all can begin the process in good faith and with good intent.

To deliberately scheme, to deliberately plan through nefarious methods, through violence, boycott and threats to nullify the decision of the highest law in the land is not only immoral, but it encourages a disregard for all laws which we do not like.

We meet the moral issue again. To write into our constitutions things that we do not intend to carry out is an immoral act. I think I am right when I say that most of our states, certainly some of them, say in their constitutions "separate but equal." But you know as well as I do that on the whole the gulf of inequality in education widened with the years. There was no serious attempt nor desire in this country to provide Negroes with educational opportunities equal to those for whites. The great surge to equalize educational opportunities for Negroes did not begin until after 1935 when Murray won his suit to enter the law school of the University of Maryland. It is also clear that the millions poured into Negro education in the last twenty years were appropriated not so much because it was right but in an endeavor to maintain segregation.

We brought this situation upon ourselves. We here in the South have said all along that we believe in segregation—but equal segregation. In 1896, in the Louisiana case, Plessy versus Ferguson, the United States Supreme Court confirmed the doctrine "separate but equal." But from 1896 to 1935 there was practically nothing done to equal. When Murray won his case in 1935, we knew we had to move toward equalization and since 1935 many suits have been won.

It would have been a mighty fine thing if we had obeyed the Supreme Court in 1896 and equalized educational opportunities for Negroes. If we had done that the problem would have been solved, because gradually the separate school system would have been abolished and we would have been saved from the agony and fear of this hour. We didn't obey the Supreme Court in 1896 and we don't want to obey it now.

Let me say again that the May 17, 1954, decision of the Supreme Court is an effort to abolish a great evil through orderly processes. And we are morally obligated to implement the decision or modify the Federal Constitution and say plainly that this constitution was meant for white people and not for Negroes, and that the Declaration of Independence, which says in essence that all men are created equal, that they are endowed by their creator with certain inalienable rights, that among these are life, liberty and the pursuit of happiness, was written exclusively for whites.

We are morally obligated to abolish legalized segregation in America or reinterpret the Christian Gospel, the Old and New Testaments, and make the Gospel say that the noble principles of Judaism and Christianity are not applicable to colored peoples and Negroes; tell the world honestly and plainly that the Fatherhood of God and the Brotherhood of Man cannot work where the colored races are concerned. We are morally obligated to move toward implementing the decision in the Deep South or to lose our moral leadership in the world. If we do not do it, we must play the role of hypocrisy, preaching one thing and doing another. This is the dilemma which faces our democracy.

The eyes of the world are upon us. One billion or more colored people in Asia and Africa are judging our democracy solely on the basis of how we treat Negroes. White Europe is watching us too. I shall never forget the day in Lucknow, India, when nine reporters from all over India questioned me ninety minutes about how Negroes are treated in the United States. I shall remember to my dying day the event in 1937 when the principal of an untouchable school introduced me to his boys as an untouchable from the United States. At first it angered me. But on second thought I knew that he was right. Though great progress has been made, for which I am grateful, I and my kind are still untouchables in many sections of the country. There are places where wealth, decency, culture, education, religion, and position will do no good . . . if you are a Negro. None of these things can take away the mark of untouchability. And the world knows this.

Recently a group of colored students from Asia, Africa, the Middle East and South America were visiting an outstanding Southern town. All the colored people, except those from Africa and Haiti, could live in the downtown hotels. The Africans and Haitians had to seek refuge on the campus of a Negro college. That incident was known to all the other colored students and it will be told many times in Europe, Asia, Africa—and it will not help us in our efforts to democratize the world.

Not long ago a Jew from South Africa and a man from India were guests of a Negro professor. He drove them for several days through the urban and rural sections of his state. The Negro, the host, a citizen of the United States, could not get food from the hotels and restaurants. His guests, one a Jew and the other an Indian, had to go in and buy food for him. The man who introduced me in India as an untouchable was right. The Negro is America's untouchable.

Two or three years ago a friend of mine was traveling in Germany. He met a German who had traveled widely in the United States. He told my friend that he hangs his head in shame every time he thinks of what his country did to the Jews—killing six million of them. But he told my friend that after seeing what segregation has done to the soul of the Negro in the South, he has come to the conclusion that it is worse than what Hitler and his colleagues did to the Jews in Germany.

Make no mistake—as this country could not exist half slave and half free, it cannot exist half segregated and half desegregated. The Supreme Court has given America an opportunity to achieve greatness in the area of moral and spiritual things, just as it has already achieved greatness in military and industrial might and in material possessions. It is my belief that the South will accept the challenge of the Supreme Court and thus make America and the South safe for democracy.

If we lose the battle for freedom for twenty million Negroes, we will lose it for two hundred million whites and eventually we will lose it for the world. This is indeed a time for greatness.

George C. Wallace

INAUGURAL ADDRESS

GEORGE C. WALLACE is Governor of the State of Alabama. Born in Clio, Alabama, in 1919, Governor Wallace attended Barbour County High School and the University of Alabama, from which he received his law degree in 1942. An athlete, as well as a politician, he held an Alabama State Golden Gloves Boxing Championship in 1936–37. Entering the U.S. Army Air Force in 1942, he saw heavy combat action in the Pacific as a B-29 Flight Engineer assigned to the 20th Air Force. He served as an Assistant Attorney General for the State of Alabama in 1946 and in 1947 was elected to the Alabama Legislature from Barbour County. He remained in the Legislature until 1952, where he was twice voted one of the most outstanding members of that body. Elected Judge of Alabama's Third Judicial Circuit in 1953, he served in this capacity until 1958. The article that follows is the address Governor Wallace made on the day of his inauguration in 1963.

GOVERNOR PATTERSON, Governor Barnett, from one of the greatest states in this nation, Mississippi, Judge Brown, representing Governor Hollings of South Carolina, Governor Dixon, Governor Folsom, members of the Alabama Congressional Delegation, members of the Alabama Legislature, distinguished guests, fellow Alabamians:

Before I begin my talk with you, I want to ask you for a few minutes' patience while I say something that is on my heart: I want to thank those home folks of my county who first gave an anxious country boy his opportunity to serve in state politics. I shall always owe a lot to those who gave me that *first* opportunity to serve.

I will never forget the warm support and close loyalty of the folks at Suttons, Haigler's Mill, Eufaula, Beat 6 and Beat 14, Richards Cross Roads and Gammage Beat . . . at Baker Hill, Beat 8, and Comer, Spring Hill, Adams Chapel and Mount Andrew . . . White Oak, Baxter's Station, Clayton, Louisville and Cunningham Place; Horns Crossroads, Texasville and Blue Springs, where the vote was 304 for Wallace and 1 for the opposition . . . and the dear little lady who I heard had made that one vote against me . . . by mistake . . . because she couldn't see too well . . . and she had pulled the wrong lever . . . Bless her heart. At Clio, my birthplace, and Elamville. I shall never forget them. May God bless them.

And I shall forever remember that election day morning as I waited . . . and suddenly at ten o'clock that morning the first return of a box was flashed over this state: it carried the message . . . Wallace 15, opposition zero; and it came from the Hamrick Beat at Putman's Mountain where live the great hill people of our state. May God bless the mountain man . . . his loyalty is unshakable; he'll do to walk down the road with.

I hope you'll forgive me these few moments of remembering . . . but I wanted them . . . and you . . . to know that I shall never forget.

And I wish I could shake hands and thank all of you in this State who voted for me . . . and those of you who did not . . . for I know you voted your honest convictions . . . and now, we must stand together and move the great State of Alabama forward.

I would be remiss, this day, if I did not thank my wonderful wife and fine family for their patience, support and loyalty . . . and there is no man living who does not owe more to his mother than he can ever repay, and I want my mother to know that I realize my debt to her.

This is the day of my inauguration as Governor of the State of Alabama. And on this day I feel a deep obligation to renew my pledges, my covenants with you . . . the people of this great state.

General Robert E. Lee said that "duty" is the most sublime word in the English language and I have come, increasingly, to realize what he meant. I *shall* do my duty to you, God helping . . . to every man, to every woman . . . yes, and to every child in this state. I shall fulfill my duty toward honesty and economy in our state government so that no man shall have a part of his livelihood cheated and no child shall have a bit of his future stolen away.

I have said to you that I would eliminate the liquor agents in this state and that the money saved would be returned to our citizens. . . . I am happy to report to you that I am now filling orders for several hundred one-way tickets and stamped on them are these words . . . "for liquor agents . . . destination . . . out of Alabama." I am happy to report to you that the big-wheeling cocktail-party boys have gotten the word that their free whiskey and boat rides are over . . . that the farmer in the field, the worker in the factory, the businessman in his office, the housewife in her home, have decided that the money can be better spent to help our children's education and our older citizens . . . and they have put a man in office to see that it is done. It shall be done. Let me say one more time . . . no more liquor drinking in your governor's mansion.

I shall fulfill my duty in working hard to bring industry into our state, not only by maintaining an honest, sober and free-enterprise climate of government in which industry can have confidence . . . but in going out and getting it . . . so that our people can have industrial jobs in Alabama and provide a better life for their children.

I shall not forget my duty to our senior citizens . . . so that their lives can be lived in dignity and enrichment of the golden years, nor to our sick, both mental and physical . . . and they will know we have not forsaken them. I want the farmer to feel confident that in this state government he has a partner who will work with him in raising his income and increasing his markets. I want the laboring man to know he had a friend who is sincerely striving to better his field of endeavor.

I want to assure every child that this state government is not afraid to invest in their future through education, so that they will not be handicapped on the very threshold of their lives.

Today I have stood, where once Jefferson Davis stood, and took an oath to my people. It is very appropriate then that from this Cradle of the Confederacy, this very Heart of the Great Anglo-Saxon Southland, that today we sound the drum for freedom as have our generations of forebears before us done, time and again down through history. Let us rise to the call of freedom-loving blood that is in us and send our answer to the tyranny that clanks its chains upon the South. In the name of the greatest people that have ever trod this earth, I draw the line in the dust and toss the gauntlet before the feet of tyranny . . . and I say . . . segregation now . . . segregation tomorrow . . . segregation forever.

The Washington, D.C., school riot report is disgusting and revealing. We will not sacrifice our children to any such type school system . . . and you can write that down. The federal troops in Mississippi could better be used guarding the safety of the citizens of Washington, D.C., where it is even unsafe to walk or go to a ball game . . . and that is the nation's capital. I was safer in a B-29 bomber over Japan during the war in an air raid, than the people of Washington are walking in the White House neighborhood. A closer example is Atlanta. The city officials fawn for political reasons over school integration and *then* build barricades to stop residential integration . . . what hypocrisy!

Let us send this message back to Washington by our representatives who are with us today . . . that from this day we are standing up, and the heel of tyranny does not fit the neck of an upright man . . . that we intend to take the offensive and carry our fight for freedom across this nation, wielding the balance of power we know we possess in the Southland . . . that *we,* not the insipid bloc voters of some sections . . . will determine in the next election who shall sit in the White House of these United States . . . that from this day . . . from this hour . . . from this minute . . . we give the word of a race of honor that we will tolerate their boot in our face no longer . . . and let those certain judges put *that* in their opium pipes of power and smoke it for what it is worth.

Hear me, Southerners! You sons and daughters who have moved north and west throughout this nation . . . we call on you from your native soil to join with us in national support and vote . . . and we know . . . wherever you are . . . away from the hearths of the Southland . . . that you will respond, for though you may live in the farthest reaches of this vast country . . . your heart has never left Dixieland.

And you native sons and daughters of old New England's rock-ribbed patriotism . . . and you sturdy natives of the great Mid-West . . . and you descendants of the far West flaming spirit of pioneer freedom . . . we invite you to come and be with us . . . for you are of the Southern mind . . . and the Southern spirit . . . and the Southern philosophy . . . you are Southerners too and brothers with us in our fight.

What I have said about segregation goes double this day . . . and what I have said to or about some federal judges goes *triple* this day.

Alabama has been blessed by God as few states in this Union have been blessed. Our state owns ten per cent of all the natural resources of all the states in our country. Our inland waterway system is second to none . . . and has the potential of being the greatest waterway transport system in the world. We possess over thirty minerals in usable quantities and our soil is rich and varied, suited to a wide variety of plants. Our native pine and forestry system produces timber faster than we can cut it, and yet we have only pricked the surface of the great lumber and pulp potential.

With ample rainfall and rich grasslands our livestock industry is in the infancy of a giant future that can make us a center of the big and growing meat packing and prepared foods marketing. We have the favorable climate, streams, woodlands, beaches, and natural beauty to make us a recreational mecca in the booming tourist and vacation industry. Nestled in the great Tennessee Valley, we possess the rocket center of the world and the keys to the space frontier.

While the trade with a developing Europe built the great port cities of the East coast, our own fast developing port of Mobile faces as a magnetic gateway to the great continent of South America, well over twice as large and hundreds of times richer in resources, even now awakening to the growing probes of enterprising capital with a potential of growth and wealth beyond any present dream for our port development and corresponding results throughout the connecting waterways that thread our state.

And while the manufacturing industries of free enterprise have been coming to our state in increasing numbers, attracted by our bountiful natural resources, our growing number of skilled workers and our favorable conditions, their present rate of settlement here can be increased from the trickle now represented to a stream of enterprise and endeavor, capital and expansion that can join us in our work of development and enrichment of the educational futures of our children, the opportunities of our citizens and the fulfillment of our talents as God has given them to us. To realize our ambitions and to bring to fruition our dreams, we as Alabamians must take cognizance of the world about us. We must redefine our heritage, re-school our thoughts in the lessons our forefathers knew so well, firsthand, in order to function and to grow and to prosper.

We can no longer hide our head in the sand and tell ourselves that the ideology of our free fathers is not being attacked and is not being threatened by another idea . . . for it is. We are faced with an idea that if a centralized government assumes enough authority, enough power over its people, that it can provide a utopian life . . . that if given the power to dictate, to forbid, to require, to demand, to distribute, to edict and to judge what is best and enforce that will of judgment upon its citizens from unimpeachable authority . . . then it will produce only "good" . . . and it shall be our father . . . and our God. It is an idea of government that encourages our fears and destroys our faith . . . for where there is faith, there is no fear, and where there is fear, there is no faith. In encouraging our fears of economic insecurity it demands we place that economic management and control with government; in encouraging our fear of educational development it demands we place that education and the minds of our children under management and control of government, and even in feeding our fears of physical infirmities and declining years, it offers and demands to father us through it all and even into the grave. It is a government that claims to us that it is bountiful as it buys its power from us with the fruits of its rapaciousness of the wealth that free men before it have produced and builds on crumbling credit without responsibilities to the debtors . . . our children. It is an ideology of government erected on the encouragement of fear and fails to recognize the basic law of our fathers that governments do not produce wealth . . . people produce wealth . . . free people; and as those people become less free . . . as they learn there is little reward for ambition . . . that it requires faith to risk . . . and they have none . . . as the government must restrict and penalize and tax incentive and endeavor and must increase its expenditures of bounties . . . then this government must assume more and more police powers and we find we are becoming government-fearing people . . . not God-fearing people.

We find we have replaced faith with fear . . . and though we may give lip service to the Almighty . . . in reality, government has become our God. It is, therefore, a basically ungodly government and its appeal to the pseudo-intellectual and the politician is to change their status from servant of the people to master of the people . . . to play at being God . . . without faith in God . . . and without the wisdom of God. It is a system that is the very opposite of Christ, for it feeds and encourages everything degenerate and base in our people as it assumes the responsibilities that we ourselves should assume. Its pseudo-liberal spokesmen and some Harvard advocates have never examined the logic of its substitution of what it calls "human rights" for individual rights, for its propaganda play upon words has appeal for the unthinking. Its logic is totally material and irresponsible as it runs the full gamut of human desires . . . including the theory that everyone has voting rights without the spiritual responsibility of preserving freedom. Our founding fathers recognized those rights . . . but only within the frameworks of those spiritual responsibilities. But the strong, simple faith and sane reasoning of our founding fathers has long since been forgotten as the so-called "progressives" tell us that our Constitution was written for "horse and buggy" days . . . so were the Ten Commandments.

Not so long ago men stood in marvel and awe at the cities, the buildings, the schools, the autobahns that the government of Hitler's Germany had built . . . just as centuries before they stood in wonder at Rome's building . . . but it could not stand . . . for the system that built it had rotted the souls of the builders . . . and in turn . . . rotted the foundation of what God meant that men should be. Today that same system on an international scale is sweeping the world. It is the "changing world" of which we are told . . . it is called "new" and "liberal" . . . it is as old as the oldest dictator. It is degenerate and decadent. As the *national* racism of Hitler's Germany persecuted a *national* minority to the whim of a *national* majority . . . so the *international* racism of the liberals seeks to persecute the *international* white minority to the whim of the *international* colored majority . . . so that we are footballed about according to the favor of the Afro-Asian bloc. But the Belgian survivors of the Congo cannot present their case to a War Crimes Commission . . . nor the Portuguese of Angola . . . nor the survivors of Castro . . . nor the citizens of Oxford, Mississippi.

It is this theory of international power politics that led a group of men on the Supreme Court for the first time in American history to issue an edict, based not on legal precedent, but upon a volume, the editor of which has said our Constitution is outdated and must be changed and some writers of which had admittedly belonged to as many as half a hundred communist front organizations. It is this theory that led this same group of men to briefly bare the ungodly core of that philosophy in forbidding little school children to say a prayer. And we find the evidence of that ungodliness even in the removal of the words "In God We Trust" from some of our dollars, which was placed there as like evidence by our founding fathers as the faith upon which this system of government was built. It is the spirit of power thirst that caused a President in Washington to take up Caesar's pen and with one stroke of it, make a law. A law which the lawmaking body of Congress refused to pass . . . a law that tells us that we can or cannot buy or sell our very homes, except by his conditions . . . and except at *his* discretion. It is the spirit of power thirst that led the same President to launch a full offensive of twenty-five thousand troops against a university . . . of all places . . . in his own country . . . and against his own people, when this nation maintains only six thousand troops in the beleaguered city of Berlin. We have witnessed such acts of "might makes right" over the world as men yielded to the temptation to play God . . . but we have never before witnessed it in America. We reject such acts as free men. We do not defy, for there is nothing to defy . . . since as free men we do not recognize any government's right to give freedom . . . or deny freedom. No government erected by man has that right. As Thomas Jefferson has said, "The God who gave us life, gave us liberty at the same time; no king holds the right of liberty in his hands." Nor does any ruler in American government.

We intend, quite simply, to practice the free heritage as bequeathed to us as sons of free fathers. We intend to revitalize the truly new and progressive form of government that is less than two hunderd years old . . . a government first founded in this nation simply and purely on faith . . . that there is a personal God who rewards good and punishes evil . . . that hard work will receive its just desserts . . . that ambition and ingenuity and incentiveness . . . and profit of such . . . are admirable traits and goals . . . that the individual is encouraged in his spiritual growth and from that growth arrives at a character that enhances his charity toward others, and from that character and that charity so is influenced business, and labor and farmer and government. We intend to renew our faith as God-fearing men . . . *not* government-fearing men nor any other kind of fearing-men. We intend to roll up our sleeves and pitch in to develop this full bounty God has given us . . . to live full and useful lives and in absolute freedom from all fear. Then can we enjoy the full richness of the Great American Dream.

We have placed this sign, "In God We Trust," upon our State Capitol on this Inauguration Day as physical evidence of determination to renew the faith of our fathers and to practice the free heritage they bequeathed to us. We do this with the clear and solemn knowledge that such physical evidence is evidently a direct violation of the logic of that Supreme Court in Washington, D.C., and if they or their spokesmen in this state wish to term this defiance . . . I say . . . let them make the most of it.

This nation was never meant to be a unit of one . . . but a united of the many . . . that is the exact reason our freedom-loving forefathers established the states, so as to divide the rights and powers among the many states, insuring that no central power could gain master government control.

In united effort we were meant to live under this government . . . whether Baptist, Methodist, Presbyterian, Church of Christ, or whatever one's denomination or religious belief . . . each respecting the other's right to a separate denomination . . . each, by working to develop his own, enriching the total of all our lives through united effort. And so it was meant in our political lives . . . whether Republican, Democrat, Prohibition, or whatever political party . . . each striving from his separate political station . . . respecting the rights of others to be separate and work from within their political framework . . . and each separate political station making its contribution to our lives.

And so it was meant in our racial lives . . . each race, within its own framework, has the freedom to teach . . . to instruct . . . to develop . . . to ask for and receive deserved help from others of separate racial stations. This is the great freedom of our American founding fathers . . . but if we amalgamate into the one unit as advocated by the communist philosophers . . . then the enrichment of our lives . . . the freedom for our development . . . is gone forever. We become, therefore, a mongrel unit of one under a single all-powerful government . . . and we stand for everything . . . and for nothing.

The true brotherhood of America, of respecting the separateness of others . . . and uniting in effort . . . has been so twisted and distorted from its original concept that there is small wonder that communism is winning the world.

We invite the Negro citizen of Alabama to work with us from his separate racial station . . . as we will work with him . . . to develop, to grow in individual freedom and enrichment. We want jobs and a good future for *both* races. We want to help the physically and mentally sick of *both* races . . . the tubercular and the infirm. This is the basic heritage of my religion, of which I make full practice . . . for we are all the handiwork of God.

But we warn those, of any group, who would follow the false

doctrine of communistic amalgamation that we will not surrender our system of government . . . our freedom of race and religion . . . that freedom was won at a hard price and if it requires a hard price to retain it . . . we are able . . . and quite willing to pay it.

The liberals' theory that poverty, discrimination and lack of opportunity is the cause of communism is a false theory . . . if it were true the South would have been the biggest single communist bloc in the western hemisphere long ago . . . for after the great War Between the States, our people faced a desolate land of burned universities, destroyed crops and homes, with manpower depleted and crippled, and even the mule, which was required to work the land, was so scarce that whole communities shared one animal to make the spring plowing. There were no government hand-outs, no Marshall Plan aid, no coddling to make sure that *our* people would not suffer; instead the South was set upon by the vulturous carpetbagger and federal troops, all loyal Southerners were denied the vote at the point of bayonet, so that the infamous, illegal Fourteenth Amendment might be passed. There was no money, no food and no hope of either. But our grandfathers bent their knee only in church and bowed their head only to God.

Not for one single instant did they ever consider the easy way of federal dictatorship and amalgamation in return for fat bellies. They fought. They dug sweet roots from the ground with their bare hands and boiled them in the old iron pots . . . they gathered poke salad from the woods and acorns from the ground. They fought. They followed no false doctrine . . . they knew what they wanted . . . and they fought for freedom! They came up from their knees in the greatest display of sheer nerve, grit and guts that has ever been set down in the pages of written history . . . and they won! The great writer, Rudyard Kipling, wrote of them, that: "There in the Southland of the United States of America, lives the greatest fighting breed of man . . . in all the world!"

And that is why today, I stand ashamed of the fat, well-fed whimperers who say that it is inevitable . . . that our cause is lost. I am ashamed *of* them . . . and I am ashamed *for* them. They do not represent the people of the Southland.

And may we take note of one other fact: with all the trouble with communists that some sections of this country have . . . there are not enough native communists in the South to fill up a telephone booth and *that* is a matter of public FBI record.

We remind all within hearing of this Southland that a *Southerner,* Peyton Randolph, presided over the Continental Congress in our nation's beginning . . . that a *Southerner,* Thomas Jefferson, wrote the Declaration of Independence, that a *Southerner*, George Washington, is the Father of our Country . . . that a *Southerner*, James Madison, authored our Constitution, that a *Southerner*, George Mason, authored the Bill of Rights, and it was a *Southerner* who said, "Give me liberty . . . or give me death," Patrick Henry.

Southerners played a most magnificient part in erecting this great divinely inspired system of freedom . . . and as God is our witness, Southerners will save it.

Let us, as Alabamians, grasp the hand of destiny and walk out of the shadow of fear . . . and fill our divine destination. Let us not simply defend . . . but let us assume the leadership of the fight and carry our leadership across this nation. God has placed us here in this crisis . . . let us not fail in this . . . our most historic moment.

You that are here today, present in this audience, and to you over this great state, wherever you are in sound of my voice, I want to humbly and with all sincerity, thank you for your faith in me.

I promise you that I will try to make you a good governor. I promise you that, as God gives me the wisdom and the strength, I will be sincere with you. I will be honest with you.

I will apply the old sound rule of our fathers, that anything worthy of defense is worthy of one hundred per cent of our defense. I have been taught that freedom meant freedom from any threat or fear of government. I was born in that freedom, I was raised in that freedom . . . I intend to live in that freedom . . . and God willing, when I die, I shall leave that freedom to my children . . . as my father left it to me.

My pledge to you . . . to "Stand Up For Alabama," is a stronger pledge today than it was the first day I made that pledge. I shall "Stand Up For Alabama," as Governor of our State . . . you stand with me . . . and we, together, can give courageous leadership to millions of people throughout this nation who look to the South for their hope in this fight to win and preserve our freedoms and liberties.

So help me God.

And my prayer is that the Father who reigns above us will bless all the people of this great sovereign state and nation, both white and black.

James Baldwin

DISTURBERS OF THE PEACE
An Interview by Eve Auchincloss and Nancy Lynch Handy*

JAMES BALDWIN was born in New York in 1924 and educated in that city, graduating from De Witt Clinton High School. His early novels (Giovanni's Room, Go Tell It On the Mountain) *won him a series of literary prizes—including the Partisan Review Fellowship, a National Institute of Arts and Letters Award, a Rosenwald Fellowship, and a Ford Foundation Grant-in-Aid. A Guggenheim Fellowship enabled him to live and work for several years in Europe. Since returning from Europe he has devoted himself to lecturing, literary criticism and work on the controversial best-seller* Another Country, *published in 1962. Mr. Baldwin is the author of three books of essays,* Nobody Knows My Name, Notes of a Native Son, *and* The Fire Next Time, *an explosive look at racial evils.* Nobody Knows My Name *was honored with a Certificate of Recognition from the National Conference of Christians and Jews and was selected by the Notable Books Council of the American Library Association as one of the outstanding books of 1961. He has also been awarded the Eugene F. Saxton Memorial Trust Award.*

EVE AUCHINCLOSS was graduated from Radcliffe College in 1944, has worked as a feature editor on several magazines, and is now on the staff of The New York Review of Books.

* The interview with James Baldwin is one of a series, called "Disturbers of the Peace," transcribed and edited for *Mademoiselle* between 1961 and 1963 by Eve Auchincloss and Nancy Lynch Handy.

NANCY LYNCH HANDY was graduated from Smith College in 1950, worked for a number of years as a staff writer and editor at Mademoiselle, *and is now engaged in free-lance writing.*

IT WAS REPORTED *somewhere recently that one of your friends—also a noted writer—said to you, in anger: "You're little, you're ugly, and you're as black as the ace of spades." But your comeback was not recorded.*

Oh, I just laughed. After all, it's true. But the point is, why, after all these years, did he have to say it? I mean, it's his problem, really, and I think it has to do with the fact that like most white liberals—though I'm not accusing him of being one exactly—he has always lied to himself about the way he really feels about Negroes.

Most people would say liberals have done more for the Negro than anybody else. Why are you so hard on them?

This has been on my mind for a long time, but it was triggered when I went on the Barry Gray show to protest the fact that the Anti-Defamation League had given a medal to Kennedy for his record on civil rights and to protest the fact that William Worthy was being indicted by the Justice Department for having re-entered his own country illegally, which as far as I know is an impossibility for an American citizen. And Barry Gray was very angry at me. What he finally said was that I should be picketing Governor Ross Barnett; I shouldn't be picketing my friends. And that made me mad, and I said that one of the hardest things anyone has to survive in this country is his friends. That made him madder. When it was over I began to feel there was involved in all this—in the case of a great many people who think they are on our side of the fence—a will to power that has nothing whatever to do with the principles they think they are upholding. They are operating in this part of the forest because this is where they find themselves, and it is easy for them—but it has nothing whatever to do with love or justice or any of the things they think it has to do with. And when the chips are down, it comes out. Their status in their own eyes is much more important than any real change. If there were no Negro problem,

I don't know what in the world they would do. Their pronouncements have nothing to do with reality, that's what I object to. Reality is involved with their relationship to themselves, their wives, their children; but this they have abdicated entirely, and use, then, me, the Negro, as an opportunity to live safely.

Does this apply to people who work for CORE and such things?

Those people, in my book, are not exactly liberals. I'm not talking about them. You can't say they're accomplishing nothing, really, because they're indispensable on a certain level. But their work has no resonance. It's all sort of meaningless, you see, like that group of anarchists in *The Secret Agent.* They're in the back room and that's where they stay.

And when the revolution comes, it doesn't come from them?

It doesn't come from them. It comes from some place you never thought it was coming from. And this is what they don't seem to know. I don't know—between the kind of sad incompetence of most workers for the Lord and the rigid egotism of the self-styled leading liberals it's very difficult to choose. Some of these liberal columnists, the professional bleeding hearts, have the public ear, but what they do with it is simply to reassure it. They sound as though they're being daring, but they're not. If reality broke into one of those columns, God knows what would happen! And when it threatens to, they get up on their hind legs and say, "Don't attack your friends!" I watched one of them in Paris one night trying to pick up the toughest, most evil, black blues singer in the world. He was drunk and weeping and she was calming him as though he were five years old. A cat who doesn't know when he's facing one of the world's top bitches! He doesn't even know it? What else doesn't he know? If you don't know that, then what *do* you know? And what good can you possibly do me? They make no connection between what they do in nightclubs and what they say in print, no connection between the ruin of their children and their public pronouncements.

Well, what's this hypocrisy covering up? You've seen Norman Podhoretz's article in Commentary, *telling how he grew up in a poor neighborhood alongside a large Negro population. And all through his childhood the Negro was someone who bullied you and beat you up on the one hand and on the other who enjoyed freedom and license no Jewish boy was allowed. And he says this animosity and envy is still buried in him.*

What Norman does in that piece is exactly what I'm asking all these high-minded white liberals to do: to tell the truth, what he really feels about Negroes—which is, as well, a confession about himself. But he is not lying about it. I'm sure that all the liberals I'm scoring off have stories very much like his, and they lie about it. But he says he hated and feared Negroes and that the little boy in him still does. The little boy in *them* still does, too, only they pretend he isn't there.

But what's the source of the bad feeling, basically?

It's very complicated, and a terrible, vicious circle, but there's no point lying about it. In any case, we all grew up with a great gulf fixed between whites and Negroes, and it makes Negroes per se exotic, strange, different, other. And whatever is "other" is frightening. The entire society reinforces this difference so that you have to be afraid of them; you aren't given much choice. And if you're afraid of them you've got to hate them. If it is so that no one really ever gets over his beginnings, then liberals are all liars, because this is true of them, too, and they pretend it isn't. And this is shown whenever you get to the personal level with them.

The sense of otherness is a fact we all recognize, anyway. But what can we do to overcome it?

In order for a person to cease to be other, you've got somehow to break through that thing which divides you and get into each other's lives. And this almost never happens. It doesn't never happen, but it almost never happens, and never at all within the liberal context, because the whole rhetoric is designed to prevent that from happening.

For instance?

Well, you certainly cannot talk to anybody in terms of great monolithic abstractions. You can't talk about The Negro Problem. What the hell are you talking about? Either we're talking about you and me, or we're not talking.

Do you ever worry that some of the things you say may only serve to reinforce feelings of guilt and fear in white people?

I think that what I feel about guilt is that it is like a festering sore that must be worked upon until it's opened and the pus can run out.

But in criticizing Native Son, *you said you felt Richard Wright had made a mistake in presenting a character who would make people feel frightened and guilty. Yet you yourself have expressed a certain amount of pleasure in the way Black Muslims frighten white people.*

I know what you mean, but as a matter of fact the Muslims frighten me very much. I consider them really irresponsible in the most serious way—irresponsible in terms of what I consider to be their obligations to the Negro community, as all racists are irresponsible. They batten on the despair of black men.

You think they have nothing to offer, really?

No. If they were organizing rent strikes among the people who live in those ghettos in Harlem right now, organizing just one block not to pay the rent until the landlords did something about the rats and the houses; if they were spotlighting concrete things, proving to Negroes that there were certain things they could do for themselves. . . .

But is there anything?

There is nothing they can do for themselves so long as they don't think there is. That's part of the price of being a Negro: you're demoralized so soon. If the Muslims were operating on that level I would have no quarrel with them, perhaps, but they're doing something else. It's just another inflated store-front church. It has that emotional value and that practical uselessness, only it's more dangerous. And another thing bothers me. I suppose it is the effect they can have on the country itself. Not so much the Muslim movement, but a whole area they represent—all the anguish that Negroes endure in this country, which no one wants to face. And the Muslims are the only people who articulate it for white people—and also for Negroes, I must say. And they frighten white people half to death. When you consider the ignorance that reigns in this country from top to bottom, it seems clear to me that the Muslim movement could act as a catalyst to turn the place into a concentration camp in no time at all.

How could that really happen?

If we'd been mad enough to go to war with Cuba, how many Negroes do you think you could mobilize out of Harlem? "Why should I go shoot Cubans? The government cannot protect me in Mississippi, but is willing to mount a whole invasion to bring freedom to the Cubans"—you really have to be an idiot not to ask that question. And God knows, if that does come about, the Muslims will not fail to ask it. You can put Elijah Muhammad and Malcolm X in jail, and maybe a couple of hundred thousand others. But if you've done *that,* then you might as well forget the war, because you've lost it.

Do you think the Negro can use the international situation as a power lever?

It depends on a great many other things, because you can use it as a power lever only to a very limited extent. The Negro situation here has not changed because of the cold war and the international situation, but the Government is aware of some things, and it is attempting to meet them by putting Negroes in the window, not to change things, but to create good propaganda. Of course, this doesn't help. What one needs is something that kids in the South are terribly aware of—some way of using such limited power as one has really to force the Government to investigate murders in Mississippi, and to bring pressure to bear on the cities to begin to deal with the Negro population.

How can it ever be done?

One's got to assume that it can be done, but how can it be done? Well, for example, in the South—which is clearer than the North—when a white man murders a black man, nothing can be done about it. But recently I went along with a field secretary of the N.A.A.C.P. in Mississippi to investigate a murder that had been hushed up. We rode around through those back roads for hours talking to people who had known the dead man, trying to find out what had happened. And the Negroes talked to us as the German Jews must have talked when Hitler came to power. It was a matter of turning the car around so that the license plate couldn't be seen from the road. And talking to people with their lights out. We had hoped to discover that the sheriff, who had forced the man to be buried without an inquest, had also murdered him. If he had, then *in principle* the Justice Department could have been forced to act. But it turned out it was not the sheriff but simply the storekeeper, who was a friend of his. And there was almost no way for the Justice Department to act, because the law-enforcement interests in the South have very strong ties with Washington, and the whole political structure in Washington is partly designed to protect the Southern oligarchy. And Bobby Kennedy's much more interested in politics than he is in any of these things, and so, for that matter, is his brother. And furthermore, even if Bobby Kennedy were a different person, or his brother, they are also ignorant, as most white Americans are, of what the problem really is, of how Negroes really live. The speech Kennedy made to Mississippi the night Meredith was carried there was one of the most shameful performances in our history.

Why?

Because he talked to Mississippi as if there were no Negroes there. And this had a terrible, demoralizing, disaffecting effect on all Negroes everywhere. One is weary of being told that desegregation is legal! One would like to hear for a change that it is *right!* Now, how one begins to use this power we were talking about earlier is a very grave question, because first of all you have to get Eastland out of Congress and get rid of the power that he wields there. You've got to get rid of J. Edgar Hoover and the power that he wields. If one could get rid of just those two men, or modify their power, there would be a great deal more hope. How in the world are you going to get Mississippi Negroes to go to the polls if you remember that most of them are extremely poor, most of them almost illiterate, and that they live under the most intolerable conditions? They are used to it, which is worse, and they have no sense that they can do anything for themselves. If six Negroes go to the polls and get beaten half to death, and one or two die, and nothing happens from Washington, how are you going to manage even to get the ballot?

It seems very hopeless.

One cannot agree that it is hopeless. But that's the way it is.

And the only hope we have is somehow to get in Washington, or *somewhere,* enough weight to begin to change the climate.

What happens to people like Meredith who put themselves in the front lines?

Aha. You can hold yourself together during all the action, but inevitably there's a great reaction somewhere. Some of them go to mental institutions. It's very hard to take. I got a taste of this only once. When I went to Tallahassee once I was living in a motel on the highway and there were trees along the road, and my room was the very last one. I would come back around midnight. Since I was the only Northern Negro in town, I was terribly visible, and my light was the only light on late at night, because I was typing my notes. I couldn't avoid thinking about the highway and those trees. I couldn't get over it by saying, "Don't be silly, Jimmy." And I was scared half to death. But I got through it and finally went to Paris. I was having lunch with a friend the day I arrived and suddenly I began to shake. And I said, "It's those trees again." And I stayed at his house for two days. I was afraid to be alone. And that taught me something about how much greater the pressure must be for those kids now. The reaction has to come, it has to come. Lately I talked to the only Negro boy in an integrated school in New Orleans. He stood and moved like a little soldier, and it was very impressive and very frightening. Because no boy his age can possibly be that controlled and not pay for it later on somehow.

Do you think school desegregation was a good place to begin? Putting all the onus of this on the children?

At this point there would be no good place to begin, really. But in another way, those beautiful children are the only people who could have done it.

Movies and beaches, all that, seem like effort lost.

Well, it isn't entirely, though. What one's trying to do is simply make white people get used to seeing you around without a broom in your hand! I think it's just as important as the schools, because the wall has been built on every single level and has got to come down on every level. The Government, for reasons of its own, prefers that Negroes in the South work on voting registration rather than try to desegregate buses or bus stations or coffee counters or stores, and, God knows, not to have any boycotts. Well, of course, the Government's being very clever about that. It will take years to get the vote, in any case, and if you're doing that and nothing else, then the vote's safe another fifty years.

What do you think of the idea that Negroes can't get anywhere until they begin to mobilize as a real group?

I don't know on what principle it would mobilize itself, that's the trouble.

But whether you like it or not, you are thrust into a sort of role as spokesman for The Negro—a group that ought not to be a group. How do you feel about that role? Maybe you didn't elect it, and yet . . .

And yet it's true.

Can you speak for those millions?

I can't. I don't try to.

The neo-Africans don't seem to think you speak for them. What about them?

They are romantic American Negroes who think they can identify with the African struggle, without having the least idea what it's about. They want to see black men in power, simply, and it's more interesting to see a black statesman in his robes at the U.N. than to consider what kind of a statesman he is.

Do they actually want to live in Africa?

They think they do, but they don't stay. The Africans don't want them. They can't *use* them. You can't deal with anybody who pretends that he doesn't come from where he comes from; you can't respect him and you can't trust him. Maybe I can go to Africa and think that I'm an African looking for my tribe—and where is it? But they hear the way I talk and see the way I walk, and they don't like me any better for pretending I don't come from Harlem. And Africans remember, though neo-Africans do not, when American Negroes would not speak to Africans. But I do feel very involved with the students in the South. I don't consider myself a spokesman for them either, but I do think that they trust me and I can't afford to fail them. That controls me more than anything else in this context, because no one else seems to be doing it, really. And kids need somebody who will talk to them, listen to them. They want you to respect their questions.

What do they ask you?

Well, they ask real questions. "What would you do if your teacher told you that instead of picketing and engaging in sit-ins, you should get an education first?" one boy asked me. And I said, "I would tell my teacher that it's impossible to get an education in this country until you change the country." And the boy said, "Thank you." And that does something for me.

To go back to our fear of the Negro, haven't you also suggested that sex is at the bottom of it?

Yes, I think it has something to do with the whole Puritan ethic, the whole idea that the flesh is something to be ashamed of. The burden that is placed on you because you're a Negro male is terrifying, and it says something about the poverty of the white cat's bed or the white chick's bed, which today is very hard to believe.

But we love to talk about sex!

That's right, and that's where the Negro comes in. If a Negro is present in a room, there's a great silence then. Sex is on everybody's mind, but nobody's going to say anything. You can see people, almost in the middle of sentences, shifting gears and making wild right turns. They wanted to talk about sex, but now they're not going to, because here sex *is,* right in the middle of the room drinking a dry martini. And it all becomes extremely polite and antiseptic. But on the other hand, at four o'clock in the morning, when everybody's drunk enough, then extraordinary things can happen. It's very hard to describe. It's something I want to do in a novel.

Why this poverty of the white cat's bed?

I have some hunches. It has something to do with Puritanism again. It has something to do with the whole role of women in this country since the country got here. Something to do with the scarcity of women and the roughness of the country. I don't mean just physical roughness, I mean the loneliness, the physical loneliness of it. When you were crossing it, it must have been terrifying.

And it has something to do with the Indians. White men married Indians, and slept with them and killed them, too.

Do you think history operates this way in people's unconscious?

I think it operates this way *actually*. This has to be so. Because when the chips are down in any crisis, what you have to draw on finally is not what happened in the time that you yourself have been on earth, but what came before you. This is what gets you through your crisis finally. And somewhere in yourself you carry all of that. You have to be in great trouble to turn to it and use it, or to suspect that you have to; but when you are in trouble, that's what you turn to, which means it must be there.

In your writing you've always been hard on everyone, white and black, but lately you seem to be getting harder and harder on white people.

What I want to do in the play I'm working on now is somehow bring that whole thing together—what white people have done and also what black people are doing. And I don't know how to put that.

Well, everything you've said about white people has been negative; yet you say that blacks have something to give us without which we'll perish.

I think that's true. If the Negro doesn't save this country, then nobody else can. And if I can find another word than Negro, it might be closer to what I mean. I don't mean the Negro as a person; I mean the Negro as an experience—a level of experience Americans always deny.

One of the most puzzling things you've said is that your darkness reminds white men of their death.

I meant what I said: if you are a Negro dealing with people all day long, all year long, all life long, who never look at you, then you have to figure out one day what they *are* looking at. Obviously it isn't you. When I was seventeen, working for the Army, I could not have been a threat to any white man alive. So it wasn't me, it was something he didn't want to see. And you know what that was? It was ultimately, yes, his own death. Or call it trouble. Trouble is an excellent metaphor for death. The white man knew he would not like to be me. People who certainly are not monsters on any other level will do monstrous things to you, semi-deliberately or deliberately, designed to protect their wives and children. This is what is meant by keeping you in your place. If you move out of your place everything is changed. If I'm not what that white man thinks I am, then he has to find out what *he* is.

Do we use status to make up for identity?

Exactly. And therefore I'm the only cat that has any identity, because it's in my skin. I've got a built-in identity for other people, which is more than they have for me, more than they have for themselves, too. And they fear and despise one for it.

How about when you look at us? Are we just blobs?

No. You never could be for me, because you all have too much power. I can be a blob for you, but you I have to study in order to survive. And this can kill you, but if it doesn't kill you it gives you a certain beat. It isn't a business of what people say. Listen to what they're not saying. A lot of Negro style—the style of a man like Miles Davis or Ray Charles or the style of a man like myself—is based on a knowledge of what people are really saying and on our refusal to hear it. You pick up on the beat, which is much more truthful than words.

They say that people deprived of the full use of their intellects make up for it with unusual powers of intuition. This would be true of the Negro, surely?

You live almost entirely by your intuition. It has to be highly developed. And the intellect, anyway, is one more way of avoiding yourself. One must find a way to get through to life or to experience, but that can't be done intellectually.

You must get a real sense of who you are, anyway. How would you define identity?

I don't know. It's some respect for the self, which has something to do—as my good friend Sidney Poitier says—with knowing whence you came. And really knowing that. And in some way, if you know that, you know something else, too. I can't tell precisely what it is you know then, but if you know where you were, you have some sense of where you are.

Evidently "whence you came" once stood between you and a sense of who you are.

It inevitably does, I think, for everybody. It has to. You have to accept it. You can't run. I know, because I've tried. And I think who you are has something to do with responsibility, too.

To whom and what?

The kind of responsibility that means that you haven't got time to weep, because you have too much to do, the pressures are too great. It's learning very soon that there are no excuses, that if you fail, it's because *you* failed. And of course it doesn't mean you won't—one way or another everybody does. Everybody has to deal with this question of who and what he is. I have to deal with it because of the kids, the students, and I have to deal with it because I'm a writer. Writers have to make use of it all, every bit of it. That's all you've got. You take it or you die.

But in a way wasn't it easier for you to find out who you were because you were a Negro and had to face your suffering?

Yes. But there's something else, too. Hannah Arendt told me that the virtues I described in *The New Yorker* piece—the sensuality I was talking about, and the warmth, and the fish fries, and all that—are typical of all oppressed people. And they don't, unluckily, she said—and I think she's entirely right—survive even five minutes the end of their oppression.

And what we think of as the Negro's innate qualities are just desperate stratagems that people who have nothing else use to stay alive?

And you make do with nothing, and you get, if you survive, a kind of authority from that. You really have to know yourself to find resources to make do with the minimum. But you wouldn't do it if you weren't forced to do it. And the moment you're not forced to do it any more, you stop doing it.

And Negro millionaires are as far removed from reality as anybody else?

Insofar as they are pretending to be white.

You said you yourself once felt that you didn't know whether you were black or white. What did you mean?

Well, I meant I didn't know who I was at all. They used to say to me, "Don't act like a nigger." Acting like a nigger meant eating with your hands or scratching yourself or cursing or fighting or getting drunk or having nappy hair—all those things. And for a long time I spent a lot of effort trying not to act like a nigger. I slicked my hair down, never raised my voice, had perfect table manners, and of course it didn't help at all.

You were just being a cultured Negro!

I was being a cultured Negro. I was always wearing a sort of iron corset. And it didn't make me white. And it didn't make me a man either. And it meant I couldn't talk to white people, because I was talking in a certain kind of way, and I couldn't talk to black people either, because I was too busy not being one of them. And I hated white people from the bottom of my heart. And I hated black people for being so common! I realized, too, that if a white man were doing any of those things I was told not to do, no one would say he was acting like a nigger. It was only me who was acting like a nigger, because I *was* a nigger. No matter what I did, I was acting like a nigger. So I decided to act like a nigger, or at least act like *me.*

What did you mean when you said that a black person should cultivate the nigger within?

Well, I mean this. If I want to beat up a doorman, maybe I don't beat him up, but I have to know that that's what I really want to do. That I'm not being the poised, controlled, civilized cat that I dream of myself as being at all. That if a policeman hits me, I'm very probably going to try to kill him. And if I don't do it, it won't be because I didn't want to. It will be because something else is operating and I know that I have to do something else. But I know it is *there.* That's my only protection against it.

And it's not a matter of black or white at all?

It's a matter of not telling any more lies than you can help. And some black people know that and some white people know that; and for the rest . . . well, there are very, very few.

Is there any hope for the body politic?

No, not now. We'd be very lucky if we had a great man in the White House right now, *if* we had a great man. We do not, but *if* we did . . .

Have you ever known anyone who seemed to you great?

James Meredith. He's a very tough and loving little man.

Still loving? Has he repressed his hatred?

On certain questions I don't think that hatred any longer operates. I don't think I hate anybody any more. It's too expensive. I stopped trying to be white. It's a law that if I hate white people I have to hate black people.

Any other people you think great?

A man named Jerome Smith. He's one of the student leaders in New Orleans and one of the veterans of Jackson, Mississippi—beaten with brass knuckles until he was entirely numb; not simply out, but numb. He's still being treated for it. He's very young. He was a longshoreman. And he is a tremendous man.

Why is he tremendous? Because he survived?

No, he's tremendous because he knows what happened. If anyone has a right to hate white people, Jerome certainly does. But he doesn't hate. He does not.

You said you used to hate yourself. How did you get over it?

Well, I think it has everything to do with my brothers and sisters. You can't be involved with that many people so young without doing one of two things: either you reject it all, or sooner or later you begin to realize that it is part of you. And I loved them very much. I didn't always. At the very beginning I did. I did—and I do. In a way you take your worth from other people's eyes. And a friend in Switzerland did something, too. In a way he saved my life by refusing to allow me to be paranoid about my color. He did it by not being sorry for me. And my mother had something to do with it, too. I think she saved us all. She was the only person in the world we could turn to, yet she couldn't protect us.

She doesn't sound like that consoling black-mammy figure that we whites are so enamored of. The maids we knew, for instance.

Yes, who's all wise, all patient, and all enduring. But it's emotionally too easy, because in fact those maids have sons who may by this time have turned into junkies because their mothers can get jobs and they can't. I'm sure all the people my mother worked for thought of her that way, but she wasn't like that at all. She was a very tough little woman, and she must have been scared to death all the years she was raising us.

Scared of what?

Of those streets! There it is at the door, *at the door!* Whores, pimps, racketeers. It hasn't changed either, by the way. That's what it means to be raised in a ghetto. I think of what a woman like my mother knows, instinctively has to know, has had to know from the very beginning: that there is no safety, that no one is safe, none of her children would ever be safe. The nature of the ghetto is somehow ultimately to make those skills which are immoral the only skills worth having. You haven't got to be sweet to survive in a ghetto; you've got to be cunning. You've got to make up the rules as you go along; there aren't any others. You can't call the cops.

What about your father?

He was righteous in the pulpit and a monster in the house. Maybe he saved all kinds of souls, but he lost all his children, every single one of them. And it wasn't so much a matter of punishment with him: he was trying to kill us. I've hated a few people, but actually I've hated only one person, and that was my father.

Did he hate you?

In a way, yes. He didn't like me. But he'd had a terrible time, too. And of course, I was not his son. I was a bastard. What he wanted for his children was what in fact I became. I was the brightest boy in the house because I was the eldest, and because I loved my mother and I really loved those kids. And I was necessary: I changed all the diapers and I knew where the kids were, and I could take some of the pressures off my mother and in a way stand between him and her—which is a strange role to play. I had to learn to stand up to my father, and, in learning that, I became precisely what he wanted his other children to become, and he couldn't take that, and I couldn't either maybe.

Did he affect your ideas of what you could do in the world?

My father did one thing for me. He said, "You can't do it." And I said, "Listen, m———— don't tell me what I can't do. I can't do it? Don't tell me I can't do it. You'll see!"

Why couldn't you do it, according to him? Because you were black?

Because I was black, because I was little, because I was ugly. He made me ugly. I used to put pennies on my eyes to make them go back.

But out of that an identity emerged.

Yes, all those strangers called Jimmy Baldwin.

Who are some of them?

There's the older brother with all the egotism and rigidity that implies. That tone will always be there, and there's nothing I can do about it except know it's there and laugh at it. I grew up telling people what to do and spanking them, so that in some way I always will be doing that. Then there's the self-pitying little boy. You know: "I can't do it, because I'm so ugly." He's still there some place.

Who else?

Lots of people. Some of them are unmentionable. There's a man. There's a woman, too. There are lots of people here.

It's been said of you that you have two obsessions: color and homosexuality.

I'm not absolutely sure I have two obsessions. They're more than that.

Whatever they are, are they interrelated?

Let's go back to where we were talking about the Negro man and sex, and let's go back again to the American white man's lack of sexual security, and then let's try to imagine what it would be like to be a Negro adolescent dealing with those people to whom you are a phallic symbol. American males are the only people I've ever encountered in the world who are willing to go on the needle before they'll go to bed with each other. Because they're afraid of this, they don't know how to go to bed with women either. I've known people who literally died out of this panic. I don't know what homosexual means any more, and Americans don't either.

You don't think it's a disease?

This is one of the American myths. What always occurs to me is that people in other parts of the world have never had this peculiar kind of conflict. If you fall in love with a boy, you fall in love with a boy. The fact that Americans consider it a disease says more about them than it says about homosexuality.

What about societies where homosexuality becomes very open, as it has here or did in Germany during the Twenties?

When it becomes open as it has here, it becomes a disease. These people are not involved in anything resembling love-making: they're involved in some kind of exhibition of their disaster. It has nothing to do with contact or involvement between two people—which means that the person may change you. That's what people are afraid of. It's impossible to go through life assuming that you know who you're going to fall in love with. You don't. And everything depends on the fashion in which you live, on the things to which you will not say no, the risks you are prepared to take.

What's going to keep black people from becoming just like white people once they've broken down the barriers?

That's what frightens me when we talk about what we call The Negro Problem. I realize that most white people don't realize the Negro is like anybody else, just like everybody else. When this situation ends, something else will begin, which may be just as terrible as what we're going through now. And what some of the students in the South know is that it's not a matter of being accepted into this society at all. It is a matter of demolishing it in some way, which has nothing to do with the Kremlin. It's a matter of transforming it; it's a matter of not making your peace with it; it's a matter really of building Jerusalem again, no matter how corny that may sound.

Wouldn't most people rather escape it than transform it?

You can't escape. You have *not* walked out of the industrial society because you say you have or because you're wearing a beard. You're still right here where you were; you haven't moved an inch.

How about your years in Europe? Was that an escape?

I'll say this: I know very well I survived as a writer by living abroad so long, because if I had not been living abroad, I would have been compelled to make more money.

Are you ever tempted to go back?

All I can do is work out the terms on which I can work, and for me that means being a transatlantic commuter. What's most difficult is that you are penalized for trying to remain in touch with yourself. I have a public life—and I know that, O.K. I have a private life, something which I know a good deal less. And the temptation is to avoid the private life because you can hide in the public one. And I've got excellent reasons for doing it, because what I'm doing is very admirable—you know, all this jazz. Except that that is not the most important thing! The most important thing is somewhere else. It always is—somewhere else. But it's not my life, and if I pretend it is, I'll die. I am *not* a public speaker. I *am* an artist.

You are stealing from the artist to pay for the Negro?

Yes. It's one of the prices of my success. And let's face it, I am a *Negro* writer. Sidney Poitier, you know, is not simply an actor; he's a *Negro* actor. He's not simply a movie star; he's the *only* Negro movie star. And because he is in the position that he is in, he has obligations that Tony Curtis will never have. And it has made Sidney a remarkable man.

Can a Negro ever talk about anything but being a Negro?

I get so tired of black and white, you know, so tired of talking about it, especially when you can't get anything across. What you have to do, I suppose, is invest the vocabulary with something it doesn't contain yet. Don't you see what I'm trying to do? I'm trying to find another word besides Negro to say what I mean, and I can't use tragedy.

Why not?

Because I haven't figured out the terms on which I can use it yet. All I know . . . I suddenly thought of all the Negroes who don't know anything either.

As we've talked now, you have translated Negro into terms which . . .

Which have nothing to do with *that*.

Which have nothing to do with that. And which is what we've really been talking about.

Which is the only thing *to* talk about. I don't know. Nothing will happen to change all that before we die—that vocabulary.

And we have to go on talking about black and white, and that's not it at all.

That is not enough, and it isn't interesting. I don't think much will happen, except disaster, to change things.

The fire next time?

Yes. People don't give things up; things are taken away from them. I'm not frightened of another war really. I'm just frightened of chaos, apathy, indifference—which is the road people took to Auschwitz.

Norman Podhoretz

MY NEGRO PROBLEM—AND OURS*

NORMAN PODHORETZ, a writer and critic, is editor of Commentary *Magazine. A native New Yorker, he was a Pulitzer Scholar at Columbia College, where he earned his Bachelor of Arts degree. He holds a Bachelor's and Master's degree in English from Cambridge University, England, where he was a Fulbright and Kellett Fellow, and a Bachelor's degree in Hebrew Letters from the Jewish Theological Seminary. Mr. Podhoretz taught English Literature and English Moral Philosophy at Clare College, Cambridge, was editor-in-chief of the Looking Glass Library, publishers of children's classics, and is currently regular book critic for* Show *Magazine. He is considered an astute literary critic and a perceptive analyst of the contemporary social scene, and his articles on the younger generation, the role of the intellectual, the shifting values in popular culture and modern literary trends have been published widely, particularly in* Partisan Review, Harper's, *the* New Leader, Esquire, *and* The New Yorker. *He has appeared on TV and radio symposia both in America and England.*

> *If we—and . . . I mean the relatively conscious whites and the relatively conscious blacks, who must, like lovers, insist on, or create, the consciousness of the others —do not falter in our duty now, we may be able, handful that we are, to end the racial nightmare, and achieve our country, and change the history of the world.*
>
> —James Baldwin

* This article is reprinted from *Commentary*. Copyright © 1963 by the American Jewish Committee.

TWO IDEAS puzzled me deeply as a child growing up in Brooklyn during the 1930's in what today would be called an integrated neighborhood. One of them was that all Jews were rich; the other was that all Negroes were persecuted. These ideas had appeared in print; therefore they must be true. My own experience and the evidence of my senses told me they were not true, but that only confirmed what a day-dreaming boy in the provinces—for the lower-class neighborhoods of New York belong as surely to the provinces as any rural town in North Dakota—discovers very early: *his* experience is unreal and the evidence of his senses is not to be trusted. Yet even a boy with a head full of fantasies incongruously synthesized out of Hollywood movies and English novels cannot altogether deny the reality of his own experience—especially when there is so much deprivation in that experience. Nor can he altogether gainsay the evidence of his own senses—especially such evidence of the senses as comes from being repeatedly beaten up, robbed, and in general hated, terrorized, and humiliated.

And so for a long time I was puzzled to think that Jews were supposed to be rich when the only Jews I knew were poor, and that Negroes were supposed to be persecuted when it was the Negroes who were doing the only persecuting I knew about—and doing it, moreover, to *me*. During the early years of the war, when my older sister joined a left-wing youth organization, I remember my astonishment at hearing her passionately denounce my father for thinking that Jews were worse off than Negroes. To me, at the age of twelve, it seemed very clear that Negroes were better off than Jews—indeed, than *all* whites. A city boy's world is contained within three or four square blocks, and in my world it was the whites, the Italians and Jews, who feared the Negroes, not the other way around. The Negroes were tougher than we were, more ruthless, and on the whole they were better athletes. What could it mean, then, to say that they were badly off and that we were more fortunate? Yet my sister's opinions, like print, were sacred, and when she told me about exploitation and economic forces I believed her. I believed her, but I was still afraid of Negroes. And I still hated them with all my heart.

It had not always been so—that much I can recall from early childhood. When did it start, this fear and this hatred? There was a kindergarten in the local public school, and given the character of the neighborhood, at least half of the children in my class must have been Negroes. Yet I have no memory of being aware of color differences at that age, and I know from observing my own children that they attribute no significance to such differences even when they begin noticing them. I think there was a day—first grade? second grade?—when my best friend Carl hit me on the way home from school and announced that he wouldn't play with me any more because I had killed Jesus. When I ran home to my mother crying for an explanation, she told me not to pay any attention to such foolishness, and then in Yiddish she cursed the *goyim* and the *schwartzes,* the *schwartzes* and the *goyim.* Carl, it turned out, was a *schwartze,* and so was added a third to the categories into which people were mysteriously divided.

Sometimes I wonder whether this is a true memory at all. It is blazingly vivid, but perhaps it never happened: can anyone really remember back to the age of six? There is no uncertainty in my mind, however, about the years that followed. Carl and I hardly ever spoke, though we met in school every day up through the eighth or ninth grade. There would be embarrassed moments of catching his eye or of his catching mine—for whatever it was that had attracted us to one another as very small children remained alive in spite of the fantastic barrier of hostility that had grown up between us, suddenly and out of nowhere. Nevertheless, friendship would have been impossible, and even if it had been possible, it would have been unthinkable. About that, there was nothing anyone could do by the time we were eight years old.

Item: The orphanage across the street is torn down, a city housing project begins to rise in its place, and on the marvelous vacant lot next to the old orphanage they are building a playground. Much excitement and anticipation as Opening Day draws near. Mayor LaGuardia himself comes to dedicate this great gesture of public benevolence. He speaks of neighborliness and borrowing cups of sugar, and of the playground he says that children of all races, colors, and creeds will learn to live together in harmony. A week later, some of us are swatting flies on the playground's inadequate little ball field. A gang of Negro kids, pretty much our own age, enter from the other side and order us out of the park. We refuse, proudly and indignantly, with superb masculine fervor. There is a fight, they win, and we retreat, half whimpering, half with bravado. My first nauseating experience of cowardice. And my first appalled realization that there are people in the world who do not seem to be afraid of anything, who act as though they have nothing to lose. Thereafter the playground becomes a battleground, sometimes quiet, sometimes the scene of athletic competition between Them and Us. But rocks are thrown as often as baseballs. Gradually we abandon the place and use the streets instead. The streets are safer, though we do not admit this to ourselves. We are not, after all, sissies—that most dreaded epithet of an American boyhood.

Item: I am standing alone in front of the building in which I live. It is late afternoon and getting dark. That day in school the teacher had asked a surly Negro boy named Quentin a question he was unable to answer. As usual I had waved my arm eagerly ("Be a good boy, get good marks, be smart, go to college, become a doctor") and, the right answer bursting from my lips, I was held up lovingly by the teacher as an example to the class. I had seen Quentin's face—a very dark, very cruel, very Oriental-looking face—harden, and there had been enough threat in his eyes to make me run all the way home for fear that he might catch me outside.

Now, standing idly in front of my own house, I see him approaching from the project accompanied by his little brother who is carrying a baseball bat and wearing a grin of malicious anticipation. As in a nightmare, I am trapped. The surroundings are secure and familiar, but terror is suddenly present and there is no one around to help. I am locked to the spot. I will not cry out or run away like a sissy, and I stand there, my heart wild, my throat clogged. He walks up, hurls the familiar epithet ("Hey, mo'f—r"), and to my surprise only pushes me. It is a violent push, but not a punch. A push is not as serious as a punch. Maybe I can still back out without entirely losing my dignity. Maybe I can still say, "Hey, c'mon Quentin, whaddya wanna do *that* for? I dint do nothin' to *you,*" and walk away, not too rapidly. Instead, before I can stop myself, I push him back—a token gesture—and I say, "Cut that out, I don't wanna fight, I ain't got nothin' to fight about." As I turn to walk back into the building, the corner of my eye catches the motion of the bat his little brother has handed him. I try to duck, but the bat crashes colored lights into my head.

The next thing I know, my mother and sister are standing over me, both of them hysterical. My sister—she who was later to join the "progressive" youth organization—is shouting for the police and screaming imprecations at those dirty little black bastards. They take me upstairs, the doctor comes, the police come. I tell them that the boy who did it was a stranger, that he had been trying to get money from me. They do not believe me, but I am too scared to give them Quentin's name. When I return to school a few days later, Quentin avoids my eyes. He knows that I have not squealed, and he is ashamed. I try to feel proud, but in my heart I know that it was fear of what his friends might do to me that had kept me silent, and not the code of the street.

Item: There is an athletic meet in which the whole of our junior high school is participating. I am in one of the seventh-grade rapid-advance classes, and "segregation" has now set in with a vengeance. In the last three or four years of the elementary school from which we have just graduated, each grade had been divided into three classes, according to "intelligence." (In the earlier grades the divisions had either been arbitrary or else unrecognized by us as having anything to do with brains.) These divisions by IQ, or however it was arranged, had resulted in a preponderance of Jews in the "1" classes and a corresponding preponderance of Negroes in the "3's," with the Italians split unevenly along the spectrum. At least a few Negroes had always made the "1's," just as there had always been a few Jewish kids among the "3's," and more among the "2's" (where Italians dominated). But the junior high's rapid-advance class of which I am now a member is overwhelmingly Jewish and entirely white—except for a shy lonely Negro girl with light skin and reddish hair.

The athletic meet takes place in a city-owned stadium far from the school. It is an important event to which a whole day is given over. The winners are to get those precious little medallions stamped with the New York City emblem that can be screwed into a belt and that prove the wearer to be a distinguished personage. I am a fast runner, and so I am assigned the position of anchor man on my class's team in the relay race. There are three other seventh-grade teams in the race, two of them all Negro, as ours is all white. One of the all-Negro teams is very tall—their anchor man waiting silently next to me on the line looks years older than I am, and I do not recognize him. He is the first to get the baton and crosses the finishing line in a walk. Our team comes in second, but a few minutes later we are declared the winners, for it has been discovered that the anchor man on the first-place team is not a member of the class. We are awarded the medallions, and the following day our home-room teacher makes a speech about how proud she is of us for being superior athletes as well as superior students. We want to believe that we deserve the praise, but we know that we could not have won even if the other class had not cheated.

That afternoon, walking home, I am waylaid and surrounded by five Negroes, among whom is the anchor man of the disqualified team. "Gimme my medal, mo'f——r," he grunts. I do not have it with me and I tell him so. "Anyway, it ain't yours," I say foolishly. He calls me a liar on both counts and pushes me up against the wall on which we sometimes play handball. "Gimme my mo'f——n' medal," he says again. I repeat that I have left it home. "Le's search the li'l mo'f——r," one of them suggests, "he prolly got it *hid* in his mo'f——n' *pants*." My panic is now unmanageable. (How many times had I been surrounded like this and asked in soft tones, "Len' me a nickel, boy." How many times had I been called a liar for pleading poverty and pushed around, or searched, or beaten up, unless there happened to be someone in the marauding gang like Carl who liked me across that enormous divide of hatred and who would therefore say, "Aaah, c'mon, le's git someone else, *this* boy ain't got no money on 'im.") I scream at them through tears of rage and self-contempt, "Keep your f——n' filthy lousy black hands offa me! I swear I'll get the cops." This is all they need to hear, and the five of them set upon me. They bang me around, mostly in the stomach and on the arms and shoulders, and when several adults loitering near the candy store down the block notice what is going on and begin to shout, they run off and away.

I do not tell my parents about the incident. My team-mates, who have also been waylaid, each by a gang led by his opposite number from the disqualified team, have had their medallions taken from them, and they never squeal either. For days, I walk home in terror, expecting to be caught again, but nothing happens. The medallion is put away into a drawer, never to be worn by anyone.

Obviously experiences like these have always been a common feature of childhood life in working-class and immigrant neighborhoods, and Negroes do not necessarily figure in them. Wherever, and in whatever combination, they have lived together in the cities, kids of different groups have been at war, beating up and being beaten up: micks against kikes against wops against spicks against polacks. And even relatively homogeneous areas have not been spared the warring of the young: one block against another, one gang (called in my day, in a pathetic effort at gentility, an "S.A.C.," or social-athletic club) against another. But the Negro-white conflict had—and no doubt still has—a special intensity and was conducted with a ferocity unmatched by intramural white battling.

In my own neighborhood, a good deal of animosity existed between the Italian kids (most of whose parents were immigrants from Sicily) and the Jewish kids (who came largely from East European immigrant families). Yet everyone had friends, sometimes close friends, in the other "camp," and we often visited one another's strange-smelling houses, if not for meals, then for glasses of milk, and occasionally for some special event like a wedding or a wake. If it happened that we divided into warring factions and did battle, it would invariably be half-hearted and soon patched up. Our parents, to be sure, had nothing to do with one another and were mutually suspicious and hostile. But we, the kids, who all spoke Yiddish or Italian at home, were Americans, or New Yorkers, or Brooklyn boys: we shared a culture, the culture of the street, and at least for a while this culture proved to be more powerful than the opposing cultures of the home.

Why, *why* should it have been so different as between the Negroes and us? How was it borne in upon us so early, white and black alike, that we were enemies beyond any possibility of reconciliation? Why did we hate one another so?

I suppose if I tried, I could answer those questions more or less adequately from the perspective of what I have since learned. I could draw upon James Baldwin—what better witness is there?—to describe the sense of entrapment that poisons the soul of the Negro with hatred for the white man whom he knows to be his jailer. On the other side, if I wanted to understand how the white man comes to hate the Negro, I could call upon the psychologists who have spoken of the guilt that white Americans feel toward Negroes and that turns into hatred for lack of acknowledging itself as guilt. These are plausible answers and certainly there is truth in them. Yet when I think back upon my own experience of the Negro and his of me, I find myself troubled and puzzled, much as I was as a child when I heard that all Jews were rich and all Negroes persecuted. How could the Negroes in my neighborhood have regarded the whites across the street and around the corner as jailers? On the whole, the whites were not so poor as the Negroes, but they were quite poor enough, and the years were years of Depression. As for white hatred of the Negro, how could guilt have had anything to do with it? What share had these Italian and Jewish immigrants in the enslavement of the Negro? What share had they—downtrodden people themselves breaking their own necks to eke out a living—in the exploitation of the Negro?

No, I cannot believe that we hated each other back there in Brooklyn because they thought of us as jailers and we felt guilty toward them. But does it matter, given the fact that we all went through an unrepresentative confrontation? I think it matters profoundly, for if we managed the job of hating each other so well without benefit of the aids to hatred that are supposedly at the root of this madness everywhere else, it must mean that the madness is not yet properly understood. I am far from pretending that I understand it, but I would insist that no view of the problem will begin to approach the truth unless it can account for a case like the one I have been trying to describe. Are the elements of any such view available to us?

At least two, I would say, are. One of them is a point we frequently come upon in the work of James Baldwin, and the other is a related point always stressed by psychologists who have studied the mechanisms of prejudice. Baldwin tells us that one of the reasons Negroes hate the white man is that the white man refuses to *look* at him: the Negro knows that in white eyes all Negroes are alike; they are faceless and therefore not altogether human. The psychologists, in their turn, tell us that the white man hates the Negro because he tends to project those wild impulses that he fears in himself onto an alien group which he then punishes with his contempt. What Baldwin does *not* tell us, however, is that the principle of facelessness is a two-way street and can operate in both directions with no difficulty at all. Thus, in my neighborhood in Brooklyn, *I* was as faceless to the Negroes as they were to me, and if they hated me because I never looked at them, I must also have hated them for never looking at *me*. To the Negroes, my white skin was enough to define me as the enemy, and in a war it is only the uniform that counts and not the person.

So with the mechanism of projection that the psychologists talk about: it too works in both directions at once. There is no question that the psychologists are right about what the Negro represents symbolically to the white man. For me as a child the life lived on the other side of the playground and down the block on Ralph Avenue seemed the very embodiment of the values of the street—free, independent, reckless, brave, masculine, erotic. I put the word "erotic" last, though it is usually stressed above all others, because in fact it came last, in consciousness as in importance. What mainly counted for me about Negro kids of my own age was that they were "bad boys." There were plenty of bad boys among the whites—this was, after all, a neighborhood with a long tradition of crime as a career open to aspiring talents—but the Negroes were *really* bad, bad in a way that beckoned to one, and made one feel inadequate. *We* all went home every day for a lunch of spinach-and-potatoes; *they* roamed around during lunch hour, munching on candy bars. In winter *we* had to wear itchy woolen hats and mittens and cumbersome galoshes; *they* were bare-headed and loose as they pleased. *We* rarely played hookey, or got into serious trouble in school, for all our street-corner bravado; *they* were defiant, forever staying out (to do what delicious things?), forever making disturbances in class and in the halls, forever being sent to the principal and returning uncowed. But most important of all, they were *tough;* beautifully, enviably tough, not giving a damn for anyone or anything. To hell with the teacher, the truant officer, the cop; to hell with the whole of the adult world that held *us* in its grip and that we never had the courage to rebel against except sporadically and in petty ways.

This is what I saw and envied and feared in the Negro: this is what finally made him faceless to me, though some of it, of course, was actually there. (The psychologists also tell us that the alien group which becomes the object of a projection will tend to respond by trying to live up to what is expected of them.) But what, on his side, did the Negro see in me that made me faceless to *him?* Did he envy me my lunches of spinach-and-potatoes and my itchy woolen caps and my prudent behavior in the face of authority, as I envied him his noon-time candy bars and his bare head in winter and his magnificent rebelliousness? Did those lunches and caps spell for him the prospect of power and riches in the future? Did they mean that there were possibilities open to me that were denied to him? Very likely they did. But if so, one also supposes that he feared the impulses within himself toward submission to authority no less powerfully than I feared the impulses in myself toward defiance. If I represented the jailer to him, it was not because I was oppressing him or keeping him down: it was because I symbolized for him the dangerous and probably pointless temptation toward greater repression, just as he symbolized for me the equally perilous tug toward greater freedom. I personally was to be rewarded for this repression with a new and better life in the future, but how many of my friends paid an even higher price and were given only gall in return.

We have it on the authority of James Baldwin that all Negroes hate whites. I am trying to suggest that on their side all whites—all American whites, that is—are sick in their feelings about Negroes. There are Negroes, no doubt, who would say that Baldwin is wrong, but I suspect them of being less honest than he is, just as I suspect whites of self-deception who tell me they have no special feeling toward Negroes. Special feelings about color are a contagion to which white Americans seem susceptible even when there is nothing in their background to account for the susceptibility. Thus everywhere we look today in the North, we find the curious phenomenon of white middle-class liberals with no previous personal experience of Negroes—people to whom Negroes have always been faceless in virtue rather than faceless in vice—discovering that their abstract commitment to the cause of Negro rights will not stand the test of a direct confrontation. We find such people fleeing in droves to the suburbs as the Negro population in the inner city grows; and when they stay in the city we find them sending their children to private school rather than to the "integrated" public school in the neighborhood. We find them resisting the demand that gerrymandered school districts be rezoned for the purpose of overcoming de facto segregation; we find them judiciously considering whether the Negroes (for their own good, of course) are not perhaps pushing too hard; we find them clucking their tongues over Negro militancy; we find them speculating on the question of whether there may not, after all, be something in the theory that the races are biologically different; we find them saying that it will take a very long time for Negroes to achieve full equality, no matter what anyone does; we find them deploring the rise of black nationalism and expressing the solemn hope that the leaders of the Negro community will discover ways of containing the impatience and incipient violence within the Negro ghettos.

But that is by no means the whole story; there is also the phenomenon of what Kenneth Rexroth once called "crow-jimism." There are the broken-down white boys like Vivaldo Moore in

Baldwin's *Another Country* who go to Harlem in search of sex or simply to brush up against something that looks like primitive vitality, and who are so often punished by the Negroes they meet for crimes that they would have been the last ever to commit and of which they themselves have been as sorry victims as any of the Negroes who take it out on them. There are the writers and intellectuals and artists who romanticize Negroes and pander to them, assuming a guilt that is not properly theirs. And there are all the white liberals who permit Negroes to blackmail them into adopting a double standard of moral judgment, and who lend themselves—again assuming the responsibility for crimes they never committed—to cunning and contemptuous exploitation by Negroes they employ or try to befriend.

And what about me? What kind of feelings do I have about Negroes today? What happened to me, from Brooklyn, who grew up fearing and envying and hating Negroes? Now that Brooklyn is behind me, do I fear them and envy them and hate them still? The answer is yes, but not in the same proportions and certainly not in the same way. I now live on the upper west side of Manhattan, where there are many Negroes and many Puerto Ricans, and there are nights when I experience the old apprehensiveness again, and there are streets that I avoid when I am walking in the dark, as there were streets that I avoided when I was a child. I find that I am not afraid of Puerto Ricans, but I cannot restrain my nervousness whenever I pass a group of Negroes standing in front of a bar or sauntering down the street. I know now, as I did not know when I was a child, that power is on my side, that the police are working for me and not for them. And knowing this I feel ashamed and guilty, like the good liberal I have grown up to be. Yet the twinges of fear and the resentment they bring and the self-contempt they arouse are not to be gainsaid.

But envy? Why envy? And hatred? Why hatred? Here again the intensities have lessened and everything has been complicated and qualified by the guilts and the resulting over-compensations that are the heritage of the enlightened middle-class world of which I am now a member. Yet just as in childhood I envied Negroes for what seemed to me their superior masculinity, so I envy them today for what seems to me their superior physical grace and beauty. I have come to value physical grace very highly, and I am now capable of aching with all my being when I watch a Negro couple on the dance floor, or a Negro playing baseball or basketball. They are on the kind of terms with their own bodies that I should like to be on with mine, and for that precious quality they seem blessed to me.

The hatred I still feel for Negroes is the hardest of all the old feelings to face or admit, and it is the most hidden and the most overlarded by the conscious attitudes into which I have succeeded in willing myself. It no longer has, as for me it once did, any cause or justification (except, perhaps, that I am constantly being denied my right to an honest expression of the things I earned the right as a child to feel). How, then, do I know that this hatred has never entirely disappeared? I know it from the insane rage that can stir in me at the thought of Negro anti-Semitism; I know it from the disgusting prurience that can stir in me at the sight of a mixed couple; and I know it from the violence that can stir in me whenever I encounter that special brand of paranoid touchiness to which many Negroes are prone.

This, then, is where I am; it is not exactly where I think all other white liberals are, but it cannot be so very far away either. And it is because I am convinced that we white Americans are—for whatever reason, it no longer matters—so twisted and sick in our feelings about Negroes that I despair of the present push toward integration. If the pace of progress were not a factor here, there would perhaps be no cause for despair: time and the law and even the international political situation are on the side of the Negroes, and ultimately, therefore, victory—of a sort, anyway—must come. But from everything we have learned from observers who ought to know, pace has become as important to the Negroes as substance. They want equality and they want it *now,* and the white world is yielding to their demand only as much and as fast as it is absolutely being compelled to do. The Negroes know this in the most concrete terms imaginable, and it is thus becoming increasingly difficult to buy them off with rhetoric and promises and pious assurances of support. And so within the Negro community we find more and more people declaring that they want *out:* people who say that integration will never come, or that it will take a hundred or a thousand years to come, or that it will come at too high a price in suffering and struggle for the pallid and sodden life of the American middle class that at the very best it may bring.

The most numerous, influential, and dangerous movement that has grown out of Negro despair with the goal of integration is, of course, the Black Muslims. This movement, whatever else we may say about it, must be credited with one enduring achievement: it inspired James Baldwin to write an essay* which deserves to be placed among the classics of our language. Everything Baldwin has ever been trying to tell us is distilled here into a statement of overwhelming persuasiveness and prophetic magnificence. Baldwin's message is and always has been simple. It is this: "Color is not a human or personal reality; it is a political reality." And Baldwin's demand is correspondingly simple: color must be forgotten, lest we all be smited with a vengeance "that does not really depend on, and cannot really be executed by, any person or organization, and that cannot be prevented by any police force or army: historical vengeance, a cosmic vengeance based on the law that we recognize when we say, 'Whatever goes up must come down.' " The Black Muslims Baldwin portrays as a sign and a warning to the intransigent white world. They come to proclaim how deep is the Negro's disaffection with the white world and all its works, and Baldwin implies that no American Negro can fail to respond somewhere in his being to their message: that the white man is the devil, that Allah has doomed him to destruction, and that the black man is about to inherit the earth. Baldwin of course knows that this nightmare inversion of the racism from which the black man has suffered can neither win nor even point to the neighborhood in which victory might be located. For in his view the neighborhood of victory lies in exactly the opposite direction: the transcendence of color through love.

* Originally published in the *New Yorker* under the title "Letter from a Region in My Mind," it has been reprinted (along with a new introduction) by Dial Press under the title *The Fire Next Time.*

Yet the tragic fact is that love is not the answer to hate—not in the world of politics, at any rate. Color is indeed a political rather than a human or a personal reality and if politics (which is to say power) has made it into a human and a personal reality, then only politics (which is to say power) can unmake it once again. But the way of politics is slow and bitter, and as impatience on the one side is matched by a setting of the jaw on the other, we move closer and closer to an explosion and blood may yet run in the streets.

Will this madness in which we are all caught never find a resting-place? Is there never to be an end to it? In thinking about the Jews I have often wondered whether their survival as a distinct group was worth one hair on the head of a single infant. Did the Jews have to survive so that six million innocent people should one day be burned in the ovens of Auschwitz? It is a terrible question and no one, not God himself, could ever answer it to my satisfaction. And when I think about the Negroes in America and about the image of integration as a state in which the Negroes would take their rightful place as another of the protected minorities in a pluralistic society, I wonder whether they really believe in their hearts that such a state can actually be attained, and if so *why* they should wish to survive as a distinct group. I think I know why the Jews once wished to survive (though I am less certain as to why we still do): they not only believed that God had given them no choice, but they were tied to a memory of past glory and a dream of imminent redemption. What does the American Negro have that might correspond to this? His past is a stigma, his color is a stigma, and his vision of the future is the hope of erasing the stigma by making color irrelevant, by making it disappear as a fact of consciousness.

I share this hope, but I cannot see how it will ever be realized unless color does *in fact* disappear: and that means not integration, it means assimilation, it means—let the brutal word come out—miscegenation. The Black Muslims, like their racist counterparts in the white world, accuse the "so-called Negro leaders" of secretly pursuing miscegenation as a goal. The racists are wrong, but I wish they were right, for I believe that the wholesale merging of the two races is the most desirable alternative for everyone concerned. I am not claiming that this alternative can be pursued programmatically or that it is immediately feasible as a solution; obviously there are even greater barriers to its achievement than to the achievement of integration. What I am saying, however, is that in my opinion the Negro problem can be solved in this country in no other way.

I have told the story of my own twisted feelings about Negroes here, and of how they conflict with the moral convictions I have since developed, in order to assert that such feelings must be acknowledged as honestly as possible so that they can be controlled and ultimately disregarded in favor of the convictions. It is *wrong* for a man to suffer because of the color of his skin. Beside that clichéd proposition of liberal thought, what argument can stand and be respected? If the arguments are the arguments of feeling, they must be made to yield; and one's own soul is not the worst place to begin working a huge social transformation. Not so long ago, it used to be asked of white liberals, "Would you like your sister to marry one?" When I was a boy and my sister was still unmarried, I would certainly have said no to that question. But now I am a man, my sister is already married, and I have daughters. If I were to be asked today whether I would like a daughter of mine "to marry one," I would have to answer: "No, I wouldn't *like* it at all. I would rail and rave and rant and tear my hair. And then I hope I would have the courage to curse myself for raving and ranting, and to give her my blessing. How dare I withhold it at the behest of the child I once was and against the man I now have a duty to be?"

Ronnie Dugger

CONFESSIONS OF A WHITE LIBERAL

RONNIE DUGGER is editor and general manager of Texas' most controversial publication, The Texas Observer, *an independent-liberal weekly newspaper published in Austin, the state capital. A graduate of the University of Texas, he also attended Oxford University under the auspices of a Rotary International Foundation Fellowship, 1947–52. A former reporter for the* San Antonio Express *and the International News Service, he has also served as a correspondent for* Time, Life *and* Fortune *Magazines. In 1952–54, he was an assistant for writing and research to the executive director of the National Security Training Commission in Washington, D.C. His articles have appeared in many leading publications, including* The Nation, Harper's, New Republic, Christian Century, The Progressive, Frontier, *and the* Southwest Review.

TEN THOUSAND PEOPLE starve to death every day in the world. One Hiroshima every ten days. A hollow-eyed young child, passing away. After his time down and out in Paris and London, George Orwell said that he did not know what should be done to help the poor, but he did know enough never again to enjoy a meal at a smart restaurant. That this was a beginning. What *can* a man's conscience do with that reproach, "Ten thousand people starve to death every day," a reproach that, once felt and accepted, never relents, and goes on existing when we are not thinking about it, just as, once we have seen and sensed them doing it, we know that the waves of the Pacific continue to caress and assail the long western coast when we are not seeing them? The quantity of the world's injustice makes conscience reel, bottoms it in the dark reality, the preventable personal pain, that ideals and pieties do not assuage. One knows of the multitudes of people who have resolved to try to be good people, who have dedicated their lives, in greater or lesser part, to trying to humanize social injustitutions (I typed it this way in the first draft, and will not change it) and who are doing what they personally can. To do what one can: there is the most exonerating thought one can force up, out of one's own equivocal and pleasure-loving being, against the oppression of ten thousand people starving today and tonight, and the other multiform reproaches from the darkling realms of exploitation, thoughtlessness, maledictions, status, and power. And even this thought, *Do what you can,* flutters unsteadily in the bedeviled illuminations of conscience like a resolution firmly adopted New Year's Eve and betrayed by New Year's Night.

When we get too close to a problem, such as contempt for Negroes, we lose some of our natural ability to know what to do, because we begin to think it is a new problem, somehow special. Racial injustice is not a peculiarly American malady, or a special kind of human malevolence; and we have within our personal and private selves its natural infections and natural antibodies. Perhaps we should look there.

The commonplace among us that sanctions much of the social cruelty and oppression we take part in is the thought, "This is the way it has been, and these are the rules I was given as I grew up. They are written into our laws and upheld by the police and the courts. I am only one person, and I cannot be blamed for going along, here where I live, with the way things have always been done." Up to a certain moment, inflicting racial injustice is just as innocent as the suffering of it; but after that certain moment, it is not. My own moral life has been a hesitant and gradual approach toward a certain objectivity about my own circumstances and personality. The most vital kind of ethical event in a person's life may be the lucid understanding that he has done, or has been doing, or is doing something that, seen objectively, is very wrong. For the duration of that understanding, if it is true, he has attained ethical objectivity about himself. From the moment it happens to him, in my opinion, a man is wholly liable for everything he does or does not do in response to improve the ethics of his personality and circumstances. As long as the owner of a ladies' clothes store thinks that, when he sends his profits to the bank in the armored car that has paused outside his store entrance, he is only doing what is right and natural, he is as innocent as a Southern white man who has never realized that he himself is acting out the life of a petty tyrant, and therefore is one. But once the proprietor realizes that the armored car protects him, not only from professional thieves, but also from the poor who need his profits much more than he does, and will starve, or get rickets, or drop out of school, or die of tuberculosis, or commit suicide, without his help, from that moment on he must answer for the pain and the death of the poor, just as, once such a Southern white man has seen the system of which he is a part for what it is, from that moment on, no matter the law, the customs, and his friends, if he is honest he must know that he is a wrong-doing man. It does not defend, that one's conscience fiercely extinguishes these occasional flushing-hot reproaches of one's self; for to the extent that a person lets himself forget the wrong he is doing, to that extent his morality is weak. For some time I have believed that inner humiliation is an event to be grateful for. With it, a man can pry his own habits loose from the rotten practices to which they have, either thoughtlessly or guiltily, adhered. Without it, and without also the will to grab and hold it still as it thrashes to submerge itself again in the brain's electrical quicksands of forgetfulness, he loses his struggle for ethical objectivity about himself, he turns from his portion of man's potentiality to be better ethically than his situation requires.

I

I've been an integrationist (if you want a label) as long as I have had social ideas, but in Texas in the forties and fifties I was not called on to practice my ideas much, you understand. Growing up in San Antonio, I had no awareness of Negroes. They were not in the schools; I must have seen them in the backs of buses, but I don't remember thinking whether it was wrong; I just accepted my advantage. At the University of Texas in 1947, as part of an attempt to find moralities to replace my failing religious ones, I repudiated segregation verbally as a matter of course. The first Negro I remember as an identity was Heman Marion Sweatt, the "test case" who was admitted to the University of Texas law school the year I edited the student paper there. I was trying out law school for a few days, and sat beside him in a law class. In walked a *Life* photographer I knew (I wonder now whether I had hoped he might), and Sweatt and I posed for him in front of the University Tower. I was pleased when the picture came out—I had such a shallow idea of what it was all about, I thought my public gestures (school paper editorials; speeches at student rallies; that picture) cleared me, you know; I thought I was great. But then I thought I was great any way I went, those days.

I know that I hoped Negro girls would come to me and sleep with me. In admiration; in gratitude. I denied the hope, it was too loathsome: to fight the good fight and then to wish to be rewarded with grateful favors for fighting it—how sickening. Still, it would be nice. . . . Eventually I conquered the fantasy, or rather it just went down deep, out of sight; I guess everyone has repressed daydreams that appear without warning: unwanted truths about the very deep motives. When later I was confronted with a person-to-person situation, at least I did not feel any entitlement to the other person; I was able to believe in and respect the reality of the other, without any flagging of this. But I became aware then of how far from adequate it is to one's responsibilities to human freedom to be correct in one's public opinions and public activities. I became aware that I had adapted myself to a racist society in many more ways than I could then admit to anyone. Putting professions of equality to the tests of private life pitilessly illuminated for me the accommodations and compromises by which I had been at the same time apparently seeking to reform, yet continuing to adapt personally to and benefit from, the social stratifications based on color. There, in fact, was my lack of real Negro friends. There, in fact, was the low-paid colored maid. There, in fact, was my inner cringing when I was first put to the test of eating at an integrated restaurant.

In subtle ways I began to punish myself for these things. I felt, and did not try to resist feeling, abasements with Negroes that would not occur in me with whites. I was going through that phase when a white understands that he personally has been wronging Negroes, that most people of his color have been, also, and that somehow he has to make corrections in his attitudes. I understood that if I made Negroes aware of these feelings of abasement, they would think them funny, or be affronted, and rightly on either score; I cannot say whether I kept them concealed or not, but I tried. I was not ashamed of them; although I did not will them and did not act on them, they were somehow meet, and they were only feelings.

And yet: "only feelings"! A person trying to break out of the racist forms ought to expect to feel confused. Because of many things that happened in me, I suspect that some confusion is almost certain to occur. One day I got on a crowded airplane and looked for a seat. It was a jackleg Texas airline, with single seats on one side of the aisle and double seats on the other. Now, I prefer to sit alone; I always have. But I came right up beside a Negro man sitting by the window on the double-seat side. I stood an instant, feeling alarmed. Then I remember deciding clearly, as I looked up toward the front, "I shouldn't sit beside him just because he's a Negro; I prefer to sit alone." Just at that moment, from up ahead of us the stewardess, damn her, indicated that there was a seat beside where she was standing. It was on the double-seat side, too. I said no, I preferred sitting on the single-seat side: was that seat at the back of the single-seat side taken? No, that was hers. I sat down beside the Negro, who turned out to be the president of a Negro college in Austin, my home town, and an intelligent man. Thinking about it later, I realized that I had done the logically right thing, but that the turmoil in my feelings meant that I was having to resist a tendency in me to conform, in this case, to the racist customs. It is just a confusion we—whether we are white or black—have to work our ways through. We have similar confusions, as a commonplace thing, when we are first talking to women we would like to make love to, or persons we are aware think they are better than we are, or very poor people whose humbleness embarrasses us. It is just something to be expected. Yet it is a part of my weakness that I felt emotional alarm that day in the aisle of that Texas plane standing at the vacant chair beside the Negro man. And it is part of the cruelty of the situation that, had there been an open seat on the single-seat side, and had I taken it, I would probably have hurt him—I would at least have left open in his mind the possibility that I did not want to sit beside "a Negro," to wit: him—and in this circumstance abides a case against acting ordinarily without concern for color when doing so results in a hurt. But I believe one should do the ordinary thing, even if at first it takes an unnatural effort to do it, because one man can believe that another man respects him only if he is honest with him.

I have less cause for *mea culpas* on this subject than most white men in Texas in this respect: from the first on the *Texas Observer,* the reformist journal I work on, I have sought to hold white liberals and their Texas organizations accountable for compromises they made with racism. I editorialized for integration, demonstrations, repeal of the miscegenation laws—the whole bit. It is easy to be upright in print, with words, but eventually you notice that not much changes. I would say to Northern, Eastern, and Western white liberals that until I had personally fronted up to the Southern reality in my bailiwick, East Texas, my racial liberalism was as farcically theoretical as Flores Magon, the Mexican anarchist, crying out from California in his paper *La Regeneracion,* "Mexicans, to war!" and then failing to fight in his own revolution.

My first experience with the racism of whites in East Texas was the Mayflower murder case of 1955. Mayflower is a rural all-Negro community near Longview. In the context of a school bond election with racial undertones, two whites, nineteen and twenty, tanked up on beer one night and drove up and down the main stem of Mayflower, shooting into mailboxes, a school bus, the school itself, and homes, and narrowly missing a Negro woman as she was kneeling by her bed saying her prayers. On the open highway they shot into a café where some Negro teen-agers were dancing, and a sixteen-year-old boy fell dying, and two little Negro girls, aged thirteen and fifteen, were hit, both in the arm. There had been similar shootings there before this, and nothing had been done—except some Negroes had been fined.

Acting on a tip from a subscriber (for the dailies gave no true idea of what had happened), I went out there to investigate. (I say "out there," because it is several hundred miles from Austin, and very much different; Austin is a bland university town.) As I drove up and down the main stem interviewing residents of Mayflower, state highway police and local cops together accosted me, rifled my car compartment, and inspected my credentials. They kept me waiting while they radioed Austin to check me out; when they got their answer, they decided not to arrest me. What if I had come down from New York? Even so, their hostility was implacable. I think about that scene occasionally: it did not happen in the free country most of us live in.

Although some weeks had passed since the murder, the driver of a Negroes' school bus still could dig a slug out of the side of the bus for me, and spent shells from the night of the shooting still lay about on the ground by the road. I took one of these shells into my pocket. In my interviewing, I got a feeling from Negroes and a few whites that a certain white youth was a prime suspect, but I found no evidence. One hot afternoon I went to the town of Tatum, near Mayflower, where he lived, and affecting a casualness that covered my fright, I went onto his porch and knocked. He came to the door, a relaxed, disingenuous fellow. Now on a hunch you can't just up and ask a man, "Are you a murderer?" I asked him (my voice came out deeper that it usually is) if he knew anything about the killing, and he said he did not; I thanked him and went on off. Before I left the area, I asked one of the sheriff's men if all the suspects had been interviewed, and he said yes. I told him I had gathered the Tatum youth was one of them: had they interviewed him? No. I went back to Austin and wrote my story.

The case agitated some people in Washington; postal authorities and the F.B.I. sent in investigators. I got a request from the highway patrol for the bullet I'd picked up, but it had been thrown away. Eventually the Tatum youth and a pal of his were indicted. At the same time, the grand jury subpoenaed me, and the district attorney accused me of suppressing evidence—that shell I hadn't come up with—and created the impression I might be indicted.

I went out a day early and revisited the school bus driver, who gladly gave me another of the wanton shells. In the grand jury room I did not fail to remark that more of them were lying around if the authorities wanted them, and that I had given them the name of the Tatum youth months before they indicted him, which was hardly suppressing evidence. Yet once again I felt the hostility; once again I felt that I was in enemy country, though I am a Texan and this is my place.

The Tatum youth was tried and given five years, suspended—he went free—and the second youth was never tried. The boy lay dead in his grave. Now comes into my mind the day I had gone to visit the boy's grandmother and guardian, the daughter of two former slaves who lived, worked, and died in the same East Texas area she'd known all her life. I wound in my car down a red-dirt road, shouldered each side by high, hot pines, and found her in a big unpainted shack in a clearing. A blue sign on the living room wall said, "God Bless Our Home and the People Therein." She was an old heavy woman, she lumbered from a life of labor and heat. She cried softly as she rocked on the front porch and talked about the boy. "I can't get myself reconciled. Just the one child she had. I thought a lot of him, I was partial to him.

"He dead. I wouldn't let them bury him with a bullet in his head even if it cost a hundred dollars to take it out. Lawda mercy, I don't think I'll ever get over it.

"We ain't got no sayso about nothin'. I ain't gonna say nothin' about nothin' 'cause I know I got to go to bed and go to sleep, an' I ain't gonna talk."

There comes into my mind, too, out of chronology, what I heard that a white liberal friend of mine in East Texas said about this later: "Here I was trying to sell subscriptions to the *Observer* out there in East Texas, and he sends out an issue with a dead nigger all over the front page!" When I heard this I laughed, too, and immediately began reflecting on the fact that I had.

An extraordinary thing happened during one of the race trials I covered in East Texas. Negroes told me, in pauses in the trial while I was standing toward the back of the courtroom in an aisle and in the courthouse lobby (and one even had me meet him outside on the courthouse steps), that the police around Marshall had been beating up Negroes on the back roads. The young man I met outside told me that his aunt had been beaten with a billy stick by a deputy he named. I made notes on what they told me, and back in Austin placed the subject on my long list of "stories to do," and filed the notes. Although I had fear, I did not doubt that I would go back and do this story; yet years passed, and I did not. I cannot find the notes now, and Negroes in Marshall tell me that beatings are not occurring.

I will say in my defense that I have not got anywhere near all those stories done, and that there were always tiring pressures getting the *Observer* out and coping with the controversiality and a not infrequent melancholy, a sense of futility in much of the work. I will say in my defense that I did not go back out there up and down those back roads and interview Negroes and then the officers charged mainly because I just did not get around to it. Granting me, if you will, this explanation, you will not have granted me much; for I had the memory of being stopped in Mayflower in me; and not having got around to coming to the defense of fellow Texans beaten on back roads for whatever reason is a terrible personal and moral failure.

There are many such failures in my life. For instance, I am told that youths in a certain corrective institution are beaten regularly and unjustly. I am told that three Negro men condemned to die in a murder-sodomy case are not guilty—by the mother of one, I am so told—and having gone some way into the case, have become discouraged that innocence could be proved, and one, or two, of the men are gone, and the third will be gone. I am told that there is much cruelty and prosecution-mania in certain jurisdictions of my state.

The Marshall beatings are but one of the many things I have not done anything about. But how could I ask those Negroes who had the courage to speak to me in the courthouse seven or eight years ago to forgive me for not getting around to them?—"You should have stopped what you were doing and come. Did you not go to a three-hour movie? And the night before—were you not reading in the history of the Great Plains? Do not your daily hours pass in a fairly quiet way? Yet we needed *help.*" I have no answer, except the resolve to do what I can, and not to despair, of myself or for those who are now abandoned by us all. Three months ago, returning from a trip to report on poverty in the Rio Grande Valley, by the Mexican border (but I had paused a day in Corpus Christi on the way down, and taken my ease), returning, I say, from that trip, and quite down from what I had seen and heard, I came upon what I thought was at last a minimum statement, from which I could salvage some hope for a cheerier daily feeling. "After," I wrote in my journal, by the side of the road—"After I have done everything I can, it would be stupid to refuse to be happy." That was a bracing thought!—until its flaw presented itself, that I can never do everything I can, and that even if I could, I do not.

I wonder if moral failure is not the given condition of man, against which he struggles, knowing that the only way he can answer this certain failure is by struggling against it, even though it is certain. The only comforting qualification I have been able to think of for Camus' principle, that we are responsible not only for what we do, but for what we do not do, is that no one of us can possibly be held responsible for everything, that we are not gods; yet the question, have you done everything for those in need that you can do?, is a terrible question for any person to put to himself. I can think of just one person in my experience who might well be able to answer Yes in total good faith, and he is regarded, by some of those he helps as well as by some of those who help him, as a fool.

Even doing as much of all we can do as we do, still we are trapped by some circumstances. When the white-conservative establishment was trying to illegalize the NAACP in Texas, a case came to trial in a Tyler court before a judge (white, of course—the thoroughgoingness of the system of oppression is so assumed, we forget how unjust it is, for example, that there are no Negro judges in the South) named Otis Dunagan. A fellow reporter for *Time* Magazine and I interviewed him in his chambers after he had ordered the NAACP thrown out of Texas. He began, in our interview with him, speaking of "Negroes." Gradually, as the simple fact that we comprehended each other's questions and answers relaxed him, he began to speak of "the Nigrahs." As we left—to assure us, in one clincher, that he really wasn't a bad fellow—he told us, "I ain't got nothin' against the nigger people!" Thus does a liberal's whiteness involve him complicitously in Southern prejudice: for as a reporter, I was enjoined not to answer the judge back, and as a man, I might have thought it too presumptuous. (These days I just make it a point to say "Negro" back to nigger-sayers.)

Along about 1958 I exchanged lessons in inverse racism with Franklin Williams, then a Negro NAACP leader in California. We spoke on a panel on race at the University of Colorado. I expressed some hope because of the emergence of some liberals in the South. I was startled when, in a friendly way, Williams called to my notice the little oversight that all the Southern liberals I had named had been whites! But he went too far then, for his part, saying, as I took his meaning, that the Negroes are the real liberals in the South—the whites are too compromised to be vaild crusaders. On the defensive, I amiably accused him of upside-down racism; he came back and accused *me* of racism. I think we were both right. Later there, we joined forces in debate against the spokesman of the Georgia Citizens' Council and enjoyed ourselves immensely, the throng of students in the amphitheater of a meeting room roaring bloodthirstily as we tore the Georgian limb from limb.

More recently I took an interest in the case of an East Texas Negro youth who had been convicted, when he was eighteen, of raping a forty-seven-year-old white woman out there, and had been sentenced to be electrocuted by an East Texas jury. In his cell in Death Row in Huntsville, the Negro told me the woman had seduced him, telling him that if he did not take her, she would holler rape. He knew what this meant, and took her. And that in a later encounter, perhaps because she feared they had been seen, she did holler rape, and a confession had been beaten out of him. In the trial, his lawyers (to whom, I confirmed, he had told this same story) advised him not to take the stand so as not to antagonize the whites by calling her a liar, and he did not. The confession was read, there was other damaging testimony, she gave her testimony that she had been raped, and that was that. I drove on north into East Texas and interviewed people who had had to do with the trial. A prosecuting attorney and one of the other lawyers asked me what other inquiries I planned, and I said I was going out to see the woman, and they each told me, in warning, deliberate ways, to be careful.

I was frightened about going out there. The woman had brothers. I was messin' with Southern womanhood, and I knew it. But of course, I felt silly, too: this was a melodrama.

I drove out to the community where the woman lived and eased slowly past the houses alongside the road until I came to hers. I was simply going to ask her about the case, whether she believed the young man should be executed, whether she had anything to add to her testimony. With pounding heart I walked onto the porch and knocked. Clothes were hanging on the line, and a car was in the driveway, but no one answered. I knocked again. I looked inside the window on the porch; it seemed bare inside the room. I called twice, loud for my conscience, and knocked again. No one answered. I went on back to Austin.

I knew I would have to go back out there to ask her these questions, yet I knew also that I might be killed for doing so, and I did not care to die. I began to weigh whether I might not be too valuable to die just now. (After all, there were those Marshall beatings to look into.) It was a long time coming, the realization I finally found, worded and waiting for me in my mind one day as I drove north to Dallas, that "This is a war I believe in." I was in Arlington, again ready to set off to interview her, but it had occurred to me (such a simple idea, I was puzzled I hadn't thought of it) that I could telephone her. I could see no reason not. I did get her on the phone; her distant voice refused to discuss the case. I did not have to go back. Even so, for a little time after my stories on the case came out, I approached callers at the front door with a little caution, and an abashed awareness of my ludicrousness.

I thought the stories, fully quoting the condemned man, made it clear there was doubt that he had had his day in court, but of course no new trial was ordered; there is something inexorable about executions, once they are decided on. He surprised me by complaining bitterly in his cell that I had quoted the mean things others had said about him. I shall never forget his execution. Never, never. He strides in and is in dignified command of himself. He will die manly. He looks at me, I feel that it is a bitter look; it is not a look of recognition, it goes through my head like a javelin. To him, I am part of the system that is killing him. They strap him in, gag him, drop a hood over his head, and kill him: The sound of breath sucked through teeth, he is lifted against the straps, his fists clench, his clothes balloon from his limbs; there is a distant sparking sound, his body is tensed against the straps for a very long time, a scene of terror. A heavy, sweetish, pungent smell that seems to touch me.

When I got home early in the dark morning after driving all night from the prison, there was a letter for me he had written two days before he died. I read it heavy with the memory of his death. About my stories he had written, ". . . the writer was real nice only if you could separate the Lies from the truth, some peoples may think my story is all a Lie, but it's not, I am right. . . . I can't understand those peoples lie to get a man killed. . . . It will come out one day and I hope it is not too late, I can't explain things like I want to in this short note, but if you can come down here for a short time that will be just fine. . . . P.S. May God Bless and Keep us all in my prayers. Hope to hear from you soon."

Can you understand how personal his careful, curlicued printing was to me? It was a letter from the dead; a letter from doubt; a letter from despair; a letter from this man; a letter from my own faulted conscience. It was a letter from everything that is human crying out against everything that is set and systematized. I could not think of anything more I could have done, than what I did do: no, perhaps I should have plowed up the whole county for new evidence. I might have found it; yes, if I had had the courage, I might have. In capital punishment, anything less than everything leaves anyone touched with the case wholly guilty of the death. I was glad when the sun came up outside my bedroom window, and I somehow had to start all over again.

Finally, all these things together caused me to need, caused my regard for my integrity to require, an act of some kind that was meaningful and that was very difficult for me to go through with. Austin's swimming pools had not been integrated. For years Barton Springs, the most beautiful natural springs public pool I have ever seen, had been the domain of whites only. I checked with my family, they were agreeable, and telephoned some Negro friends, two Negro secretaries agreed to come; and together one day (after some delay, some on my part, and some on the Negroes') we all went swimming at Barton's. The authorities stopped us at poolside and told us they'd call the police if we went in. I told them to go ahead, and call the mayor while they were at it; he was a Democrat I knew, who'd never been heard from much on race. I remember that a white lady made it a point to swim across the pool to talk to us. We swam about an hour and a half and went on to our respective homes—in the different parts of town, you know. Another two years passed before Negroes really began using the pool. Now they do, a little.

II

It is a comment on the twists the racial situation has taken that one day, after some prolonged readings in James Baldwin, I was visited, while driving down a one-way street, with the angry thought, "It's not my fault I was born white! I was born to my place and color as helplessly as you were, Baldwin, and have come but slowly toward an objective seeing of my circumstances. That's the way it is with each of us."

On the fourth of July, 1963, I spent the sunny afternoon at Barton Springs with my family. There were Latin-American and Anglo children, and a few Negroes; the young were rolling varicolored balls down hills and riding the child-size trains through the pecan groves by the creek, and running and dreaming as children do. I sat watching a group of white children playing, innocents, beautiful and lively; and the thought came upon me with great force, "You, Baldwin, you, Negroes, you may not blame these children for being whites, you may not feel hostility toward them, counting their color against them."

It is surprising that this thought was surprising. It is well established that parents' sins may not be visited on their children. Closely considered, I do not think Baldwin would do it. Yet the racial wrongs of American life have so sickened our consciences, some of us who are white have found ourselves gradually accepting the idea of our "racial guilt." We may not, for exactly as the belief in the individuality of the human occurrence is the basis of our abhorrence of the oppression of any person because of color, so also is it the basis of every individual's innocence of all the wrong he has not personally done. No group, ethically, exists at all; guilt or innocence cannot physically occur, cannot be located, anywhere but in the person, the self and the doings and the failures to do, of a one.

This is more burdensome than it is absolving, for it means that a person may never plead absolution from personal guilt on grounds that, realizing he was doing a wrong, he was going along with a group—the Stalinists, the Nazis, Hiroshima atom bombers, Southern whites, Black Muslims. But neither may a man be accused of guilt, save on evidence that applies separately and personally to him. In what way is whites' despising Negroes different from blacks' despising whites? If I will not consent that a white class a Negro by color, I will not either permit a Negro to class me by my color; or my son, by his. Here are my confessions. I am guilty to an extent, and purged to an extent, not because I am white; I am, because I am I.

I think of three white women in East Texas.

One told me that she resents my feeling the way I do about her section because I do not have a right to such feelings. She herself has left her little home town there, to work in the city; but listen to her:

"None of the boys I thought would amount to anything went

back. The only girls who are still there are the ones who married in high school and can't leave. That's the truth!—they all leave.

"I can't talk calmly about it. When I go home, it's the same: I'm going to be grown up about it, and I break down and cry. When you've gone off to school—you don't go back.

"It's not the lack of activity. When I was there I went to games in Dallas, and you drive to other towns for a movie—there's a lot of activity. Everybody has a car."

Why do they leave? She would not say. "You're not saying why out of loyalty," I told her. "That's right," she said. "When I read your pieces on East Texas, I feel, 'He can't feel that way. He doesn't live there—he doesn't know.'

"Take my father. He's a fine, wonderful man, but he thinks like all the rest of them do on—the Negro. We've supported a Negro family since I can remember. We buy their false teeth, pay their bills—everything. We even went without Christmas presents one year to buy them a house. And we didn't even have a house. But they'd got in some trouble, signed some wrong papers to somebody taking advantage of them.

"The mother comes in to wash the dishes. But they stay in their place—period, you can't discuss it, that's all. And they come in to wash the dishes on Sunday. They stay in their place."

I told her that when I go into East Texas, I feel that I'm going where there's something rotten, and that I'm going where it's very beautiful.

"I know. But you can't feel that way. I don't know, I haven't analyzed how I feel. You either go off to college and don't come back, or you go back and are torn up for the rest of your life. I couldn't change a thing. Things may change, but I can't change them. About all I can do is endorse every crook and reactionary who runs and maybe Dad'll vote for him."

I don't know exactly what she meant by that last; but I think I have since understood her resentment of me. I was traveling in East Texas on a bus and watched things from that high vantage point, without having to drive distracting me. What I saw was the apparent solidity of the culture. The way old men sit on the railings by the plate glass window of the general merchandise store, and walk slowly across the street, in the sun, in their khakis and suspenders, Saturday morning. The mass of the fields. The strawberry shed along the highway: the innumerable little accepted arrangements for prevailing, for profiting, or for sustaining oneself. The cultural envelope. The very fixedness of the streets, lawns, homes—the frightening implications of a bright green tricycle in a white man's yard. The fact that everyone who is an accepting beneficiary of the social apparatus *owes* it; is *of* it; as in a family. Thus, a white man, about thirty-five, driving along Saturday morning in a new but musty-green Bel-Air, his big-eyed boy looking over the top of the almost closed window. The black-and-sparkle-uniformed white policeman with the gun high in his holster, the brown-worked ivory handle switching a little as he walks past the Safeway.

I think also of a young matron in a modern East Texas city. Prominent socially, she is a Southern girl, the kind you can be candid with, but with the Southern reserve. She says very seriously, "I am a just woman. What I mean is, if I owned those houses, they wouldn't leak, and they'd have plumbing, and. . . ." Later she drove me through the rich sections; then to the slum quarters where her maid lives. "That house back there. You see it? There's not even a screen on the door!" Her indignation seemed very genuine. She blamed the landlord; she did not seem to connect her maid's plight with what she was paying her, and I felt that it would be simply too rude to tell her. She had let the thought sink out of sight, if she had ever had it. I told her instead that I would not let her get away with saying she is a just woman; that justice is not a condition, but a doing of things continuously.

Then I think of one of the cagiest woman politicians I have ever met: an East Texas Democrat who knows everything that makes her city tick and has keys, or wax impressions of them, to every skeleton closet of any interest at all. She told me on one occasion many things about her town I knew nothing at all about. We did not discuss race, but she let me sense her liberal views, and as I left she said something that caused me to think a good deal after her meaning: "If you want to last in politics in this county," she said, "you walk in tennis shoes and tread with a light step, and you carry a good, sharp knife, and it may be a year or three before you get in close, but when you do you give 'em a good stiff blow. That may sound . . . but it's the way you *do* it."

III

Granted, then, the individualness of guilt and innocence, I nevertheless believe that the future of personal liberty in the South, and therefore to an extent also in the world, rests presently in the hands of Southern white people.

Today we know from our intuition, and also from a great deal of indirect evidence, that many Southern whites must have decided in the privacies of their consciences that the Negroes are morally right in their cause. Realism has impelled most Southern whites to see that the Negroes' movement, backed by more and more whites and by the federal government, has taken on the aspect of something almost irresistible. All over the South, mostly behind the scenes, many whites of good faith have been turning their energies to the tasks of revising their own and their region's traditions.

But, what is going to happen, as to the inner tranquility of Southern towns, when a nearer approach is made to equal opportunities for Negroes, and the hostilities of die-hard whites toward whites who have helped make this approach come into active personal play? We could be in for a serious time. There have been robed, cross-burning Klan revivals in Alabama and Georgia. The *New York Times* reports (ominously without elaboration) that one part of the fierce Danville, Virginia, resistance to any integration is "retaliation against those in responsible positions who waver toward moderation." As Negroes begin to vote in better proportion to their numbers; as, better-educated and better-organized, they begin to compete more effectively with whites for the available jobs; as they begin to be able, economically, to break out of the housing ghettos in the cities—as they become full citizens, in other words—it will be logical for them to enter into political coalitions with moderate and liberal whites, with one of their conditions being public positions of honor for Negroes. This has already happened in Texas in what is called the Democratic Coalition. The populist movement collapsed in the South in the 1890's, as is well known, because Southern whites in that movement would not, or could not, accept the implications of a political liaison with Negro voters. The people W. J. Cash describes as the old Confederate captains, the mill-owners, and the landowners were all too willing to use the poor whites' need to believe in their racial superiority against those very whites' own economic and political interests. That willingness is evident among Southern conservatives again, in the Citizens' Council movement, for example, and in the Klan revival.

Generally speaking, Negroes in the South have proven their courage. It would take a bitter man, indeed, to deny the courage of the children who have walked to school through mobs, and of the college youths who have sat in at lunch counters and beaches and churches and have been spat upon and insulted and arrested. These are brave folk. It does not detract from their bravery to observe that it proceeds from the desperateness of their condition. However (and of course I apply this to myself), I think that many Southern whites of moderate and liberal bent on race are also in a desperate condition: their consciences are. Inheritors of a segregated social and economic system evolved from the time of slavery, they find it now anathematized by national law and world opinion. Re-examining it, they find it wanting. It has been possible for many of them to effect some accommodations without becoming openly identified among the whites with the Negro cause, but that cause is insistent on its full arrival, and presently Southern whites will not be able to do their good works in private, for it is of the essence, it goes to the tender core of racial humiliation, that a man cannot be acknowledged to be a man in private, and denied in public; equality cannot be clandestine. It is my thought that the deepest question abiding now in the racial matter is the courage of Southern whites of moderate or liberal views on race as the moments arrive, local scene by local scene and private conscience by private conscience, that call for it.

I would say, subjectively, that heretofore the three great domestic crises of our national life have been these: our genesis, in revolution and constitutional government; the war that ended slavery; and the New Deal that made floors for poverty. Just when this, our fourth great domestic crisis, really began, no one seems able to say—perhaps with television; or Martin Luther King's bold and pioneering bus boycott in Montgomery in 1955–56; or the first sit-ins in 1960. As the *Times,* I think it was, observed, it is expressive of the authenticity and intensity of the crisis that there was no great precipitating event, and that the unrest has persisted and proceeded from energies within the Negro people, less a march than a moiling, less an explosion than a ceaseless turbulence. That it is a crisis, no one can deny, but for my part I do not feel any sense of resentment or burden. Once again, these are the times that try men's souls, but what is a man for if not to be tried? We are given now our chance to be a part of the historic American pursuit of an elusive dream. As our nation competes abroad against a new form of ancient European totalitarianism, we hasten at home to undo inherited Old World wrongs, so that the idea of personal liberty, of this band of people living together in freedom and plenty, may spread around the world and be known in every clime among people of every kind and color as the idea we preach and the idea we practice; as the American idea. Just as Negroes these last few years have had to decide whether they will risk everything for their beliefs, and just as Negroes have been clubbed down in the streets, kicked before the altars of churches, bitten by dogs, hosed down by police, and jailed by the thousands, so will Southern whites who wish to purge their consciences of discrimination have to decide whether they will risk everything for *their* beliefs, and tell the men they work beside, or practice law with, the bankers they borrow from, the wholesalers they buy from, the customers they sell to, the politicians they vote for, or don't vote for, that Negroes are men and women and children, and have the same rights as us all, that it is not for us whites benignly to give them these rights, but that it *is* for us whites to stop withholding these rights from them. I know I have felt the call of this crisis as it has turned upon me, and I have felt within me, as I have told you, the alarm of it; and I guess men have all over East Texas, and all over the South, and all over the country, for these are the times. These are the times. And John Donne told us, "No man is an island, entirely of itself; every man is a piece of the continent, a part of the main; if a clod be washed away by the sea, Europe is the less, as well as if a promontory were, as well as if a manor of thy friends or of thine own were; any man's death diminishes me, because I am involved in mankind; And therefore never send to know for whom the bell tolls; It tolls for thee."

Francis E. Kearns

OLD MYTHS AND NEW DIALOGUE

FRANCIS E. KEARNS, a New Yorker, is currently an Assistant Professor of English at Georgetown University in Washington, D.C. He holds degrees from New York University, the University of Chicago and the University of North Carolina. He has served as Editor of the Chicago Review *(1954), Case Officer for the U.S. Central Intelligence Agency (1955–56), and an English Teaching Fellow at the University of North Carolina (1954–55; 1956–60). In 1960, he served as Assistant Director of the Georgetown University Writers Conference. His articles have appeared in such publications as* America, Carolina Quarterly, Chicago Review, Commonweal, *and the* Journal of the History of Ideas. *He is currently working on two books: an edition of the letters of Margaret Fuller to Ralph Waldo Emerson (under a grant from the American Philosophical Society), and a study of* Three Transcendentalists *(Margaret Fuller, Bronson Alcott, and Orestes Brownson).*

PERHAPS THE GREATEST PROBLEM standing in the way of a solution to America's race problem is the residue of myth and stereotype which still clouds our thinking on the problem. Even though the 1954 Supreme Court decision on segregation in the schools laid the foundation for the various court appeals, which are breaking down the wall of legal barriers between the races, a court decision can do little to dispel the distorted notions which prevent an honest, personal meeting between Negro and white.

One of the tragic facts about the Supreme Court decision is that it occurred during the 1950's, a period which has been called America's "placid decade." In 1954 Americans were interested in learning do-it-yourself techniques for maintaining the various gadgets and appliances piled up by the post-war shift to production of consumer goods. In national politics it was a time for the platitude and the grin, a time for the eschewal of eggheads. And the abiding influence of Senator McCarthy made it clear to newspaper and magazine editors that timidity was still a prudent course.

Yet the decision reached by the Supreme Court was an epochal one—it represented one of the first serious attempts by the federal government since Reconstruction days to implement the guarantees of the Fourteenth Amendment. The Court was aware of the epochal nature of its decision and recognized the revolutionary changes in regional tradition which compliance would entail. Thus, according to Lenoir Chambers, former editor of *The Virginian Pilot,* the Court took many steps toward easing the problems of local compliance. For example, it invited the participation of attorneys general from states besides those directly involved in *Brown v. Board of Education.* Moreover, contrary to many Southern myths about the highhandedness of Earl Warren and the Supreme Court, the fact that the Court separated its decision in principle from its decision as to compliance by a full year, indicates the careful consideration given by the justices to this problem of compliance.

Despite the responsible attitude displayed by the Supreme Court, the legislative and executive branches of the federal government failed to respond with similar farsightedness. As Walter Lippmann and other observers have pointed out, what was needed in 1954 was a national program, involving step-by-step procedures and carefully-thought-out priorities, for implementing the Court decision. When President Eisenhower and the Congress refused to accept responsibility for working out such a program, the difficult task of enforcing the Court's decision was left almost entirely to litigation initiated by Negro civil-rights organizations. The "cquality" achieved by such litigation has been limited ("tokenism" is a tragically inadequate response to both the decision of the Court and the demands of our time) and has come about in heartbreakingly slow fashion. Thus the 1954 decision was epochal in another sense —it marked the beginning of the Negro's awareness that true equality would not be achieved through the courts. Out of the Negro's frustration with the slow and hodge-podge process of litigation have come the programs of non-violent action by Dr. Martin Luther King and the Congress of Racial Equality, the development of such techniques as the sit-in, and, finally, the massive demonstrations in Birmingham and elsewhere.

The new Negro, the Negro who has been with us since about 1960, has accomplished something that could never have been achieved in the courts—he has dealt a shattering blow to those illusions about Negroes on which the South and the rest of the nation have fed for generations. Whether sitting patiently at a lunch counter in Greensboro or standing firmly against a police dog in Birmingham, the new Negro has demonstrated that he is not content with his lot, that the white Southerner does not have a priority in understanding him, and that he is not incapable of intelligent leadership. Throughout the South one can see the crumbling of those classic myths, stereotypes, and rationalizations which the white man has traditionally used to deceive himself about the gap between his American equalitarian creed and his actual treatment of the Negro.

Yet for several decades the sociologists and psychologists (for example, John Dollard, in *Caste and Class in a Southern Town;* W. J. Cash, in *The Mind of the South;* Gunnar Myrdal, in *An American Dilemma;* Gordon Allport, in *The Nature of Prejudice*) have told us that these illusions are of vital importance to the white Southerner. Not only do they help him avoid seeing the disparity between creed and practice, but, more important, they give him a sense of status. The ability to have respect for one's own position in the social hierarchy, the necessity to have someone lower in the pecking order, is particularly important in the society of the South, a society deficient in those educational and economic opportunities which allow vertical social mobility. In effect, myths and stereotypes about the Negro are important to the white Southerner in that they enable him to define himself.

Even among white Southerners who no longer cling to such illusions as a matter of conviction these myths and stereotypes have an important influence. Despite the glorification of independence and self-reliance in our Southern literature, the "Southern way of life" exacts a high degree of conformity. It must be remembered that the population of the South is still largely small-town or rural, that the local religion is likely to be an evangelical form of Protestantism with great stress on worldly appearance, and that Southern family relationships are usually more formal and tradition-bound than those in other parts of the country. Given this set of circumstances, it is no wonder that the South should produce an "other-directed" mentality. As a result, a problem often encountered by civil-rights workers in the South is not so much that local merchants and political leaders firmly believe in segregation but rather that these leaders are unwilling to assume leadership in changing local prejudices. One could cite for example the reaction of Birmingham department store owners at Martin Luther King's attempt to desegregate lunch counters. Moreover, having been both a student and teacher in the South, I could point to the fact that many of the more enlightened Southern college students find themselves adopting two sets of notions and vocabulary in regard to the race problem—one for the university town and another for the home town and family. Recently a white high school teacher in Birmingham eloquently summed up the dilemma of the enlightened white Southerner for *Life* reporter Bill Wise:

> All this time we've done nothing to prepare these kids for social change. All these years there should have been some effort to prepare them for this. But we've been forbidden to even mention it. They could have been taught about the worldwide aspirations of all peoples for equality, and there should have been social exchange between colored and white children. . . . To me the solution is simple: just treat human beings as human beings. But to many of these people Negroes are not human beings. Please don't use my name with this. I am ashamed to ask you not to. If you do I will lose my job. The fear that prevents people from saying what they want to say is a terrible thing.

Ironically, while Dr. King and other Negro integration leaders have to run to keep pace with a rank and file which is constantly moving forward from under their leadership, potential opinion makers in the white community often maintain a tight-lipped silence out of fear of retaliation by the white man in the street.

But, as I have indicated, Southern illusions about the Negro are rapidly crumbling. And the important fact is that this loss of illusions has come about not through education or through compliance with a national program of desegregation but through the face-to-face confrontation forced by the activist "new Negro." It is the suddenness of this "shock of recognition" that the Negro will no longer consent to be a "nigger" that is so terrifying for the white Southerner. As Joseph Conrad recognized, a large part of civilized restraint lies in the familiar, in the ability to take for granted the predictability of one's neighbor's reactions. But when a man is faced with the unfamiliar and the unpredictable, when he is unable to find an adequate role in his repertory of social poses, then the veneer of social restraint may crack and a man may revert to barbarism and violence. Thus there is both danger and genuine pathos in the inadequacy of Governor Wallace's desperate attempt to answer the recent Birmingham demonstrations by reviving the worn-out myth of the "outside agitator" through an invitation to the House Un-American Activities Committee to investigate Communist influences on the demonstrations.

But the white Southerner is not the only one caught up in this horrifying inability to depend on old preconceptions. Many Negroes are also troubled. It must be remembered that having been required for generations to accept the white man's stereotype of himself, the Negro has also learned to use this stereotype for his own advantage. An indication of the extent to which Negroes have come to rely on the white man's stereotype may be seen in James Baldwin's essay "Equal in Paris." Here Baldwin tells how he had been arrested and sent to a Paris jail after mistakenly being accused of stealing some hotel bed linen. What was so terrifying for Baldwin was his discovery that the French police regarded him not as a Negro but as an American. Suddenly he found himself cast in a strange new role he had never been allowed to play back in New York. Unable to predict the attitude of the French police, and unable to determine what should be his own reaction, Baldwin found the few days spent in a Paris jail among the most miserable in his life.

Thus in today's South both Negroes and whites find themselves faced not only with the problem of desegregating public facilities but also with the more profound problem of developing a new set of roles and attitudes toward each other. Regardless of the rear guard actions taken by Governors Wallace and Barnett and regardless of whether the Negro takes a gradualist or extremist course, desegregation is coming and it is coming fairly soon. Whether it comes about with some harmony will depend largely on whether the two races are able to attain a view of each other which is more honest and truthful. But to be honest in one's view of another is not easy, for it involves the development of personal communication with the other. And, more than that, it involves the risk of being honest with one's own self. In the end, we are faced with a simple, even platitudinous, truth frequently underlined by James Baldwin: the final solution to the race problem, a solution which goes beyond mere desegregation, depends on the development of man's capacity to love.

In dealing so far with myths and stereotypes, I have been concerned primarily with the Southern variety of such illusions. I do not mean to imply by such an approach that the South is the only area of the country blinded by distorted notions of race. Indeed, the fact that the North can practice race discrimination and at the same time congratulate itself for its tolerance is indicative of the presence in the Northern mentality of illusory notions perhaps even more grotesque than those held in the South.

There are many racial stereotypes and myths in the North, but the particular type of myth I wish to deal with here is one held by many Northern whites—and Southerners too, for that matter—who regard themselves as liberals. An examination of the racial stereotypes maintained by such whites is of particular importance today, since many Negro spokesmen, ranging in responsibility from James Baldwin to Adam Clayton Powell, have recently expressed an increasing skepticism about the help offered by white liberals in the struggle toward racial justice.

The specific white liberal illusion about the Negro I want to examine is one that Baldwin alluded to in his recent book *The Fire*

Next Time.[1] Here Baldwin expressed his disgust with the failure of white liberals to relate their doctrines to their perceptions and actions. And he charged that white liberals could "deal with the Negro as a symbol or a victim but had no sense of him as a man." Ironically enough, this very need to deal with the Negro as a symbol was vividly illustrated in the violent reaction by many liberals to a recent *Commentary* article by Norman Podhoretz published at the moment that *The Fire Next Time* was coming from the press.

In the February, 1963, issue of *Commentary,* Podhoretz' essay, "My Negro Problem—and Ours,"[2] told how the author had developed a thoroughly confused attitude toward Negroes while growing up in a Brooklyn Jewish ghetto which bordered on a Negro neighborhood. Although Podhoretz believed that Negroes were victimized and persecuted—he had read this in newspapers and an infallible older sister had told him so—in his actual neighborhood experience "it was the Negroes who were doing the only persecuting I knew about—and doing it, moreover, to *me.*" Thus he was "repeatedly beaten up, robbed, and in general hated, terrorized, and humiliated" by Negroes. As a result of these experiences Podhoretz came to hate Negroes as much as they hated him. Today, as an adult liberal, he has not been completely able to overcome his feelings of fear, envy, and hatred toward the Negro, even though he has learned to appreciate the injustices suffered by Negroes, and even though he now feels self-contempt for his inability to suppress such emotions.

Trying as an adult to discover the reasons for such racial hatred in the neighborhood of his youth, Podhoretz cannot fully accept the explanations of either James Baldwin (the Negro hates the white man because he knows him to be his jailer) or of the psychologists (the white hates the Negro in compensation for guilt feelings he suffers over the way he has exploited the Negro):

> How could the Negroes in my neighborhood have regarded the whites across the street and around the corner as jailers? On the whole, the whites were not so poor as the Negroes, but they were quite poor

[1] New York, Dial, 1963.
[2] See pp. 210–225.

enough, and the years were years of Depression. As for white hatred of the Negro, how could guilt have had anything to do with it? What share had these Italian and Jewish immigrants in the enslavement of the Negro?

Podhoretz sees a fundamental sickness at the heart of the feelings of American white and Negro for each other, and the root cause of this sickness lies deeper than either Baldwin or the psychologists suspect. What the nature of that cause is Podhoretz does not pretend to understand. But he feels that an ultimate understanding and solution will come about only when both white and Negro are willing to engage in a candid examination of the tangle of emotion and conviction underlying their own attitudes toward the race problem. Thus, in telling the story of his own twisted feelings about Negroes and of how such feelings conflict with the moral convictions he has since developed, Podhoretz is doing something more than writing a liberal's true confession. He wants "to assert that such feelings must be acknowledged as honestly as possible so that they can be controlled and ultimately disregarded in favor of the convictions."

The reaction to Podhoretz manifested in the correspondence columns of the April and May issues of *Commentary* represents an interesting cross section of liberal opinion. Many readers congratulated him for his honesty and courage. John Fisher, editor of *Harper's,* hailed both "My Negro Problem" and *The Fire Next Time* as important steps toward the development of a new humane dialogue between Negro and white. Fisher hoped that the new willingness to speak and write candidly about one's deepest feelings on race relations would contribute to "a much wider realization that the country's racial problem involves emotional issues which cannot be solved by legislation, lawsuits, or police action; that the fault is not all on one side; and that the first step toward resolving such issues is to bring them into the light of honest discussion." On the other hand, Podhoretz was vehemently denounced by many readers as a "bigot" or "racist." This negative reaction could be seen outside the correspondence columns of *Commentary* too. Thus an article in *Congress Bi-Weekly,* published by the American Jewish

Congress, termed Podhoretz' essay a "witch's brew of fear turned to hatred, characteristic of those who require scapegoats in life." And Chuck Stone, editor of the Washington *Afro-American,* labeled the piece "about as viciously anti-colored a polemic as I've ever read."

The reason for the vehemence of this attack on Podhoretz is that he has questioned one of the most recurrent liberal myths of our time—the myth that every Negro is a noble savage or a natural man who functions as a symbolic sacrificial victim suffering for all the sins of a bourgeois and generally corrupt white society. This myth is not widely held by those white liberals who have taken an active part in programs of racial justice and thus entered into a personal relationship with the Negro. But it is an important myth for those persons of liberal conviction on racial matters who have never quite allowed their conviction to result in sacrifice or risk. The myth of the Negro as noble savage seems to function in two ways for such liberals. On the one hand, it works as an excuse for those who fail to act out of lethargy. After all, who can get excited over whether a noble savage enjoys equal employment opportunities? On the other hand, the myth provides a flavorful emotional relish to the not inconsiderable number of liberals who enjoy the exquisite pleasure of working themselves into a frenzy of self-guilt over the race problem. One can take an increasingly dramatic view of one's assumed guilt in proportion to the innocence and nobility ascribed to the person one has supposedly sinned against.

Podhoretz seems to have realized that an honest approach to the race problem would offend such liberals, for at one point in "My Negro Problem—And Ours" he points out that help toward a solution to the race problem will not come from "the writers and intellectuals and artists who romanticize Negroes and pander to them, assuming a guilt that is not properly theirs . . . the white liberals who permit Negroes to blackmail them into adopting a double standard of moral judgment, and who lend themselves—again assuming the responsibility for crimes they never committed—to cunning and contemptuous exploitation by Negroes they employ or try to befriend."

The myth of the Negro as noble savage is a long-standing one in

America and has been accepted by some of our first-rate writers. In *Huckleberry Finn,* Mark Twain demonstrates the difficulty faced by a post-Civil War Southerner in straightening out his Negro stereotypes. At the beginning of the book Nigger Jim is presented as the typical stage darkie of vaudeville with the usual characteristics, including laziness, boastfulness, servility, and superstition. However, once Huck and Jim are united on the raft and have temporarily escaped the corrupting influences of adult society, Jim emerges as one of the most noble of natural men in American literature. Huck comes to rely on Jim's nature lore and good judgment and thus the escaped slave becomes a type of spiritual father to the run-away white boy. Nevertheless, when, toward the end of the novel, Jim is recaptured and held prisoner by the Reverend Silas Phelps, he reverts to the role of minstrel darkie he played at the book's opening ("Ya'sah, Mars Tom"). Critic Leo Marx has pointed out that the last fifth of the novel represents Twain's compromise with the genteel tradition and respectability. Reverend Phelps, who might have stepped directly from a Norman Rockwell *Saturday Evening Post* cover, stands for exactly the hypocritical social and religious values that Huck had earlier been fleeing. But now Twain presents these values as thoroughly wholesome. Phelps is a charitable and conscientious Christian, but neither he nor Twain seems to think that Christian principle is violated in holding Jim prisoner. Marx compares Reverend Phelps' moral insensitivity to that of the middle-class German families who lived near Buchenwald or Dachau and yet managed throughout the war to remain undisturbed by the activities at such camps. One might up-date Marx's analogy and make an interesting comparison between Reverend Phelps and the eight ranking white religious leaders of Alabama (including C. C. J. Carpenter, Bishop of the Protestant Episcopal diocese of Alabama; Joseph A. Durick, Auxiliary Bishop of the Roman Catholic diocese of Mobile-Birmingham; and Rabbi Milton L. Grafman, of Temple Emanu-el) who recently issued a statement that termed Negro demonstrations in Birmingham "unwise and untimely" and commended the white community, the local dailies, and "law enforcement officers, in particular, on the calm manner in which these demonstrations have been handled."

A more modern Southern writer, William Faulkner, manifests a similar difficulty in balancing stereotypes. In his frequently anthologized story, "The Bear," Faulkner presents Sam Fathers, half-Negro, half-Indian, as a thoroughly noble aristocrat of the woods. Like Twain's Jim, Sam Fathers possesses a great stock of nature lore, and he brings about an initiation into the formal code of the hunt for Ike McCaslin, a white boy from whose point of view the story is told. As his last name indicates, Sam too serves as a spiritual father to a white boy who rejects the ways of his elders. Nevertheless, though Faulkner resents the injustice that the completely noble Sam suffers in Mississippi, he warns us in the same story that the attempts of outsiders to remedy that injustice must be rejected. Thus, in clinging to his mythical view that the sin of segregation is somehow a part of the mystique of the South and must be expiated—"but not now"—by Southerners, Faulkner invokes another old myth—the myth of the "outside agitator." For Faulkner to have considered the view of other Southerners, such as Ralph McGill of the *Atlanta Constitution,* that the only progress toward civil rights in the South has been that brought about by the "outside" pressure of the Federal Government, would have been to run the risk of losing his romantic concepts not only of the Negro but also of himself. Moreover, such a realistic view would involve the risk of losing what Hawthorne regarded as one of the primary assets of the writer of romance (and romance is the literature of myth): a country where there is "a picturesque and gloomy wrong."

The foremost contemporary literary exponents of the Negro-as-natural-man myth are the beat writers, among whom, according to Podhoretz, in a *Partisan Review* essay entitled "The Know-Nothing Bohemians," "there is positive adulation for the 'happy, true-hearted, ecstatic Negroes of America.'" It is this beat version of the racial myth that Kenneth Rexroth has termed "crow-jimism." Thus in Kerouac we find the following passage:

At lilac evening I walked with every muscle aching among the lights of 27th and Welton in the Denver colored section, wishing I were a Negro, feeling that the best the white world had offered was not enough ecstasy for me, not enough life, joy, kicks, darkness, music, not enough night.[3]

To point out the continuance in American literature of the myth that the Negro is more elemental and noble than the white man is not to deny the existence of another important view, or non-view, of the Negro in our literature. There is the tradition of the Negro as the man who isn't there, or the "invisible man." James Baldwin frequently refers to the fact that white men refuse to look at Negroes. They regard Negroes as faceless and as not entirely human, and it is this refusal to regard the Negro as someone that, according to Baldwin, makes all Negroes hate white men. In Fitzgerald's *Great Gatsby* there is a brief but revealing scene that could serve to illustrate Baldwin's point. Nick Carroway, the narrator, and Gatsby, the embodiment of the American Dream, are driving on the Queensboro Bridge. Nick is an American intellectual—he is a Yale man and he studies the stock market—and earlier in the novel he has scoffed at the irrationality of a racist tract entitled *The Rise of the Colored Empires;* but at this point he tells us:

As we crossed Blackwell's Island a limousine passed us, driven by a white chauffeur, in which sat three modish negroes, two bucks and a girl. I laughed aloud as the yolks of their eyeballs rolled toward us in haughty rivalry.[4]

The two cars speed on to their separate destinies in the city, Nick and the Negroes never having known or touched each other. Again, in *Tender Is the Night,* Fitzgerald's spokesman, this time Dick Diver, has a fleeting glimpse of the colored man when a shabby American Negro comes to his Paris hotel room for a handout. This Negro is later murdered by another mysterious Negro and his body is found dumped in the suite of Rosemary, an American movie star whom Dick loves. Dick saves both Rosemary and the hotel from embarrassment by having the Negro's body quietly removed by Paris police. We learn nothing of the private tragedy of the

3 *The Subterraneans* (New York, Grove, 1958).
4 New York, Scribner, 1925.

shabbily dressed Negro, for he passes quietly out of the novel when the white man disposes of his body.

In writing of the stereotyped views of the Negro maintained by white writers, I do not mean to imply that the business of racial stereotypes is a one-way affair. Even a work of such great eloquence and intense personal honesty as James Baldwin's *The Fire Next Time*[5] is permeated with such stereotypes. Thus Baldwin can term Negroes "the only genuine aristocrats this country has produced." And in describing the American white man he can ask: "How can one respect, let alone adopt, the values of a people who do not, on any level whatever, live the way they say they do, or the way they say they should?" Moreover, in certain sections of *Fire* Baldwin offers us precisely the same stereotyped view of the Negro as the upright barbarian, and vital primitive, which so offends him in those white liberals who can see the Negro only as symbol. It is interesting to compare the following description by Baldwin of Negro parties and music to the passage from Kerouac quoted earlier:

> . . . we ate and drank and talked and laughed and danced and forgot all about "the man" [i.e., the white man]. We had the liquor, the chicken, the music, and each other, and had no need to pretend to be what we were not. This is the freedom that one hears in some gospel songs, for example, and in jazz. In all jazz, and especially in the blues, there is something taut and ironic, authoritative and double-edged. White Americans seem to feel that happy songs are *happy* and sad songs are *sad,* and that, God help us, is exactly the way most white Americans sing them—sounding, in both cases, so helplessly, defenselessly fatuous that one dare not speculate on the temperature of the deep freeze from which issue their brave and sexless little voices.

It is Baldwin's own difficulty in overcoming stereotypes that, I believe, results in the great sympathy for the Black Muslims displayed in the same book:

[5] Baldwin, *op. cit.*

Elijah Muhammad has been able to do what generations of welfare workers and committees and resolutions and reports and housing projects and playgrounds have failed to do: to heal and redeem drunkards and junkies, to convert people who have come out of prison and to keep them out, to make men chaste and women virtuous. . . .

Ironically, Baldwin fails to perceive that the Black Muslim's severe proscriptions on credit purchases, liquor, tobacco, and sex all tend to lead towards one end: the re-making of the Negro in the image of the white Puritan, a re-making which, incidentally, also seems to be accompanied by the Puritan's general intransigence and hostility toward outsiders. A further irony in Baldwin's view of the Black Muslims is the fact that he can blame the indifference of white Christians for the rise of the Third Reich and its atrocities toward Jews while at the same time remaining unaware of, or indifferent to, the revival of old Jewish stereotypes and the increasing use of the Jew as scapegoat by the Muslims.

In the end the ultimate myth that the Black Muslim tries to feed the American Negro is that he can find freedom only by separating himself from the white man and establishing a separate society somewhere on the American continent. Yet the very idea of freedom in America, that radical and perennial idea which now inspires the "new Negro" but which we whites have so long taken for granted and so frequently betrayed, has from the beginning been based on three antecedent concepts: liberty, equality, and fraternity. The new myth taught by the Black Muslims is that the Negro can have liberty and equality without fraternity. And, in its way, the new Muslim myth is just as insidious as the old Southern myth that the Negro could have liberty and fraternity (or at least friendship) without equality. But Baldwin is aware of the fundamental irrationality of the Muslim notion that the American Negro can separate himself from our national dilemma, for despite his great sympathy with the Black Muslims, he concludes in *Fire* that the American Negro "has been formed by this nation, for better or for worse, and does not belong to any other—not to Africa, and certainly not to Islam."

One of the chief difficulties with *The Fire Next Time* is that Baldwin further obscures the already thoroughly complicated race problem by attributing to racial prejudice certain universal human ills that existed long before the first slave ships sailed from Africa. For example, Baldwin presents an eloquent picture of the absolute misery endured by him and his friends in Harlem, and he attributes this misery to the fact that Negroes are taught by the white community to despise themselves from the moment their eyes open on the world. Yet in *The Diary of a Country Priest* Georges Bernanos presents a strikingly similar picture of the misery of the French poor and he too finds at the root of their misery the fact that they are taught by society to despise themselves for being poor. In the end, though, Bernanos pushes the question of responsibility further and finds French Christians to blame for this misery because they have compromised Christian principle by accommodating it to a capitalist economic system. One might ask whether there is not a more fundamental sickness than race prejudice in Baldwin's society that causes men to despise themselves for being themselves—and to ask such a question is not to gainsay the moral irresponsibility of whites for allowing the misery of Harlem to develop and continue.

In the same way, both Baldwin and Podhoretz seem to be obsessed with the question of love versus power as solutions to the race problem. Podhoretz tries to expose his emotional feelings toward Negroes in order that he might love them with rational conviction. But at the same time he admits "I cannot restrain my nervousness whenever I pass a group of Negroes standing in front of a bar or sauntering down the street. I know now, as I did not know when I was a child, that power is on my side, that the police are working for me and not for them. And knowing this I feel ashamed and guilty, like the good liberal I have grown up to be." In a similar vein, throughout *Fire* Baldwin alternates between a belief that love will provide the only real solution to the race problem and a realization that the only progress the Negro has made toward equality in America has come with the acquisition of political power by the new African states. "The only thing white people have that black people need, or should want," Baldwin asserts, "is power—and no one holds power forever." Again, one might see this difficulty in balancing love against power in a wider context than the race issue. Both Arnold, in *Culture and Anarchy,* and Newman, in the *Apologia,* were aware that one of the most pressing problems in the modern mass democracy would be the growing separation of the intellectual, with his culture, order, and love, from the source of raw political power. Moreover, Baldwin's dichotomous view that the race problem will finally be solved by either the white man's acquisition of the capacity to love or else the black man's acquisition of the power to retaliate is not fundamentally good psychology. Hans Morgenthau has written a very perceptive essay, "Love and Power," in which he points out that these two basic drives are organically connected. They are inseparable in human relations since the desire for both is rooted in the universally human experience of loneliness.

One final criticism I must make of *Fire* is that I do not think Baldwin can denounce the cowardice of the white liberal without also denouncing the cowardice and indifference of America's Negro bourgeoisie. Moreover, I am not quite convinced that the leading spokesmen in the new Negro criticism of white liberals are the Negroes most qualified to take such a stand. Adam Clayton Powell, for example, was a reliable supporter throughout the fifties of an Eisenhower administration largely indifferent to racial matters. And I know some bitter Negro intellectuals who regard Baldwin, because of his Guggenheim and his access to the pages of *Harper's, Esquire,* and the *New Yorker,* as a "white man's Negro."

But in criticizing several of the points made by Baldwin in *The Fire Next Time,* I do not mean to obscure the book's many merits or its great importance. Part of its significance is that it reflects the growing mood of desperation and frustration felt by today's Negroes. As Baldwin says, the time is rapidly coming when a bill will be presented that he fears America is not prepared to pay. Moreover, his suggestion that there are some American wars in which the Negro is not prepared to fight has come as a much needed jolt at a time when Robert Kennedy is ready to congratulate the Negro on the progress toward integration he has already achieved. Indeed, the very overstatement of Baldwin's case, to which I have pointed, is indicative of his desperateness.

Baldwin's chief contribution, however, lies in the fact that he has, despite some exaggerations and inconsistencies, been exceedingly honest and intensely personal in his approach to the race problem. Moreover, I have no doubt that, as in the case of Podhoretz, his honesty has been achieved through considerable pain and courage. And it is this honest and personal approach that forms, as John Fisher has written, the basis of a promising new dialogue between white and black on the race question.

But we must not forget that it is possible to become too "personal" in dealing with the race issue. Most whites I know who are involved in interracial activities find themselves caught in a dilemma something like this: Are they to regard their colored acquaintances as Negroes or human beings, as abstractions or persons? To regard the Negro as a Negro, as a victim of oppression, is to render indistinct his essential human traits and obscure the fact that he is, after all, one of us, sharing our common human destiny. On the other hand, to approach the Negro as just another human being, as one of us, is in a way dishonest, for it involves overlooking the fact that in actuality the Negro is not just like us: he is denied our freedom and many of our opportunities.

It is also possible to be too "personal" in our approach to race relations in another way. Thus Baldwin in *The Fire Next Time* reveals many deeply personal concerns which are not particularly germane in a treatment of the race problem but which inevitably confuse his view of that problem. There is, for example, his early religious crisis and his struggle to overcome the youthful sense of utter depravity with which his evangelical religion had filled him. (Is it possible that Baldwin's early feelings of worthlessness as a Negro stemmed not only from the treatment accorded him by whites but also from this religious notion of man's depravity?) There is his eventual rejection of Christianity and his hatred for his father. (Is it possible that Baldwin's view that all Negroes hate white men results partly from his difficulties with his father? A large part of his youthful emotional reserve was spent in rejecting his father, the chief authority figure in his life at that time. Consequently much of Baldwin's adult attraction for Elijah Muhammad seems to stem from his quest for a substitute father, and some of his feeling toward whites seems to arise from the fact that whites have replaced his real father as symbols of authority and repression.)

The most important of the personal concerns revealed in *The Fire Next Time,* however, is Baldwin's search to find himself, to define himself. Thus Baldwin finds he is unable to answer when Elijah Muhammad asks him, "What are you now?" And throughout *Fire* there runs like a leitmotif the question "Whose little boy are you?"—the question asked of him by the pimps and racketeers on the Avenue, by the kindly woman minister who helped bring about his conversion, and by Elijah Muhammad. Certainly the quest to know oneself is the noblest of all human quests, but I am not quite convinced that it is a good reason for enlisting in the struggle against racial intolerance, or that the civil-rights battlefield is the place where one should go to flee one's own inner turmoil. As Podhoretz implies, one must try to overcome one's inner emotional conflicts in order to work for racial justice with rational conviction. Moreover, to use the racial struggle as a form of group therapy is to belittle the grand aims of that struggle. And to expect that out of a solution to the race problem will come new men magically made whole and a new world suddenly perfected is to doom oneself to bitter disappointment.

Furthermore, to anticipate that out of the racial struggle will come a new definition of the human person is, in a way, a betrayal of that struggle because the struggle is itself based on a pre-existing definition of the person. Among the chief sources of this definition are the doctrine of the Mystical Body of Christ, contending that all men are equal members of the spiritual body of God with all the dignity that accrues to such membership, and the Declaration of Independence, asserting that all men are endowed by God with natural rights and that they have sufficient reason to construct a government which will guarantee these rights. The freedom toward which the Negro marches is clearly then a freedom involving a definition of man as sanctified, dignified, and rational. The fact that the Negro must now endure imprisonment and assault by police dogs, for reminding us of what we have always believed, is evidence not of the failure of our beliefs but rather of our shortcomings as human beings.

In the end, the honest and personal approach to the race problem demonstrated by Baldwin and Podhoretz has made possible a promising new dialogue that may yet sweep away the old myths and stereotypes. Yet the importance of this dialogue is not so much that it will help to bring about desegregation—desegregation is coming, and coming soon, regardless of what we think or write—but that it will help to bring desegregation with some harmony. However, in carrying on this new "personal" dialogue we must always strive to maintain that difficult and tenuous balance between personality and personhood. We must strive to balance our uniquely personal sense of frustrations, shortcomings, and talents, on the one hand, against, on the other hand, our abstract sense of being persons with dignity, natural rights, and reason.

Lillian Smith

THE MOB AND THE GHOST*

LILLIAN SMITH achieved immediate literary recognition with her first published book, the prize-winning Strange Fruit. *One of the South's most celebrated writers, Miss Smith has been a dedicated student of race relations all her life. Co-editor of* South Today *for more than a decade, her books, in addition to* Strange Fruit, *include* Killers of the Dream, The Journey, Now Is the Time, One Hour, *and her gay memoir of childhood,* Memory of a Large Christmas. *Her articles have appeared in leading periodicals, both in this country and abroad. A volume of selected articles and speeches is scheduled for publication in 1964. Miss Smith is currently working on a book called* The Mysteries of Autobiography *and two new novels.*

THE SOUTH is a heavy word, dark with misunderstandings, edged with defenses, streaked with love and hate. I shall not begin with it. I shall instead return to my childhood where one little white girl can be watched as she runs into ghosts, as she asks unanswerable questions, as she searches for the poet and shies away from the demagogue and the mob that hover on the edge of White Town.

It was born on the rim of that mysterious terrain which spills over from Georgia's Okefenokee Swamp into Florida. As a child, I walked on earth that trembled; the only way it could be done was to run fast, never look anywhere, and get to solid ground as quick as you could. There was Shaky Pond where we had picnics: the edge of that pond, extending back twenty, thirty feet from the water,

* This article is reprinted from *The Progressive,* December, 1962.

trembled if a child stepped on it. There were other ponds with no bottom. As a child, before going to sleep, I used to travel down, down with those who had gone under. I knew at six years that space has no edge and journeys sometimes never end.

There were other fabulous things: a river that, now and then, disappeared into the earth and came up thirty miles away. Suddenly it happened: the fish were feeling secure and comfortable, then *whsst!* there they were, left wriggling on white hot sand with no water within miles. I learned early not to stake much on security; if fish didn't have it, why should I? And there were the sinks: a piece of land, ordinary land, was there today, with perhaps a house on it; tomorrow, sunk into the earth forty feet down. Today, solid fact; tomorrow, emptiness. I learned my lessons early, those the existentialists have been reminding us of in recent decades. Kierkegaard would have felt at home in my region. My childhood landscape could have been designed for *Fear and Trembling.*

I think what impressed me most was this: On that trembling earth of the Great Swamp, although a child could scarcely walk on it, heavy trees and jungled growth were supported by it. Is it not a superb image of civilization: all that men have dreamed and created, springing out of and supported by massive uncertainties? In this mythic and surreal place I lived as a child. In a world full of not only spiritual but physical ambiguities, each casting a shadow on the other. Eyes and muscles and heart knew them long before I heard that word. I knew chasms; I knew things that were here and not here; I had seen invisible walls; I had felt ghosts pull at me, let go, pull again. I moved freely for days in my town, my culture, then suddenly ran head-on into Something, was bruised by it, yet never knew its name.

I do not remember when I first heard the word segregation, but I knew its meaning from babyhood. I learned it the hard way, for I was separated from people I loved by death. These were my first lessons in segregation. Other lessons came quickly. I learned of the segregation that cuts one off from knowledge. There were things I wanted to know which no one would tell me; questions no one would answer. What is death? I needed to know but no one could explain it. I asked about time and eternity; I wanted to know when eternity ended. People told me to go play dolls; and my Sunday school teacher said if I asked about eternity again she would not let me come to her class.

Eight years old: hugging great questions which burned as they touched me. But all children want to know what cannot be known, what words cannot say. Science was just creeping into our town; new doubts were blowing even in that small place. But I dared not say them aloud. I doubted God, yet at the same time I feared Him. This was another ambiguity I was learning to live with. How could part of me question the existence of God and another part be aware of His presence? I kept worrying the idea of time and eternity as a kitten plays with a ball of yarn—getting myself more and more entangled in it. I laughed at the absurd whenever I saw it, as all children do; but my spine ached with the burden of silence as I asked: *Where did I come from? Where am I going? Who am I besides a name?* And no one answered.

Then came another question, more and more often, that concerned me every day: the question about race and its ritual of segregation.

My first concern with it was because it affected *me,* not because it affected Negroes. I just did not like to be segregated. I wanted to be free to ask questions, free to seek answers, free to learn about the mysteries of birth, death, the human body and soul; free to question God, free to love Him, free to run away from Him and deny Him; I wanted also—a want closer to my consciousness—to choose my own friends. I did not like being restricted to members of the white race. Some of the most interesting and daring and skillful youngsters in town were my colored friends to whom I secretly attached myself. This hurt: the secrecy hurt, the fact that they were not welcomed on our street. I wanted the people I loved to come through the front door. I was taught to love freedom, to love the dignity of men, to consider other people's comfort and rights, to respect the human being, to believe in Christian brotherhood, to admit mistakes, and to speak the honest word. My family taught me these things; and yet, there was always the quiet, gentle, back door treatment of the dark people we loved. Love without dignity: the thought chilled me.

I was also taught to go to church, to listen carefully and to believe what the preachers said. Of course, those questions curled up in my head shot like rockets through the discrepancies in this intertwining mesh of family lessons and church lessons and street lessons and school lessons. Everything contradicting everything else, and I knew it. But gradually I "adjusted" better; I grew the third skin which all white Southerners finally grow, and it shut off the quick pain, the sudden glimpse of horror, the ever-pressing whispers of conscience. I got used to my colored friends living in shacks on the edge of town while I lived in a big, fine house on the "best" street. I got used to playing with them on my way home from school but never inviting them to my house. I got used to seeing an all-white congregation in our church, although I asked questions before I grew silent. I got used to being split apart inside, conscience segregated from reality, body segregated from heart, mind separated from the knowledge it craved.

My earth was trembling—not only out near Big Swamp but in the bigger swamp of my interior life. And yet, there were rich experiences, fine glimpses of knowledge and art and poetry; there was love, there was compassion. But beneath it all were not only the unchangeable uncertainties on which the human condition is based, but another uncertainty that *need not be*. It was this that hurt me, this knowledge that racial separation does not belong in the category of the archetypal and unchangeable separations: birth, death, a universe which we can never know save in small fragments, a God whose existence we can never prove, a *why was I born?* which even a man's vocation does not answer in full. This separation was different; it could be *changed*.

And yet, others seemed to accept it as unchangeable. Their families told them they were members of the white race and that was enough for anybody to be; their demagogues told them this superiority gave them the right to treat Negroes like things and animals and they need not listen when their conscience did not agree. They became solid with certainty; hard, undifferentiated in their mystique of whiteness. Faces took on a bleak surety which frightened me as a child more than even the ghosts I could not name. I would run to the security of a home where such racial hate talk never took place, though my family were long-time Southerners; where no man was considered less than a human being; where dignity was acted out by my parents in their relationships with their children. And because of this retreat, this peaceful cloister, I never accepted "the Southern way of life." I knew someday it could be changed; and so my loyalties never became too tied up with "the South." I love the South not for its sins but because it is home, where my memories hover; I love its climate, its strange and beautiful jungles, swamps, beaches, forests, hills, mountains; I love the softness of voice; I still cherish the easy kindnesses, even though I know that many of these "kind" people have cared little about Negroes' rights or welfare.

The small acts of grace can sometimes blind you to the large cruelties. For the cruelties keep distance. Most white Southerners have never seen a lynching, have never seen a Negro wounded or whipped, have never heard a dark scream of pain, never come close to the awful humiliation which colored women endured for so long from many white men; have never visited a Negro school; have never asked what happens to Negroes when they get sick; never looked hard at a starving face or a crippled mind; never whispered the sorrow and shame of a love without esteem. Most knew these terrors only remotely, never letting them creep into consciousness. They thought of them, often, as "exaggerations"—or lies. They blamed the worst of them on "outsiders" even though the outsiders might live on their street. And until recently, they pulled the silence tight around their hearts and made like they felt nothing. The third skin has had its uses even for the best of us in the South (as well as in Germany); and yes, let me say it: in those Northern cities where few of the privileged have ever visited *their* dark ghettos. The wound is unhealed in all of us, but we cover it with sweet-smelling salve and pretend the stench comes from somewhere else. Each of us in our own way has to struggle to step back a few inches and look, really look, at our home town and its cruelties and blindnesses and pitiful, tragic lies.

I have never been sure that racial segregation has hurt the Negro more than the white. I am not certain that physical lynching of the few is worse than the spiritual lynching of many white children by their own parents and school and church. There is a spiritual lynching of black children, too; different, but perhaps no more terrible than that of the white children. What segregation has actually done is to destroy spiritually and mentally millions of its children of both races. Arrogance, or shame—which do you prefer that your child feel? A mind deadened to knowledge, or a body shut out of a decent school? An indifference to the suffering of others, or suffering itself? The choice is hard to make for all these things will dehumanize the child.

Neither Negroes nor whites have fully realized that segregation is a two-edged sword, that it cuts both ways and cuts to kill. If this could once be seen clearly, if white people could for one hour stare at the faces around them, could peer even for one minute into the hollow souls they work with and play with, they could not say, "It must come slowly; a little token sanity, yes, but not too much sanity, not too much compassion, not too much fairness—just a moderate amount." To hear thoughful men speak of postponing decency, postponing excellence, postponing the return of rights they have stolen from Negroes and from their own children, leaves me gasping in astonishment. How can our people be so blind?

We need someone to blame. We cannot bear our anguish if we know it springs from our own hearts. We look around; some name our own U.S. Supreme Court as the mortal enemy; others blame "the North" or the National Association for the Advancement of Colored People or the Communists. But besides ourselves, we can blame the immediate trouble today only on the demagogues (the racist politicians) and the ghosts which the demagogues whistle back—those old guilts and memories, the consciences we killed but which never died, the children we maimed, the souls we destroyed. Now they are sent forth as maenads by the demagogues to cut the head off of every Orphic truth, to whip and lash every one who dares to disagree, to speak what is right, to measure and examine reality.

And we let them. The churches let them, the preachers let them, the businessmen let them, the unions let them. All? No. There has been a small minority of mute dissenters since the Civil War; there has been a small minority of soft speakers since 1925; there have been more and more who have spoken and written clearly, persuasively, in recent decades, but the maenads torment them: tongues lash, houses are burned or dynamited, friends shun, critics destroy not only books but status, reviewers sneer (not only in the South but in the North, too), saying, "This writer is angry; he is excited; too disturbed." I say in reply, "How under God's heaven could a sane, observant, sensitive human being be less than disturbed over a region that has sacrificed its children to a white Moloch? How could a deeply religious person feel anything but anguish at the springing up of idolatries not only in this South of ours but throughout the country and the world? How can we, with gentlemanly decorum, accept for one minute the philosophical implications of "gradualism" and the caution of racial "moderates"?

And yet, many do. Many others are so glazed over, so frozen by fear, so toughened by this third skin of ours that they obey the demagogues and run from the ghosts, or chase them, as ordered. Otherwise, how could we have had Little Rock? Or those jeering women persecuting children in New Orleans? Or those students mobbing one lone girl at the University of Georgia? Or those deaths at Oxford, Mississippi? And worst of all, the dreadful silence of the good, the respectable, the prominent: the collapse of the poet in each of us.

I was close to the mob at Athens, Georgia; not in the town but close enough to watch it build (even a year before it exploded). It was not surprising to many Georgians when a mob of two thousand students (helped by the Klan) attacked one girl. But the point that few have seen is that the mob was not attacking a real girl named Charlayne Hunter but a symbol, a ghost into which they had stuffed noisome memories, guilts, and words from the white supremacy ritual. They had never met Charlayne Hunter, would not have recognized her on the streets, yet their rage was tremendous and uncontrolled. They felt they must kill Something, Something that had haunted them a long time, Something that kept them split and torn and confused.

When we see this kind of thing happening, when we see a governor of a state act like a mad fool, when we watch students go berserk as if they were in psychotic flight, when we see responsible men of a community turn dumb and mute as if they were cowed animals, when suddenly crowds of people begin to lie, to blame on mythic outsiders what they themselves brought to pass—when such outbursts occur, we can be sure we are not dealing with reasonable problems such as poverty or a one-party political system or the memories of a war fought a century ago which no living man knows anything about from personal experience, or an outmoded peonage system of sharecropping. Although all have their effect and all exacerbate the situation, the cause for such turmoil is not on rational levels of men's thinking.

We shall more likely find the answer in lower depths of personality, lower—and higher. A look at the charismatic power of the demagogue should warn any observer that depths, not surfaces, are being stirred. Ghosts are on the loose and one somehow knows it. Ghosts are, of course, breathing symbols; they are symbols with a half-life; they are memories that cannot end their story and in restlessness keep haunting men's minds with unfinished business; they are guilts that have never asked forgiveness. Above all else, they are powerful, for they can turn men into things and things into men. How could Hitler have killed millions of Jews had not the Nordic ghosts helped him turn them into things? But—and this we need to remember—the ghosts could not have done the bloody, grisly business alone. They had to have a witch doctor to free them—for ordinarily ghosts are segregated—and then direct them to do their work. The demagogue understands this; so he uses incantation and hypnotic gestures to loosen the ghosts from the mythic level of men's minds where they ordinarily stay. In the South he repeats words that are close to men's bodies, words that have taken on symbolic meanings: *blood, white, black, menace, mixing, mingling, white, black,* and with these words he creates, actually makes, a new situation that does not exist in terms of facts but exists, nevertheless; and men, listening, react to this mythic situation as though it were literally real.

The racists dehumanize the man, Negro, into the thing, Negro.

On this mythic level where the reason's categories and logical processes are never found, it is easy to ask why the Negro (now a fetish, a symbol) should have human rights. Why should a *thing* be protected by the Supreme Court and the Department of Justice? There are people who actually cannot grasp the fact that a Negro is not an object but a human being.

The demagogue knows he can force people into this primitive state by the skilled use of the ghosts and by the freeing of demonic impulses from the restrictive covenants of conscience. The demagogue, speaking with the authority of a priest, tells the crowd they are justified in doing anything in the name of white supremacy. They believe him. And because of the release he gives them, they give him obedience.

In this slave condition, reason won't work. For decades, demagogues have fattened on this powerful bit of knowledge. Reason cannot undo magic tricks once they have been performed. Only physical force can control the external violence; and only the poetic truth can subdue the inner turmoil. The poet, therefore, is the demagogue's mortal enemy—for he and he alone can overcome the evil state of men's minds. The poet can do this not only because he, too, uses ghosts—"the good ghosts"—but because he has power over the poetic, truth-seeking levels of the mythic mind. This is why the silence of the poet in all of us is so dread a thing when the mob begins to merge. This is the moment when only truth can kill the lie, when only love can weaken hate: reason cannot do it, nor common sense, nor logic; but poetic truth spoken to people with compassion and beauty has the strange power to arouse their good feelings and desires.

The mythic mind is, above all else, highly creative: it can create lies and demons and mobs and riots; but it can also create art and poetry by careful addition of heart and intelligence and the proper use of symbols and ghosts. What the demagogues do is to change gold into straw; what the poets do is to change straw into gold; their purpose is different, their grasp of knowledge is different, their procedures are different, but they use the same magic. They both know the power of metaphor; they both know how to change a person into a thing or a thing into a person; they both understand that "holy" can be the holiness of devils or the holiness of God. A demagogue by his tricks melts a thousand people into a mob. A poet by his "tricks" builds bridges among those people, separating them a little so they can feel their own edge, yet drawing them closer by the new relationship to truth he gives them. Can you not see that "rational man" with his logic and his scrupulously collected facts does not have much chance with the people in crisis who are chasing ghosts, who are acting symbolically? Reason must do its work *before the crisis comes.*

Mobs and demagogues, riots and hate slogans, are also symptoms of a collective illness. The South is suffering from such a malaise. The illness is by no means limited to the South or to our country. It comes not primarily from racism (racism is a symptom, not the disease itself); it comes from two centuries of Western man's misunderstanding of science and over-esteem of proof and from his unnecessary subjection to the machine he created. Combined, these have caused him to misinterpret religion, have pushed him toward the facts of the laboratory and away from the truth found in poetry. And now, most men no longer believe that there is something bigger than a man, that spiritual laws exist which no one can disregard without destroying himself.

This is the heart of the matter. To understand the compulsive fury of people caught in racial stress, we must understand not only the mechanisms they use but their emptiness; and to understand the emptiness we must understand their basic, often unverbalized, rejection of God and the terrible hunger that is a consequence of this rejection. No wonder men in a bi-racial situation have seized upon color (their own) and made of it a fetish. They need and must have something to worship. What now—if God is dead? Who will be our new God? Who will be our new priests?

The ignorant, the culturally stunted, and a small but noisy group of psychotics are the demagogue's natural audience. The strain of living in both a spiritual vacuum and a scientific world which is totally beyond their comprehension is eased by this frank regression to more primitive ways. They love the demagogue's ghost stories; the threat of "the Negro" is more titillating than terrifying; it helps them forget the atom bomb; they feel by casting a vote or taking part in a riot they can "do something about the Negro," but they can't do anything about those missile bases. Substituting a spurious menace for a real one and promising security plays a big part in the demagogue's success. These deprived people were once pitiable, but with the vote, with jobs, with spending power, they grow dangerous; dangerous because a large group of them are addicts who for years have given themselves kicks with the drug, white supremacy; and they will not give up their "white powder" without a nasty struggle.

Of all our Southern sins—and we have plenty—the persistent, blind ignoring of the needs of our poor and ignorant whites is perhaps the worst; our culture has fed them lies—not folk wisdom; our power structure, instead of giving jobs, gave them for decades a false and ridiculous sense of superiority, teaching them that excellence lay simply in possessing a white skin. These people heard nothing about dignity, human growth, relationships; they heard nothing of the myths and poetry by which Western man has become great. You can know the wisdom of the poets without reading poetry if other men will speak of this wisdom, but the uncultivated white Southerner, for eighty years, has heard nothing except lies about white superiority, skin color, mongrelization.

Now, suddenly, they are told to obey the law. What law, they ask in astonishment—for they had been told they could break any law that protected a Negro; that no one could have civil rights in this country unless his skin was white. Now they are told to obey: to obey not because the laws are good and right but because they are The Law. This is supposed to be a clever way out, a face-saver for politicians and the power structure and for certain editors who have exclaimed editorially for years that nobody but a fool would question segregation. Now, the new slogan is, "Even though we despise the Supreme Court's decision, we must obey."

It is not the truth but a half-lie, and we shall suffer from it. The ignorant white can take the truth, if the truth is spoken in kindness. I know face-saving is sometimes expedient—I did not live in China for three years without learning this—but in a time of deep stress and spiritual turmoil, to try to settle for a half-lie is dangerous. People must change their ways and their values, but to do so without breaking to pieces physically and spiritually they must *change inside*. They must fill the hollowness with the full Orphic truth; only in this way can they master their ordeal as men. And now, our leaders are once more offering them only face-saving subterfuges.

One could weep. Like the old Greek warriors one could lift one's face to the sky and weep. When the sharecroppers in Arkansas were thrown out in snow and ice by the plantation owners, an old Negro prayed, "Break their hearts, O God; give them tears." I heard him pray and ever since it has haunted me with its pathos and its truth.

Things are changing, but much too slowly; the "old forms are breaking," and we are beginning to "feel the new things"—but much too slowly. Our leaders have not yet faced the truth that we, too, must hurt, we must suffer with the poor white and the Negro, not only to be redeemed from our past but to find the wisdom to create our future.

We must say with Aeschylus: "Cry sorrow—and let the good prevail."

John LaFarge, S.J.

THE NEGRO'S IDENTITY IN TODAY'S SOUTH

The late JOHN LAFARGE, S.J. (1880–1963) was Associate Editor of America, *the National Catholic Weekly Review, and authored many books, including* The Race Question and the Negro, An American Amen, The Manner Is Ordinary *(an autobiography), and* Reflections on Growing Old. *Father LaFarge was for sixteen years a country pastor in Southern Maryland, for both whites and Negroes, and initiated many educational projects in that area. He was founder and chaplain emeritus of the Catholic Interracial Council of New York, Inc., and honorary chaplain of the National Catholic Conference for Interracial Justice.*

ANY DISCUSSION of the Negro in the South, or in the other parts of the country for that matter, will naturally start from the question of identity.

Who—or what—is it that we are talking about?

The white man is ready with his self-identification by birth and region, by profession or vocation. But how does the Negro identify himself? For if a person cannot establish his own identity, he is confused and frustrated.

Others, of course, are ready to do the job for him. In point of fact, the Negro finds an identification all prepared, without any question of his agreement or consent. Yet, it is utterly unreal to believe that he will accept it. For identification, except for inmates of a prison camp or other compulsory institution, must be something the person willingly accepts: that he *can* accept without doing violence to his own personality.

In order to live with some degree of peace in a racist-minded community, the sole identification a Negro can adopt is that of an unquestioning, ever-faithful servant. In earlier days, it was possible to accept this permanent, absolutely servant status, since there was nothing else to look forward to, save for a few far-seeing individuals, and the question of citizenship was only remotely raised. But two world wars and their consequences, plus an immense, tranquil interior effort of self-development, have raised the question of citizenship-identity to an acute and drastic form.

In the present armed forces, the Negro simply cannot continue to be identified as a second-class human being: one essentially, by rigid laws of nature, irrevocably condemned to be inferior or second-class in any branch or at any level of human existence, except the most abject and servile. For his obligations, the duties of service that are exacted from him, in the Army or Navy or Air Force, or in any civilian occupations connected with these services, are precisely the same as those of any other person, of any other race, color or national origin.

No *exception* is made in the armed forces to any person because of his or her race. When the rules of the armed services are explained to new recruits, I do not see any instance where they are informed, in a paternal and kindly fashion, that of course, since we are Southerners, we "understand" you, and therefore do not require quite the same exacting standards of excellence that we would of people of white American, or Irish, or Italian, etc., descent. No, to my knowledge, no such paternal and kindly explanation is made. Hundred-per-cent identification is expected, or else. . . .

Yet, when you return to your home town, you must by no means identify yourself with the status expected and required of you in the armed forces. You will accept completely, uncomplainingly, your prior status. You must even accept it *within* yourself, by an act of interior submission, or be gravely suspect. And this line of submission, incidentally, is to be practiced in a country, in a present-day culture and civilization, which is going more or less mad on the subject of social status, as the be-all and the end-all for ambitious youths and maidens. Even the cigarette you light must denote your social status. You are known as socially having "arrived" if you light up a Dromedary or an Essex.

The Negro youth of today is bluntly informed that (a) he must be ready to shoulder the full burden of citizenship, even if it means offering his life and limb, in the service of the only country he knows or—in the majority of cases—his ancestors have ever known. But (b) he is not to exercise these duties, or enjoy the privileges that are elementary for every United States citizen who is not disqualified by crime or insanity.

We may theorize to our hearts' content about the type of identification the Negroes or any other people in our community *ought* to accept. But Negroes are no exception to the rule that all peoples need their own identification, and that it is as meaningless when imposed by others as was the identification imposed by Egypt's Pharaoh upon the people of ancient Israel.

The painfully plain fact remains that if American Negroes are refused the opportunity to identify themselves with the very country in which they and their ancestors for generations back were born, if they are told, as they not infrequently are: you can't leave here, but you belong here, on any but totally unacceptable terms; then, being ordinary human beings, they will turn to other means of self-identification.

Recently I received a letter from the superintendent of a large state prison in the Far West, asking me if I could suggest for the Negro prisoners a course of study in the history of the American Negro. The superintendent was disturbed by the fact that Elijah Muhammad's Black Muslim movement was being, as he said, systematically organized among Negro prisoners around the United States. Without endeavoring to appraise this movement—described briefly, but vividly, by James Baldwin in *The Fire Next Time*—it is certainly a response to the Negro's elementary demands for some type of self-identification. The ignoring of such a demand can only lead to harmful frustration and demoralization. The office of self-identification has been partly fulfilled in the past by the autonomous Negro Protestant churches and their web of social activities and institutions. But that type of self-identification cannot suffice for the world in which Negro youth today grows up.

If the Negro today cannot consider himself a full-fledged citizen, he may be offered the wholly specious substitute of communism: the plea being that here is an opportunity for him to identify himself with the workers and oppressed classes of the whole world. Communist sales-talk snared for a decade or so its feckless victims among the Negro intellectuals between the world wars. But its dupes soon discovered how hollow was the offer. Communism, they learned, is a white man's job, invented by whites and controlled by whites, and interested in Negroes purely as a means of gaining political power. When the communist pretenses were exploded, its siren appeal soon fell on indifferent ears. Yet the appeal of Cuba, communism right at our doors, and within shouting distance of the sacrosanct Deep South, is not so easily passed over. The American Negro has learned long ago that neither Soviet Russia nor Red China has anything to offer him, except where some individual consents to be a pawn in the interests of specialized Red propaganda. But Cuba is another matter. Negroes, Spanish-speaking, are an integral factor in all of Cuba's historical movements, and they are welcomed today with open arms if they make their way there from the United States. Africa, too, offers today certain possibilities for self-identification, in quite a different fashion from that of earlier epochs, when African ancestry was felt to be a reproach, a reminder of former slavery, rather than an honor. No matter how little enthusiasm the American Negro may feel for the ever-increasing number of aspiring African students who win scholarships and come to our shores, he can derive a grim satisfaction from the perplexities African aspirants cause when they knock upon the doors of institutions that hitherto have been closed to any but white applicants.

The question, then, that underlies any discussion of the future of the Southern Negro is above all, and primarily, How far does any young Negro, growing up under present conditions, feel any inclination, indeed see any possibility, to identify himself or herself with the growing and developing Southern community? Is the South simply a place to get out of, if you possibly have the chance—save perhaps for a few happily circumstanced or marginally situated individuals? Or does the South, the dynamically expanding, progressive South, offer a corresponding opportunity to young and rationally ambitious Negroes? There will always be room, I imagine, for the type of person who is content to settle down to a life of mere service at the white man's convenience, and the future may bring him a little more honor in that respect than he was able to command in the past. There will, presumably, always be demand for waiters and for garage helpers. But what does the New South offer for youth who share the generally progressive spirit of the age, who honestly want to grow with a growing region, and be a part of that growth, as they are already a part of its very existence? For the most part they know that the New South after all could not have come into being were it not for their labors—as yet unrequited, say the Black Muslims—in the past.

I have stated this question crudely and in a very general form. Yet the question must be answered with the utmost honesty. Neither Sunflower County nor Leflore County, Mississippi, has the answer. The question cannot be answered as long as Sunflower County or Leflore County holds the reins of political power and shapes the world in which Negro youth is called to mature. And the alternative to an honest answer is the empty logic of despair.

The question, like the various attempts to answer it, is not new. Can—or will—the intelligent and normally progressive Negro identify himself with the future South?

I know that for certain types of mind such a question is vexatious. A good deal of ingenuity is employed in order to present the case for the South, and indeed the "case" can be thoroughly convincing if offered as an abstract proposition. But we are not living in an abstract world, and both elements in the bi-racial picture are obliged to face the actual facts of life. Any practical answer to the question will, of course, depend upon how far the South expects to identify itself. Before we speculate as to the part of the Negro, we will naturally need to inquire as to what the South in general expects itself to be. And "South in general" is an enormously comprehensive and heterogeneous term.

Such an inquiry, of course, is not new. It has been made in great sincerity and with much detail by accomplished and devoted leaders—Southerners themselves, with the addition of some Northerners who have joined with them. A lifetime of thought and action was devoted to the problem by men like the late Will W. Alexander and the galaxy of distinguished scholars, philanthropists, educators and public servants that he gathered around him during the course of his long and active career. Most of these were deeply concerned about the Negro: his prospects, his outlook for the future. I need only mention Julius Rosenwald, builder of countless country schools and patron of scholarships; James Hardy Dillard, of Charlottesville, Virginia; George Foster Peabody, Robert Russa Moton, Thomas Jesse Jones, John J. Eagan, Anna T. Jeanes, Mary McLeod Bethune, Dr. Charles S. Johnson, Charlotte Hawkins Brown, and a host of other famous names, both living and dead. They battled heroically with poverty, ignorance and massive discontent. Rockefeller's General Education Board, with its immense resources, sincerely believed that the racial problem could be solved through a nobly and generously conceived plan of education, but still implicitly on the separate-but-equal line. The good accomplished by these pioneers in philanthropy, with their manifold approaches to the mixed problems of ignorance, poverty, political corruption and racial prejudice, is incalculable. Were it not for their foresight, their patience, and the projects they initiated and supported, we would have no starting point for our present discussion.

It was they who laid a solid groundwork for the New South. They stubbornly refused to look upon the Negro as a mere problem; an unfortunate heritage left over from unhappy earlier times, as a weight hung around the neck of the progressive South. They saw in the South's Negro population sources of great strength, bedrock wisdom. Yet they still left unanswered the basic question: What will be the Negro's part in a new civilization that still denies him the very first requisites of humanity, which still confronts him with barriers that no diligence, no degree of virtue, no known or tangible prescription can possibly cross?

Many Southerners, as I have known them, seem to feel that if the Southern Negro is accorded his full civil rights, if he is treated as an equal citizen, by this very act the whole fabric of Southern culture is swept away. Perhaps that is true. It may be that the only rational course to follow with old Colonel Cotchipee, of *Purlie Victorious* fame, is decently to inter him and thereby to obliterate his very memory. But is this necessarily the case? When the venerable Cotchipee manor is broken up into houselots, or selected for a rayon factory, employing white and colored with equal opportunity, why should the memory perish of everything that was truly worthwhile about the old estate? There is a nobility and grandeur about the old myths, and I am not certain of any reason for their total demolition. The Civil War, from whichever side you approach its memory, "won freedom," in the words of Bruce Catton of Gettysburg College. If the Stars and Bars once floated proudly from the family flagpole, why not let them continue to float? The memory of the brave men who died for them—and of Negroes who were loyal to their brave masters in the time of their disaster—is imperishable, like that of my former aged Negro housekeeper, who in her youth brought soup clandestinely to dying Confederate soldiers in the fever-stricken Federal prison at Point Lookout, Maryland—even if today we can no longer flourish such memories as an excuse for manifest, present-day injustices.

The question I have raised here has put itself from time to time when I was called to speak to young Negroes graduating from high school. What could I say to them that would be honest, and not merely conventional recommendations to industriousness, worthy ambition and fear of the Lord? To all of them, in the North or the South, I could frankly say: Work for what you believe you can be and want to be, at your highest capacity. I could recall individual instances of Negro boys and girls whose hopes and ambitions for the future were not bounded by the limited outlook of their parents or the society around them, but were determined by the knowledge of their own talents and highest inclinations. "Don't hesitate and ask: what places will be open for me?" I told my classes, "ask rather, what do I want to do, and work for that place, whether it be open or not."

But can one go further, especially if you are addressing Southern Negro youth, and tell them that a new world of opportunity is opening up? Can I say to them, that a New South is inviting them;

that this New South is not simply tolerating them, as a sort of grim necessity, but, on the contrary, is looking to them to join in the building of a new and better world, on the terms of true American citizenship? Can I bring home the idea that they are needed, that were it not for the gifts of their talents and personalities, the New South would suffer an indescribable loss? For they are needed from the aspect of mere man and woman power; and, moreover, they are needed for what they are, for their own personalities. They *are,* in great measure, the New South.

How far can we speak such words to young people with absolute sincerity? How far can they look forward to a different South than that which confronted their own parents, if or when these were deliberating about their own future? The point is that for the young Negro of today it is no longer intelligible that such a deliberation should be necessary. The slow pace of certain gradual steps of upward progress to which Negroes were more or less willing to accommodate themselves has taken on a sinister aspect in view of violent racist propaganda set on foot in recent years, for the clear purpose of preserving at all costs the existing political power structure.

Yet, Dr. Stephen J. Wright, president of Fisk University, speaking in Detroit before the National Catholic Conference for Interracial Justice in August, 1962, does not abandon all hopefulness:

> The New Negro in the South, with his new instruments of pressure, his increasing self-confidence, and new leadership which is *earning* the right to lead, will inevitably make significant changes in his status, despite the stiffening resistance of the white South. In assuming this new posture, he has placed himself in a position to be helped a great deal more by both the "moderate" and the liberal white Southerners, as well as by many others who understand the national and international significance of the stakes involved in this struggle.

Dr. Wright makes certain hopeful predictions. He believes the existing racial demagogues can be retired, and recent elections in South Carolina, Georgia and elsewhere seem to confirm his view. He believes:

That with better economic and educational opportunities, the New Negro in the South will do much to help raise the economic level of the South. The system has forced large numbers of Negroes to be a part of the problem of poverty in the South, rather than a part of the answer to its eradication. . . . The nation will be the beneficiary of the talents and genius of many thousands of young Negroes who, under the system, either fell because of undevelopment or atrophy. This is a luxury which this nation in these demanding times cannot afford.

Among the factors that will speed the fulfillment of these predictions, President Wright lists as principal:

(1) *The role the federal government will play.* Since he spoke, the series of dramatic events concerning the admission of Negro students to the Universities of Mississippi and Alabama have unfolded, and have set a precedent for other forms of federal action.

(2) *The attitude of Northern business operating in the South.* Southern business is almost inextricably interwoven with Northern business. Northern chain-store and restaurant concerns have been shocked into recognition of this phenomenon of national responsibility by the sit-in's and other forms of protest, and, at the date of this writing, I notice that practically every one of the member-chains of the Howard Johnson Restaurants has now abandoned the practice of racial discrimination.

Dr. Wright also lists elements that are decisive in determining the direction of the New South: such factors as (3) *National public opinion,* and (4) *The emergence of a new Southern leadership.* He said:

There are leaders in the South who recognize the incomparable damage the system does to whites and Negroes alike, as well as to the nation in the eyes of the rest of the world. They recognize also the ultimate futility of the effort to defend it and the hypocrisy which its defense involves. The question is, when will a new crop of political and business leaders begin to make these facts their platform? Take any group of human beings and provide them with inferior education; deny them the right to vote; deny them equal job opportunities; force them to live in ghettos; and exclude them from hotels, public eating places and even hospitals, and developed under such conditions, they will scarcely be able to compete as first-class citizens, unless they are supermen.

I have spoken of the ambivalent future that still confronts young people who graduate from American high schools. They still confront a world of racial handicaps. How painful and far-reaching those handicaps can be, it takes the drastic experience and the frank language of a John Howard Griffin to enable us to some degree to realize. What, then, of the future that faces the ever-mounting multitude of our teenage drop-outs? Unless they are rescued in a few months' time, the world of gangsterism and perverted criminality offers them its solicitations.

The drop-out problem is due to elements in our national educational situation which go beyond the question of racial discrimination. Our entire national and, to some extent, international social system is involved, making peculiarly futile any attempt to deal with such a question upon purely sectional and regional lines. For the sixteen-year-old country boy, the temptation is apt to prevail to abandon school and somehow to place himself at the wheel of a speeding car.

If the years bring a special conviction to the student of the racial scene in the United States—or elsewhere—it turns on the consciousness that no single phase of our social life can be studied without reference to all the others. If this is true at all times, it is vastly more worthy of emphasis today, for a nation which bears the reputation of being the most mobile in the world; where the influence of central or national economic decisions reaches down into the remotest crossroads. This is not said in order to discourage a reasonable degree of regionalism. On the contrary, we shall best serve the interests of a particular region when we see it clearly in its relation to the rest of the nation.

But regional interests can go only so far. It is our general, national view of the nature, for instance, and obligations of the human family, which is bound to influence the standards we set up for a particular locality. The national view, for better or worse, is conveyed to us daily by all the ample means of intercommunication that beset the modern scene. If certain matters are to be declared wrong and objectionable with regard to the sanctity of married life—divorce, adultery, neglect of children, premature and casual unions—the basis for our declaration must be the solid religious and moral truths that hold for all mankind and all races and places, and are not subject to the whims of local politicians, selfish property holders, or enterprising real-estate brokers.

Deep at the heart of this problem lies the fundamental question of the moral issue as regards any successful political or social construction, which involves the influence of religious faith upon the racial scene.

The ultimate word on human identity rests with our religious teachers. In times of slavery and oppression the preaching of the Gospel, and enthusiastic worship that accompanied that preaching, did convey to the American Negro a most unusual message. Negroes identified themselves in spirit with the people of Israel struggling against their Egyptian and Babylonian oppressors. The Catholic Negroes, a small island in the great Protestant sea, were taught their identity with the universal church: a fact that gave great strength to individuals, but for the most part the message stopped there, and did not proceed to its logical consequences in the area of public and social life.

Today, upon all the religious bodies, Catholic and Protestant and Jewish alike, rests the burden of a new proclamation addressed equally to all races, regions and localities. This message is one of full responsibility and recognition of individual worth, regardless of race, color or creed; and the identification of the individual with the entire nation. Hence the obligation for all to contribute, as far as humanly possible, in order to convey this message to a divided and tension-burdened country.

This was the message of the memorable meeting in Chicago (January 14–17, 1963) of the religious leaders of the principal religious groups—Protestant, Jewish, and Catholic—the National Conference of Religion and Race, concerning the "unfinished business" of the anniversary year of the Emancipation Proclamation of January 1, 1863. The declaration of that meeting:

We seek a reign of courage so that the people of God will make their faith in God their most binding commitment, so that their religious faith becomes the norm by which all human customs, civil law, and legal precedent are judged and accepted. In the strength of God, our Father, to join those who suffer in the cause of justice and love becomes indeed blessed. We desire to see our churches and synagogues lead, not follow; to offer an example of justice, fair treatment, initiative and love to other areas of human life.

I believe that the South's culture consistently isolates its people from considering the problem of the neglected Negro, largely because the Negro has practically no way to express his problems without having to resort to methods of attracting attention that straightway take on the appearance of subversion. The primary requirement in certain parts of the country is that you do not talk of such things, and if you do—and if you vary from an accustomed formula—it is because of some sinister "outside" influence. As a consequence of this general tactical agreement of silence, the Southern Negro has developed a certain protective appearance: to use a current expression, the Negro says what he thinks it is safe to let the white man hear.

The ultimate sufferers from the present state of affairs are the young white people, just as much as the Negro youth. The "open contempt" of moral values, as demonstrated by those elements in the community to which we naturally look for courageous leadership—our local, county and state leaders—has a disastrous effect that ultimately results in the weakening of our entire social structure. Most instructive in this respect will be the experience of intelligent Southern youth when they come directly in contact with the grave social problems of the non-white peoples abroad.

The general overriding problem has been stated eloquently by Ralph McGill in his book, *The South and the Southerner.** In the chapter entitled, "The Conscience of the South," he writes:

"The solution is really relatively simple if we would but admit it to ourselves. It is no longer as complex as it was. Much of the undergrowth of myth and self-deceit has been cleared away. The

* Boston, Little, Brown and Co., 1963.

clamor of mongrelization of race, of supremacy, and of tradition has not ceased, but more and more it is known to be noise, not fact. The problems were aggravated because they were made into more than they were. The remedy is no longer as difficult. It is to grant the Negro the rights and privileges of full citizenship. It is to look at the Negro and see another human being."

Bradford Daniel

WILLIAM FAULKNER AND THE SOUTHERN QUEST FOR FREEDOM

BRADFORD DANIEL, a native Texan, is a former white editor of Sepia *Magazine. During his tenure with that publication he had, at 25, the distinction of being the nation's youngest executive editor of an internationally distributed magazine. While at the University of Texas, from which he graduated in 1959, he was for two years an editor on* The Daily Texan, *the university daily newspaper. In addition to having written for many leading American periodicals, he served as editor on the now-defunct magazine,* Collegia. *He is currently working on a first novel.*

"LOVING ALL OF IT even while he had to hate some of it. Because he knows now that you don't love because; you love despite; not for the virtues, but despite the faults. He was born of it and his bones will sleep in it." Thus, the late novelist William Faulkner described himself, his native Mississippi and the South in a *Holiday* Magazine article several years ago.

This statement, perhaps more than any other Faulkner made, helped to shed light on a question that had long puzzled many Southerners: Did Faulkner hate Mississippi and the South?

"Faulkner didn't write the truth about Mississippi," an Oxford citizen told me in Leslie's Walgreen drugstore in July 1962, only hours after Faulkner's funeral. "His books depicted our state in a false and perverted manner. Mississippi isn't like he wrote at all. Not at all! We'll be a long time living it down." When asked if he had read all or most of Faulkner's twenty-five books, he replied, "Only one or two of them."

The Oxonian, like a majority of Faulkner critics, apparently didn't understand or appreciate what the Nobel Prize-winning author attempted to do throughout his entire body of work; in all their anxious criticisms and repudiations his constant critics refused to accept Mississippi as merely the background against which he analyzed and evaluated universal problems and truths.

Faulkner had a deep love of the South, despite the criticism that had labeled him over the years as a "South hater." Ignoring the vestiges of moonlight and magnolia blossoms, he pictured the South as a way of life that had disappeared forever, a region haunted by memories and fearful of a commercialized future that Faulkner believed would make life impersonal and depthless.

He loved the South as much as any man, yet he was never afflicted with the Southern malady of being blinded by its prejudices and faults. In a letter written in 1955, Faulkner noted: "And those of us who were born in Mississippi and have lived all our lives in it, who have continued to live in it forty and fifty and sixty years at some cost and sacrifice simply because we love Mississippi and its ways and customs and soil and people; who because of that love have been ready and willing at all times to defend our ways and habits and customs from attack by the outlanders whom we believed did not understand them, we had better be afraid, too—afraid that we have been wrong; that what we had loved and defended not only didn't want the defense and the love, but was not worthy of the one and indefensible to the other."

He must have loved the South, for he never left it. Instead, except for brief trips away, he chose to spend his life in Oxford where his "bones sleep" now in the red clay of St. Peter's Cemetery, shaded by a cluster of ancient oaks.

Many dismissed his work as being too labored for popular enjoyment, for branding the South with a false image, or out of simple reading difficulty: a failure on their part to grasp his long sentences, multiple meanings and negative phrasings.

Calling him "Probably the most famous Mississippian of his generation," the Jackson (Miss.) *Clarion-Ledger,* in an editorial that appeared on July 7, 1962, the day following his death, commented:

> It is only honest to say that he was a prophet who was but partly honored in his home country, while being accorded the topmost honors the literary world could pay. . . .
>
> Faulkner wrote of a South of decadence which appeared headed for doom, and he so ably pictured this land that the entire literary world believes it to be, in part at least, a mirror of the Mississippi of yesterday, today and tomorrow, where the land and the people are exploited and dying by degrees. We think this is not an accurate picture of our commonwealth of today, a distortion of yesterday, and a fallacious forecast of tomorrow. What a pity this great talent could not have caught the inspiration of the flowering of our really superior youth, many of them at Ole Miss, so close at hand to him. Then he could have lightened and brightened the reflection of our state which he painted with an ability that truly was genius.

(If Faulkner could have lived a year or so longer he undoubtedly would have seen "the flowering of our really superior youth, many of them at Ole Miss"—seen them as they flowered into violence, as they turned one of America's most beautiful campuses into a battlefield of rioting chaos that left two men dead and hundreds injured, as the night of September 30, 1962, blasted its way into the annals of American history.)

On the same day as the *Clarion-Ledger* article, the *Jackson Daily News* contained an editorial headed "William Faulkner's Greatness":

> Faulkner was a superlative storyteller and he made his characters around mythical Yoknapatawpha County spring to life and created a wicked, sordid image of Mississippi around the globe.
>
> Faulkner was a man of the world. How else could a man who thought pure, lofty thoughts all his life create such a prolific outpouring of sin, rape, perversion, violence and downright trash? . . .
>
> While we rejoice in his far-flung fame and recognize the fact that he reached the pinnacle of applause for his literary accomplishments, William Faulkner was also a dirt dauber. He dealt in and pros-

pered from filth, seemingly the first requisite for a successful book peddler in these days.

Perhaps the newspapers and the elected state officials of Mississippi, who saw fit not to attend his funeral, knew only too well that Faulkner painted, contrary to their public statements, an essentially true picture of Mississippi. Or, as Lon Tinkle, Book Editor of the *Dallas Morning News,* so cogently pointed out: "Faulkner allowed his readers the dignity of distinguishing the truth from mere facts, which in themselves can be untruthful."

It has been generally believed that Faulkner equivocated about racial justice, that he carefully averted any controversy over the conflict of the Negro in the South. Claiming that he was a molder of words, not political opinion or policy, Faulkner sometimes did ignore controversial skirmishes.

However, in a rarely-publicized and little-known series of letters to Frank R. Alhgren, editor of the Memphis (Tenn.) *Commercial Appeal,* following the historic United States Supreme Court ruling on school desegregation in 1954, Faulkner carried on an extraordinary personal crusade in which he denounced segregation and demanded unrestricted educational opportunity for all.

With the assistance of the librarian at the *Commercial Appeal* offices, I was able, with considerable squinting over the small type on the microfilm, to assemble the letters. Their importance was immediately apparent. For Faulkner speaking—in any form—be it through the pages of a book, in a speech, or the "Letters to the Editor" columns of a newspaper, is a part of the South speaking. The original letters have been retained for posterity by Paul D. Flowers, Book Editor for the *Commercial Appeal.* (Mr. Flowers is a close friend of the Faulkner family and was considered one of the late writer's favorite "literary friends," of whom he claimed few.)

His letter, published March 20, 1955, and headlined "Faulkner Says Mississippi's Schools Not Even Good Enough For Whites," read:

To the Commercial Appeal:

We Mississippians already know that our present schools are not good enough. Our young men and women themselves prove that to us every year by the fact that, when the best of them want the best of education which they are entitled to and are competent for, not only in the humanities but in the professions and crafts—law and medicine and engineering—too, they have to go out of the state to get it. And quite often, too often, they don't come back.

So our present schools are not even good enough for white people; our present state reservoir of education is not of high enough quality to assuage the thirst of even our white young men and women. In which case, how can it possibly assuage the thirst and need of the Negro, who obviously is thirstier, needs it worse, else the Federal Government would not have had to pass a law compelling Mississippi (among others, of course) to make the best of our education available to him?

That is, our present schools are not even good enough for white folks. So what do we do? Make them good enough, improve them to the best possible? No. We beat the bushes, rake and scrape to raise additional taxes to establish another system at best only equal to that one which is already not good enough, which therefore won't be good enough for Negroes either; we will have two identical systems neither of which are good enough for anybody. The question is not how foolish people can get, because apparently there is no limit to that. The question is, how foolish in simple dollars and cents, let alone in wasted men and women, can we afford to be?

This letter, signed "William Faulkner, Oxford, Mississippi," naturally attracted much attention. Letters of support and protest poured into the newspaper. One of the protest letters was from State Representative Dave Womack of Humphreys County, Mississippi. Representative Womack wrote, in a letter published March 27, 1955:

To the Commercial Appeal:

I read with interest a letter from William Faulkner published in your March 20, 1955, issue, wherein he expresses his views about the schools of Mississippi. Of course, we are only mortal men and not Nobel Prize winners, and we bow to his higher intellect. However, we feel that being a true citizen of the state of Mississippi, which I am sure he is, if he has a better plan than those proposed by some of our legislative leaders, he should come forward with it.

We are looking forward to hearing any suggestions that he may have. Also, we would like to know how many degrees he holds from these inferior Mississippi schools of which he writes.

Representative Womack, in a later letter published on April 10, 1955, wrote, "What other state can boast a sixth grade graduate as a Nobel Prize winner?" in an obvious dig at Faulkner.

Another letter, also published in the March 27, 1955, issue, and signed C. J. Martin of Greenwood, Mississippi, dissented:

To the Commercial Appeal:

Mr. Faulkner's letter in the Commercial Appeal of March 20 poses a question as to the advisability of promoting the dual system of schools. He creates an impasse while offering no concrete solution.

The theme of the letter seems to suggest a concentration on improvement of the present schools without building new Negro schools, with the subsequent integration of the races.

As lofty as the aims of an idealist may be, reality must be faced. Call it prejudice, antipathy, or tradition, the fact remains that the white people of Mississippi do not wish to attend school with the Negroes. Legislation and Supreme Court rulings do not abolish nor alter the feelings of a people dedicated to the preservation of their established culture. The rightness or wrongness has no bearing on the immediate solution of this problem. Mississippi is taking the only course it can under existing circumstances. Mr. Faulkner has, however, performed a service in the stimulation of our thinking about this problem and the righteous questioning of methods.

Faulkner's answer to these and other letters appeared on April 3, 1955, under the title, "Faulkner Tells Why He Believes Equality in Education Is Essential":

To the Commercial Appeal:

I have just read the letters of Mr. Neill (*another dissenter*), Mr. Martin and Mr. Womack in your issue of March 27, in reply to my letter in your issue of March 20.

To Mr. Martin and Mr. Womack's first question: whatever the cost of our present statewide school system is, we will have to raise that much again to establish another system equal to it. Let us take some of that new fund and make our present schools, from kindergarten up through the humanities and sciences and professions, not just the best in America but the best that schools can be; then the schools themselves will take care of the candidates, white and Negro both, who had no business in them in the first place.

Though I agree that this only solves integration; not the impasse of the emotional conflict over it. But at least it observes one of the oldest and soundest maxims: If you can't beat 'em, join 'em.

Then the rest of the new fund could establish or improve trade and craft schools for the ones whom the first system, the academic one, had already eliminated before they had had time to do much harm in the terms of their own wasted days and the overcrowded classrooms and harried underpaid teachers which result in a general leavening and lowering of educational standards; not to mention making the best use of the men and women we produce. What we need is more Americans on our side. If all Americans were on the same side, we wouldn't need to try to bribe foreign countries which don't always stay bought, to support us.

To Mr. Womack's last question: I have no degrees nor diplomas from any school. I am an old veteran sixth-grader. Maybe that's why I have too much respect for education that I seem unable to sit quiet and watch it held subordinate in importance to the color of the pupil's skin.

Under the heading, "Faulkner Would Fit Schooling to Students' Ability and Interest," published April 10, 1955, Faulkner wrote:

To the Commercial Appeal:

I have read Mr. Murphy's letter in your issue of April 3. I also received one from Dr. Flinsch, Dean, School of Engineering, Mississippi State College, along the same line. If my letter stated or implied any facts which are incorrect, I retract and apologize.

My aim was not to injure our present school system, but to take advantage of whatever changes in it the future holds, to improve our schools from their present condition of being a sort of community or state-supported baby sitters, where the pupil is compelled by law or custom to spend so many hours of the day, with nobody but often-underpaid teachers to be concerned about how much he learns.

Instead of holding the educational standard down to the lowest common denominator of the class or grade group, let us raise it to that of the highest.

Let us give every would-be pupil and student the equality and right to education in the terms in which our forefathers used the words equality and freedom and right; not equal right to charity, but equal right to the opportunity to do what he is capable of doing, freedom to attain the highest of standards—provided he is capable of it; or if he is not competent or will not work, let us learn early, before he has done much harm, that he is in the wrong occupation.

If we are to have two school systems, let the second one be for pupils ineligible not because of color but because they either can't or won't do the work of the first one.

Faulkner's letter to the *Commercial Appeal* on April 17, 1955, was inspired by an April 10, 1955, letter, signed merely "Student, Dorsey, Mississippi." The student's letter, headlined "Faulkner Was Right," noted:

To the Commercial Appeal:

It is about time someone spoke the truth about the educational system like the greatest person in our state and America's greatest author did recently in his letters to this paper.

I do think we have one great institution in the state of Mississippi. Ole Miss, to me, is one of the greatest universities in the United States.

I plan to enter Ole Miss next year and I favor Negroes entering that school and other public schools of Mississippi. So long as the races are pulling against each other (educationally, that is) they will succeed only in pushing both races down. For both to pull together we can raise the standards of both races.

I only hope the people of my state will wake up to the fact if they lower the educational standards of the Negroes as they seem to be now doing they will lower the standards for the whites as well.

Long live Mr. Faulkner.

Faulkner's letter of April 17, "Faulkner Urges Student Survey: Wants Them Questioned About Integration," stated:

To the Commercial Appeal:

I would like to say "well done" to the writer of the letter signed "Student" from Dorsey, Mississippi, in your issue of April 10th. Let us make a canvass of the young people of Mississippi who are attending our present schools and will attend the integrated ones if or when they come, for their opinion of it; they are certainly interested parties.

We in the South are faced by two apparently irreconcilable facts: one, that the National Government has decreed absolute equality in education among all races; the other, the people in the South who say that it shall never happen.

These two facts must be reconciled. I believe there are many young people, too, in Mississippi who believe they can be, who love our state—not love white people specifically nor Negroes specifically, but our land; our climate and geography, the qualities in our people, white and Negro both, for honesty and tolerance and fair play, the splendors in our traditions and the glories in our past—enough to try to reconcile them, even at the risk which the young writer from Dorsey took, despite the fact that he didn't sign his name. And what a commentary that is on us; that in Mississippi communal adult opinion can reach such emotional pitch that our young sons and daughters dare not, from probably a very justified physical fear, sign their names to an opinion adverse to it.

In his letter on February 20, 1955, Faulkner's subtle wit was at its best. In a letter captioned, "Faulkner Solves Rat Hole Puzzle; Just Enough To Go Round Once, He Discovers," he lashed out at unfair criticism of the Southern Negro:

To the Commercial Appeal:

I have read with interest the "Letter to the Editor" of Mr. Wolstenholme, of Hohenwald, Tenn., in your issue of Sunday, the 6th, in which he suggested that the Negro inhabitants of Memphis slums could nail up their ratholes if they were not too shiftless to do it; and that the white investigating groups would do much better to come to Lewis County, where they could find plenty of white people deserving of their offices.

Does this mean that, for every rathole Shelby County Negroes have, Lewis County white folks have two? Which can't be right, since white folks, not being Negroes, are not shiftless; and therefore, for every rathole which a Shelby or Lewis County, Tenn., or a Lafayette County, Miss., Negro has, a Shelby or Lewis County, Tenn., or Lafayette County, Miss., white man can't have any, which won't hold water either, since, for the simple reason that there are more rats than people, there is some inevitable and inescapable point at which the white man, no matter how shiftless, is going to have one rathole.

So, at what point on the scale of the Negro's non-ratholes does the white man gain or earn one or anyway have one rathole? Is unshiftless twice as unshiftless as shiftless, giving the white man twice as many ratholes as the Negro man, or does this get us into the old insoluble problem in amateur physics about how much is twice as cold as zero?

A strong plea for equal right to opportunity for all races in the South was made by the author in a 1955 address before the twenty-first annual meeting of the Southern Historical Association at the Peabody Hotel in Memphis. The text of that address presented valid arguments that our embattled Southland—indeed, our entire nation—might well consider:

For the sake of argument, let's say that, as a white Southerner or maybe even any white American, I too curse the day when the first Yankee ship-master bought the first penful of Negro captives from the Arab dealer and brought them across the middle passage into American slavery.

Because that doesn't matter now. To live in the world of A.D. 1955 and be against equality of race or color is like living in Alaska and being against the snow. We have already got the snow; what we must do now is plan how to live with it. Live with it, not just beside it, because the day when that would have been enough is past, too.

Only this snow is a good deal more serious than the denial of an accomplished fact. To stand against equality on grounds of race or color can invite a situation in which the whole white and-or free world as we know it can disappear.

We think of the world situation today as a precarious and explosive balance of two irreconcilable ideologies confronting each other; which precarious balance, once it totters, will drag the whole world into the abyss along with it.

That's not so. Only one of the forces is an ideology, an idea. Because the second force is the simple fact of man, the simple belief of individual man that he can and should and will be free. And if we who so far are still free, want to continue to be free, all of us who are still free had better confederate fast, with all others who still have a choice to be free—confederate not as black people nor white people nor pink nor blue nor green people, but as people who still are free with all other people who still are free; confederate together and stick together, too, if we want a world or even a part of a world in which individual man can be free, to continue to endure.

And we had better take in with us as many as we can get of the non-white peoples of the earth who are not completely free yet but who want to be and intend to be, before that other force which is opposed to individual freedom, befools and gets them.

Time was when the non-white man was content to—anyway, did—accept his instinct for freedom as an unrealizable dream. But not any more; the white man himself taught him different with that phrase of his—the white man's—own culture which took the form of colonial expansion and exploitation based and morally condoned on the premise of inequality not because of individual incompetence, but of mass race or color.

As a result of which, in only ten years, we have watched the non-white peoples expel, by bloody violence when necessary, the white man from all of the Middle East and Asia which he once dominated. And into that vacuum has already begun to move that other and inimical power which people who believe in freedom are at war with—that power which says to the non-white man: "We don't offer you freedom because there is no such thing as freedom; your white overlords whom you just threw out have already proved that to you. But we offer you equality; at least equality in slavedom; if you are to be slaves, at least you can be slaves to your own color and race and religion."

We, the Western white man, who does believe that there exists an individual freedom above and beyond this mere equality of slavedom, must teach the non-white peoples this while there is yet a little time left. We, America, who are the strongest force opposing communism and monolithicism, must teach all other peoples, white and non-white, slave or (for a little while yet) still free.

We, America, have the best chance to do this because we can do it here, at home, without needing to send costly freedom expeditions into alien and inimical places already convinced that there is no such thing as freedom and liberty and equality and peace for all people, or we would practice it at home.

The best chance and the easiest job, because our non-white minority is already on our side; we don't need to sell them on America and freedom because they are already sold; even when ignorant from inferior or no education, even despite the record and history of inequality, they still believe in our concepts of freedom and democracy.

That is what America has done for them in only 300 years. Not to them, for them, because to our shame we have made little effort so far to teach them to be Americans, let alone to use their capacities to make ourselves a stronger and unified America—the people who, only 300 years ago, were eating rotten elephant and hippo meat in African rain-forests, who lived beside one of the biggest bodies of inland water on earth and never thought of a sail, who yearly had to move by whole villages and tribes from famine and pestilence and human enemies without once thinking of a wheel, yet in only 300 years in America produced Ralph Bunche and George Washington Carver and Booker T. Washington, who have yet to produce a Fuchs or Rosenberg or Gold or Greenglass or Burgess or Maclean or Hiss, and for every prominent communist or fellow-traveler like Robeson or Richard Wright, there are a thousand white ones.

I am not convinced that the Negro wants integration in the sense that some of us claim to fear he does. I believe he is American enough to repudiate and deny by simple American instinct any stricture or regulation forbidding us to do something which in our opinion would be harmless if we did it, and which we probably would not want to do anyway.

I think that what he wants is equality, and I believe that he too knows there is no such thing as equality per se, but only equality TO—equal right and opportunity to make the best one can of one's life within one's capacity and capability, without fear of injustice or oppression or threat of violence.

If we had given him this equal right to opportunity 90 or 50 or even 10 years ago, there would have been no Supreme Court decision about how we run our schools.

It is our white man's shame that in our present Southern economy, the Negro must not have economic equality; or double shame that we fear that giving him more social equality will jeopardize his present economic status; our triple shame that even then, to justify ourselves, we must becloud the issue with the purity of white blood.

What a commentary that the one remaining place on earth where the white man can flee and have his blood protected by law, is Africa—the source and origin of the people whose presence in America will have driven the white man to flee from defilement.

Soon now all of us—not just Southerners nor even Americans, but all people who are still free and want to remain so—are going to have to make a choice. We will have to choose not between color nor race nor religion, nor between East and West either, but simply between being slaves and being free. And we will have to choose completely and for good.

The time is already past when we can choose a little of each, a little of both.

We can choose a state of slavedom, and if we are powerful enough to be among the top two or three or ten, we can have a certain amount of license—until someone more powerful rises and has us machine-gunned against a cellar wall. But we cannot choose freedom established on a hierarchy of degree of freedom, on a caste system of equality like military rank.

We must be free not because we claim freedom, but because we practice it. Our freedom must be buttressed by a homogeny equally and unchallengeably free, no matter what color they are, so that all the other inimical forces everywhere—systems political or religious or racial or national—will not just respect us because we practice freedom. They will fear us because we do.

Addressing the graduating class of the Oxford, Mississippi, High School in the summer of 1951, Faulkner issued another strong statement on freedom and human dignity. He told the graduates:

. . . So never be afraid. Never be afraid to raise your voice for honesty and truth and compassion against injustice and lying and greed. If you, not just you in this room tonight, but in all the thousands of other rooms like this one about the world today and tomorrow and next week, will do this, not as a class or classes, but as individuals, men and women, you will change the earth. In one generation all the Napoleons and Hitlers and Caesars and Mussolinis and Stalins, and all the other tyrants who want power and aggrandisement, and the simple politicians and time-servers who themselves are merely baffled or ignorant or afraid, who have used or are using, or hope to use, man's fear and greed for man's enslavement will have vanished from the face of it.

July 7, 1962

Knowing fully that he was mortal, and forgetting it, too, I had thought he would endure forever; then the dreaded reality of accepting the news; that it was true, that it had happened, the sad fact placing itself in my mind: that William Faulkner was dead.

Mrs. Richard Elliott, wife of the mayor of Oxford and owner of a jewelry store in the main square of the town, tells of an incident that occurred a few days before his death. Faulkner, so she recalls, was standing in front of her store looking at items in the display window. Three Negro children walked by and he stopped them; then they all four stood talking and laughing about an animated jewel box in the window. "I can't ever remember him looking any happier than he did with those children, all of them laughing," she says.

In keeping with his own wishes, he is buried in a plain wooden coffin; he disliked metal ones. One reporter quotes a local citizen as saying: "They'd have brought Bill to the cemetery in a farm wagon pulled by a team of mules if he'd had his way."

Mrs. Walter Rogers, wife of a teacher at Oxford's Negro Training School, brings up an interesting point about the funeral services. "Why, you know," she said, "his funeral was just like the one he held for Aunt Callie Clark." (Aunt Callie was the Negro nurse who helped raise Faulkner and his three brothers.)

"Aunt Callie was about one hundred years old when she died," Mrs. Rogers continued, "she had worked for the Faulkners for years. Now here's something that'll show you how Mr. William treated people: the last fifteen or twenty years that Aunt Callie lived she was sickly and Mr. William saw that she had everything she needed—medicine, anything! He paid the rent for the little house she lived in. When she died, he held her funeral in his own parlor."

Mrs. Mabel McEwen, a native of Oxford and a funeral director for twenty years, told about Aunt Callie's last rites: "The Faulkners all loved Aunt Callie. They gave her a splendid funeral. They had a choir to sing and everything was beautiful." Mrs. McEwen related that Faulkner himself delivered a eulogy at the funeral. Some of the words that she remembered him saying were: "Mammy knew me before I knew myself. Although she never entered a school room, her intelligence exceeded that of many a person holding a college degree. We taught her to read and write.

Mammy taught me many things not found in books. I learned many facts of life from her."

Aunt Callie lies in the same cemetery in which Faulkner is buried, only a narrow dusty road and a short distance separating them. (Oxford is one of the few Southern towns where whites and Negroes share the same cemetery.) On her tombstone are these words:

CALLIE CARR CLARK
1840–1940
Mammy
Her White Children Bless Her

Reverend W. N. Redmon, pastor of Burns Methodist Church, one of Oxford's largest Negro churches, described Faulkner in this manner: "He was one of the finest Southern gentlemen that it has been my pleasure to know. We've not only lost a great talent, but we have also lost a close, warm-hearted friend. Mr. Faulkner was a friend to the Negro. He did not believe in delegating second-class citizenship or rights to anyone."

"Mr. Bill shot straight from the hips," James O. Buford, owner of Buford's Radio-TV Service said, "you could always count on him to mean what he said; otherwise, he wouldn't have said anything. In many ways, he was *too honest for this community.*"

W. R. Wiley, a colored shoe repairman, put it this way: "Faulkner was an honorable and gentle man. If every white person in the South was as respectful of other peoples' rights as he was, there would be no problem."

Mrs. Evelyn Calloway told of Faulkner as a youth: "I knew him ever since we were kids together. I remember when I was ten or twelve, maybe younger, we were all out in back of his grandfather's house playing like a bunch of wild Indians. He flew the first kite I'd ever seen. He didn't mind my being a Negro, nor did he in the years that followed."

"You won't find any colored person who didn't respect him," Oscar Rivers reminisced. "Of course, I knew William, I'm almost eighty-five years old. He and Dean and John and Murray [Faulkner's brothers] used to ride in a wagon I drove for his daddy and grandmother. He was about the finest man you'd hope to meet."

I learned that a large percentage of Faulkner's $30,000 Nobel Prize award was spent to help needy students, both white and Negro, achieve higher education. This philanthropy was done without publicity and was relatively unknown until recently. In December, 1960, the William Faulkner Foundation was established. Dedicated to "advancing the understanding of literature," the organization awards a prize each year for the most outstanding first novel; recipient of the first such award was John Knowles for *A Separate Peace*. In addition, the Foundation provides stipulations for scholarships to deserving students, principally for "Negro students in the Deep South."

October 12, 1963

Oxford, today, is a town that seems content in its own activities, complacent in itself, and wary of any strange face. The very exterior of the town and its inhabitants seem to reflect the word "Caution."

Most of the people don't want to discuss Faulkner, and they stare at visitors who ask questions, as if to satisfy themselves, without asking, who are you?, where are you from?, what do you want?, and why?

They don't want to discuss Governor Ross Barnett.

They cringe at the name of John F. Kennedy.

They smile, sardonically, at the name of Edwin A. Walker.

They stare, then walk away from you at the mention of James H. Meredith.

There are exceptions in the town, of course, but they are few.

They mirror the expression: "We might have worked out our own problems if 'outsiders' had left us alone." They seem to say: "We're good people, we work hard, we sweat under the sun for our dollars, why all this fuss? Why all this fuss about a writer? About a nigger? Why was our serene Oxford turned into a battleground over one person?"

It was to these people and to this land that William Faulkner gave his very life. If his messages and attitudes made little impression on this town, it is due to the fact that so few read him. What seems so utterly inexplicable and saddening is that these people lived next door to genius—some all their lives—without his wisdom and concern for honor and charity rubbing off on them, even a little.

Oxford is not a town that likes questions. If they must be asked at all, they must be put silently to get any visible response. Nor is it a town that likes hatred, as some have written. Hatred has a strange odor. This odor is not present here. But you can smell the slow decay of tradition, you can sense the rotting away of customs. And, as Faulkner questioned in 1955: *are these traditions and customs worth holding onto?*

Oxford feels the Federal Government has abused it. It is doubtful that many Oxonians are familiar with Faulkner's speech before the Southern Historical Association. But, if they were, would his words make sense to them: "If we had given him [the Negro] this equal right to opportunity 90 or 50 or even 10 years ago, there would have been no Supreme Court decision about how we run our schools"?

Perhaps the town's lack of concern for Faulkner lies in the fact that they understood how he felt, that they accepted him as a "rebel" to their way of thinking and, not agreeing with him and his beliefs, chose to ignore him.

Would the battle of Oxford have been avoided if Faulkner, in the role of prophet nine years ago, had been heeded? I think so. (In the early part of 1962, Faulkner, commenting on the upcoming registration of Meredith in September, said that trouble in Oxford would come from the people who lived in Beat Two, a rougher element in the town. This prediction came true.)

But Faulkner was guilty of telling the truth, something that Southerners, and especially Mississippians, often want to dispel.

They say Faulkner cursed their state, distorted it to the world. They cannot comprehend that his books posed *universal* truths and problems.

In his first published work, a six-stanza poem entitled "Portrait" that appeared in *The Double Dealer,* a now-extinct literary magazine, in June, 1922, Faulkner seemed to sum up his life, his philosophy and these stubborn native sons. The poem contained these lines:

Profoundly speak of life, of simple truths.
The while your voice is clear with frank surprise.

A